curious
fragments

BOOKS BY DALE L. WALKER

The Lost Revolutionary (1967) with Richard O'Connor

The Fiction of Jack London: A Chronological Bibliography (1972) with
James E. Sisson III

C. L. Sonnichsen: Grassroots Historian (1972)

The Alien Worlds of Jack London (1973)

Jack London, Sherlock Holmes, and Sir Arthur Conan Doyle (1974)

Death Was the Black Horse: The Story of Rough Rider Buckey O'Neill
(1975)

curious fragments

Jack London's
Tales of Fantasy Fiction

Edited by Dale L. Walker
Preface by Philip José Farmer

National University Publications
KENNKAT PRESS / 1975
Port Washington, N.Y. / London

Permission to reprint the following works is acknowledged to Mr.
Irving Shepard, Literary Executor of Jack London:
        Goliah © 1908
        War © 1911
        The Red One © 1918
        The Scarlet Plague © 1912

Manufactured in the United States of America

Published by
Kennikat Press Corp.
Port Washington, N.Y./London

Library of Congress Cataloging in Publication Data

London, Jack, 1876–1916.
    Curious fragments.

    (National university publications)
    Bibliography: p.
    1. Fantastic fiction, American.   I. Walker, Dale
L.   II. Title.
PZ3.L84-6Cu3   [PS3523.046]   813'.5'2   75-29450
ISBN 0-8046-9114-2

CONTENTS

FOREWORD

What was the influence of Jack London's early twentieth-century science fiction on modern science fiction? I have seen no studies on this, though I would welcome one. I do not know how many of those who rank as today's major science fiction writers read London in their formative years. From my personal knowledge of such men as Isaac Asimov, Arthur C. Clarke, Robert Heinlein, and many others, I would say that all were well acquainted with London in their late childhood and early youth. Most science fiction authors (the ones I've known, anyway) are voracious readers. They were as eager as London himself to read every book on which they could lay their hands.

I know that I was. Perhaps it is not too speculative to suggest that they were influenced by the same characteristics in London's fiction which influenced me. These were awe of the vastness, harshness, and indifference of nature set against a fierce admiration of man's fighting spirit and intellect; man's insistence on saying Yea in the face of the inevitable Nay; London's melding of fantasy with reality, so that the two seem to be one; his basic dictum (anticipated by Heraclitus but as true now as then) that character determines destiny; the striving by men of awareness to prove that, though they came from the apes, they were more than apes; the importance of using vivid physical detail to exemplify a philosophical basis; the importance of telling a story as if it were fuel for a fire.

A prolonged reading of Jack London's works in one's childhood (the fatherhood of the man) insures that these elements of London become ingrained in one's consciousness and unconsciousness. (The latter is the real writer in the writer; the former, the editor.)

In addition to these, I myself drew from London a gusto, a sense of the ridiculous and the absurd, and a realization of man's cruelty and injustice to man and beast alike.

It is no exaggeration to say that every time I write, London, to some effect, is directing my pen.

CURIOUS FRAGMENTS

Jack London is chiefly noted in academic circles as the writer of some semiclassic Far North and sea stories, of the novel *The Sea Wolf*, and some "socialist" autobiographical accounts. A number of London's stories are, however, considered by science fiction aficionados to be science fiction classics. The most prominent candidates for this are *Before Adam* and *The Star Rover*. In my opinion, these two will eventually be admitted into the canon of mainstream classics.

Some of London's best works, such as those two novels mentioned, have been reprinted many times since their first appearance. Regrettably, a number have not. The present editor, Dale L. Walker, has performed a long-needed service by collecting some out-of-print short fiction pieces for Kennikat Press. Some are minor items but still worth reading. "The Red One" and "War" are especially noteworthy, and I believe that reissue of these will result in their being hailed as "long-lost" science fiction classics. These, with some of the others in this collection, exhibit all the features which have insured the permanence of his science fiction novels *The Star Rover* and *Before Adam*.

"The Red One," my favorite, conceals beneath its blood-sweat-dirt-beauty tale of South Seas adventure the "impenetrable," the unconquerable mystery of things beyond man's ken. This theme is the same as that much used by the Polish science fiction writer Stanislaw Lem. But in his stories man goes to the stars, whereas in London's the stars come to man, and he can, as in Lem's stories, make nothing of them.

Death comes, too, in London's tale, though he shows that it is man's driving curiosity—inherited from his apelike ancestors—that forces him to investigate the inevitably fatal—or the fatally inevitable.

A few comments on some of the other tales included in this collection might be in order. The title story, "A Curious Fragment," is an example of London's belief that literacy would free the unlettered from poverty and oppression. He was applying his individual experience as a mass principle, and as a principle it is correct. Rather, half correct. Literacy is one of the tools which enable the masses to gain political and social benefits and economic improvement. But reading and writing, and the modern media of radio and TV, can also be tools to enslave the masses, to manipulate and exploit. Note also that London used *his* literacy to break the chains of manual labor and poverty only to be chained in another type of slavery: wealth and fame and all the troubles and heartbreak they can bring. There is no doubt, however, which type he opted for.

FOREWORD

"A Thousand Deaths" is a curious little tale, one of which a Freudian could make much. The villain is the protagonist's father, and the protagonist, like London himself, is unrecognized by his father. It might be stretching interpretation too far to say that London is portraying in physical form the thousand deaths he suffered from his non-acknowledgment by his putative father, Professor Chaney. But London does, in a sense, anticipate in this fantasy what would happen in reality. He was to free himself from the stigma of illegitimacy and from the back-breaking, mind-deadening prison of manual labor. And he would find that the wide world lay before him. Nevertheless, each of the thousand deaths had left its scar in him.

"The Shadow and the Flash" contains London's unspoken, but evident, warning: See what the abuse of science can do. Whether there is any symbolism in the darkness of one major character and the paleness of the other, I do not know. Perhaps London was saying something about yin and yang, about the death and destruction and waste that occur when science is not balanced by reason and love. It could be significant that the two "villains" are twins in mental attitudes and physical appearance except for their pigmentation.

"A Relic of the Pliocene" is an amusing example of the Paul Bunyan type of tall tale. London, who shared many characteristics with the mythical French logger, knew how to tell such tales. Even with its facileness, however, it carries a certain seriousness. Man, as represented by Thomas Stevens, is the therocide, the great killer of animals, great or small. He is also the superior beast, outwitting and surpassing in ferocity and physical endurance the behemoth.

My second favorite in this collection is "War." As Dale Walker points out, this story bears some resemblance to Ambrose Bierce's "An Occurrence at Owl Creek Bridge." The resemblance is not in incident but in attitude, in style, and in portrayal of the inevitability and pitilessness of nature, the world's and man's. And in irony. It's a classic that should be better known.

The Scarlet Plague is not the first story by any author to describe a post-catastrophic world. Nor will it by any means be the last. Nor is it the first or last to describe the effects of a mutation in bacterial life. It may be the first in which the author implicitly approves of the effects. I think that London really preferred the low-population, back-to-the-Stone-Age world he depicted. In its simple society he would have been the chief of a tribe; his physical and mental strength, his drive and charisma and articulateness would have insured that. He would, however, have grieved over its illiteracy. He loved books.

CURIOUS FRAGMENTS

Jack London was a message sender. But in these tales he subordinates message to the story. When he did that, he was among the best of storytellers.

And is.

Philip José Farmer

curious fragments

INTRODUCTION

Jack London is, of course, best known today as a writer of stories about the Far North, the South Seas, and socialism. Significantly, he wrote fantasies in all three settings, and examples of each are to be found herein: the Far North—"Even unto Death" and "A Relic of the Pliocene"; the South Seas—"The Red One"; socialism—"A Curious Fragment" and "The Strength of the Strong." But for all his reputation as a claw-and-fang realist, he always had his eye on the stars, a keen sensitivity for the infinite mysteries of life and the universe, for the unknown, the outré, the occult, the otherworldly—the regions of fantasy.

London's idealistic and imaginative preoccupations seem decidedly out of tune with the presumably rational and scientific approach to things he found and embraced in his self-educational steeping in Darwin, Spencer, and Karl Marx. But London was forever a man of philosophical contradictions (his individualism versus his socialism being the most critical in any thorough examination of his career), and his periodic experimentation in fantasy fiction is perhaps not so extraordinary as it is a neglected aspect of his contributions to American literature.

The fourteen short stories and one novelette comprising this collection are intended to shed light on this aspect of London's spectacular career: Jack London the fantasy and science fiction writer. Of the first four of these tales, two have never been reprinted since their original appearance in periodicals long since defunct; the first two have seen publication rarely, and never in book form.

Some definition of terms is in order. The word "fantasy" in the context of fantasy fiction is generally considered to describe writings about events apart from common experience, and ideas totally imaginary and "fantastic." Into this grab bag go such types of fiction as ghost stories, tales of ESP and the occult, horror fiction, weird tales, and a host of other off-beat writings, including what has come to be known as "science fiction." Science fiction is most often construed as a more circumscribed

3

type of fantasy, as the following definition by the science fiction historian and anthologist Sam Moskowitz makes clear:[1]

Science fiction is a branch of fantasy identifiable by the fact that it eases the "willing suspension of disbelief" on the part of its readers by utilizing an atmosphere of scientific credibility for its imaginative speculations in physical science, space, time, social science and philosophy.

While the present collection contains a few stories fitting the more rigid category of science fiction ("A Thousand Deaths," "The Unparalleled Invasion," and "The Shadow and the Flash") by reason of London's self-proclaimed "pseudo-scientific" accouterments, in the main we are dealing here with the broader category—Jack London's tales of fantasy fiction.

In the light of his fictional output—188 short stories and 22 novels published in a period of but twenty-one years (1895-1916)—it is clear by the numbers alone that the selection of fifteen works in this collection represents a significant proclivity on London's part for fantasy writing. But the numbers tell only part of the story, for the fact is that fantasy is *pervasive* in London's fiction, even in his works most popularly acclaimed and critically examined for their realism.

Examples of this consistent pulse taking of the unknown, the magnetic pull London experienced toward the alien and fantastic and away from the everyday and explainable, are legion. A few will suffice to make the point.

Describing a poem by the tragic George Sterling-patterned Russ Brissenden, London writes in *Martin Eden* (1909):

. . . : swung in the majestic rhythm to the cool tumult of interstellar conflict, to the onset of starry hosts, to the impact of cold suns and the flaming up of nebulae in the darkened void; and through it all, unceasing and faint, like a silver·shuttle, ran the frail, piping voice of man, a querulous chirp amid the screaming planets and the crash of systems.

Of the pup exploring outside his mother's cave in *White Fang* (1906):

---

1. Moskowitz, *Explorers of the Infinite*, p. 11.

4

. . . After that he sat up and gazed about him, as might the first man of the earth who landed upon Mars . . . . Without any antecedent knowledge, without any warning whatever, that such existed, he found himself an explorer on a totally new world.

Of Margaret Henan in one of London's short story masterpieces, "Samuel" (1913):

She was as alien as a far journeyer from some other star.

Even London's best-known book, *The Call of the Wild* (1903), deserves special mention for its fantastic elements, something which the London scholar Earle Labor has brilliantly examined. *"The Call of the Wild* is London's version of 'The Heart of Darkness'," Professor Labor has written, "which lies beneath the protective layers of civilization, society, and super-ego within all men." Labor says that "The 'uncharted vastness' penetrated by John Thornton's party near the end of the book is enveloped appropriately in the atmosphere of the dream world; it is the timeless landscape of myth."[2]

He refers to Chapter Seven of *The Call of the Wild* in which John Thornton, two other men, Buck and a half-dozen other dogs form a party seeking a fabled lost gold mine in the trackless country east of the Yukon, an area "steeped in tragedy and shrouded in mystery" where have been found "nuggets that were unlike any known grade of gold in the Northland." The description of the trek continues:

They went across divides in summer blizzards, shivered under the midnight sun on naked mountains between the timberline and the eternal snows, dropped into summer valleys amid swarming gnats and flies, and in the shadows of glaciers picked strawberries and flowers as ripe and fair as any the Southland could boast.

Then in a passage of surpassing beauty and fantasy London writes:

In the fall of the year, they penetrated a weird lake country, sad and silent, where wild-fowl had been, but where now there was no sign of life—only the blowing of chill winds, the forming of ice in

---

2. Labor, Ed., *Great Short Works of Jack London,* p. xii. See also Labor's *Jack London* (1974), pp. 69-81.

sheltered places, and the melancholy rippling of waves on lonely beaches.

This "landscape of myth" continues to the end of the book. Buck, in the lassitude of long hours at the campfire, is pursued by a recurring dream, a vision of a "short-legged hairy man" from a time-lost world who, nostrils flared and ears twitching, swings effortlessly through the trees. And, after John Thornton is murdered by the vicious Yeehat Indians, Buck returns to the wild, coming back in summertime to the weird lake country where his beloved master had been slain:

> He crosses alone from the smiling timber land and comes down into an open space among the trees. Here a yellow stream flows from rotted moose-hide sacks and sinks into the ground, with long grasses growing through it and vegetable mould overrunning it and hiding its yellow from the sun; and here he muses for a time, howling once, long and mournfully, ere he departs.

Even in his "notes for future work" which he compiled in 1911, London's great affinity for fantasy is clear, and while he did not, unfortunately, write "The Far Future," he clearly envisioned it as a science fiction type of fantasy, heavy on the science and utilizing the device of the earth itself as a giant spacecraft hurtling through space.[3]

> Why not a series of past and future novels? . . . 'The Far Future,' the perfected and perishing human race . . . .
> Farthest Distant
> Radium Engines, etc., for energy—See Atoms and Evolution, in Saleeby's 'The Cycle of Life.' Collision of dark body from out of space (not large), one-tenth the size of sun.[4] And earth learns of coming by perturbations of outer planets. Then rush the earth away from the sun.
> When earth travels through space, all must be inclosed; and they must use stored heat of some sort. The oceans freeze, etc. A great preparation. See Direction of Motion chapter by Herbert Spencer. The initial momentum they have. The momentum in a straight line that is altered to a curve around the sun by the pole of the sun.

---

3. Charmian London, *The Book of Jack London*, 2:218-19.

4. At one-tenth the size of the sun, London's proposed dark body from outer space would be anything but "not large." It would be about the size of the planet Jupiter, which is eleven times the diameter of the earth.

Nullify the pole of the sun, select the right moment, and sail off into space to reach nearest neighbor sun.

What is clear from the contents of *Curious Fragments* and from such pàssages as those quoted above is that there exists in London's prodigious fictional output an enormous conflict: the realist fleeing from reality. In truth, London fled from it all his life. He was the son of a strange pair of square pegs who had united briefly in common-law marriage. Jack's mother, Flora Wellman of Massillon, Ohio, was an ardent spiritualist; his putative father, William Henry Chaney of Maine, was an itinerant astrologer who left Flora before their son was born. Raised by a kindly but ill-starred stepfather, John London of Pennsylvania, John Griffith ("Jack") London could never quite face up to his probable status as bastard child (though he admitted to his daughters that he felt certain Chaney was his father).[5] As for the spiritualism of his childhood, he would write: "I was born amongst spiritualists and lived my childhood and boyhood life amongst spiritualists. The result of this close contact was to make an unbeliever out of me."[6]

Yet he would make use of spiritualism in some of his fiction; for example, in such an early tale as "Who Believes in Ghosts!" the opening story of this collection. That story, in fact, is a perfect illustration of London's flight from reality and is worth placing in its proper setting.

When London entered Oakland, California, High School the frenetic pattern of his life had been established. At age nineteen he had already worked in a cannery and jute mill, as a coal shoveler, and on both sides of the law on San Francisco Bay, where he had been skipper of the sloop *Razzle-Dazzle*, raiding the bay's oyster beds, then an officer in the fish patrol, engaged in the dangerous business of arresting oyster pirates such as he had been, shrimp poachers, and similar bay thieves. In 1893 he had spent several months on the sealing schooner *Sophie Sutherland* in the North Pacific and Bering Sea, and in that same year made his literary debut by winning first prize in a San Francisco newspaper's essay contest with his entry titled "Story of a Typhoon Off the Coast of Japan." In 1894 he had joined the western detachment of "Coxey's Army" to march to Washington, D.C., had deserted its ranks in the Midwest to ride the rails eastward, earning the nicknames "Sailor Jack" and "Frisco Kid," and had

---

5. In a 1966 conversation, Joan London, Jack's eldest daughter (who died in 1971), told the editor her father had no serious doubts that Chaney was his father. She herself had no doubt whatever and had undertaken a serious study of Chaney's life and astrological work.

6. Shepard and Hendricks, *Letters from Jack London*, p. 444.

served a month in the Erie County Penitentiary in Niagara Falls, N.Y., for vagrancy.

But despite the aura of danger and vagabondage that clung to this handsome young man with his sunburned face, wad of chewing tobacco, and sailor's rolling gait, London was determined in entering Oakland High to be a "brain merchant" not a "work beast." Specifically, he wanted to be a writer, and no sooner had he enrolled than he sought out the school literary magazine, the *High School Aegis*. There he launched his writing career in earnest, publishing twelve stories and essays in the magazine between 1895 and 1901.

"Who Believes in Ghosts!" was the seventh of those twelve contributions and his fourth published work of fiction. Though it is a remarkable performance in several ways,[7] the story's relationship to reality, to London's own experience, is at best marginal. "Sailor Jack," who grew up in suffocating poverty and neglect, a youngster who knew the deadening toil of the fish cannery and jute mill, whose boyhood friends were the toughs and roustabouts of the waterfront—this young man writes of wealthy young fops, their names drawn from Roman mythology, who speak of "Chaldean necromancy," "sophistry," and "chimeras" and who utter words like "Forsooth!" and "Preposterous!", who play chess, read *Trilby* and Lecoq's *Emile Gaborieau* and who have a friend "deep in Gray's *Anatomy.*" But there is that connection with London's life, for all the contrived fakery of the characters and their utterances. The spirits of the old mansion, the ghosts of Birchall and Duinsmore, were in a very real way significant creations sprung from that "boyhood life amongst spiritualists."

Prof. Earle Labor, the most eminent Jack London scholar in America, wrote in 1974 that one element of London's writing "which he did not mention and which, indeed, he seemed hardly aware of—a genius for myth—made his achievement ultimately something more lasting than popular success."[8] In these pages the reader can readily discern this genius.

Labor also wrote in his brilliant critical study of London that "For very lately the realization has come to me that the full magnitude of London's achievement persists in eluding us. My great hope is that the coming critical generation will have the understanding and the resources to

---

7. Irving Stone, for example, writes of its "innate sense of story structure" (*Sailor on Horseback*, p. 78).

8. Labor, *Jack London*, p. 43.

8

assess him justly and fully."[9] It is hoped that the fifteen rare selections in this volume, making available to the general reader and literary scholar the best and most important of London's short fantasy fiction writings, will stand as one of those "resources" and that this book will contribute to that assessment of one of America's best-loved and perenially popular writers which Labor—and the editor—believe must result in the recognition of Jack London as a major figure in American literature.

A NOTE ON THE SELECTIONS

The intent in gathering the selections for this volume has been threefold: to include rare, seldom (and in some cases never) reprinted stories; to provide a chronological cross section of works between the years 1895 and 1916—the period of London's writing career; and to present as wide a selection from a thematic standpoint as possible.

Among short stories which could have been included in *Curious Fragments*, "The Man With the Gash" (1900) was omitted because it would duplicate a Klondike setting already represented in another 1900 tale in this volume, "Even unto Death." The latter has never been reprinted until now, while "The Man With the Gash" has appeared in many London story collections. There was a momentary temptation to include the 1906 tale "Planchette," a long (17,000 words), wooden, and excessively melodramatic story of ouija and spiritualism. It was sacrificed for these reasons and because, for its length it would have added little that the earlier, shorter, "Who Believes in Ghosts!" does not illustrate. Moreover, "Planchette" can be found in the 1906 collection *Moon-Face & Other Stories* which has been reprinted many times.

The knowledgeable London reader may wonder at the omission of all or any part of the three London novels which fit the description "fantasy"—*Before Adam* (1907), *The Iron Heel* (1908), and *The Star Rover* (1914), the first and third of which Philip José Farmer (and the editor) believe will become "mainstream classics."

The decision not to include either a portion or all of *Before Adam* was based on the fact that the novel remains in print, is available in an inexpensive paperback edition, and is widely known. Moreover, as a

9. Ibid., [7].

prehistory type of fantasy work, the novel would have added little, as an illustration of atavistic fantasy, that the short story "The Strength of the Strong" has not depicted.

The Iron Heel is omitted because it is a fantasy only in the sense that its "Foreword" and running footnotes are ostensibly written by an editor far in the future—"Anthony Meredith" writing in the city of Ardis on November 27, 419 B.O.M. ("Brotherhood of Man"). For this reason it is impossible to carry a meaningful portion of the book.

The Star Rover was difficult to omit but it is a synoptic novel of great length, impossible to excerpt for purposes of illustrating its fantastic elements. Darrell Standing's adventures in time and space are meaningless apart from the integration London gave them by having this transmigrating hero cinched in a straitjacket in San Quentin prison, able to move only with his mind. Furthermore, the novel is in print and is more familiar to most readers than The Scarlet Plague. The latter also has the virtue of being novelette in length and is the perfect example of support for Earle Labor's observation (in his Jack London, p. 69) that "the simple truth is that he [London] was a born sprinter who never acquired the artistic stamina of the long-distance runner."

WHO BELIEVES IN GHOSTS!

As noted in the introduction, this story is London's fourth piece of published fiction and his first published fantasy story. *The High School Aegis* provided young London a "market" for his first six short stories—his entire fictional output for 1895.

"A remarkably good one—for you; but I know of one that beats—"

"No, no, Damon. I know you always have a story to cap the last one; but I meant this in all honesty, and if you doubt its truth, at least believe my sincerity in telling it."

"George! You don't mean to tell me that you really believe in ghosts? Why, the very idea is absurd, and to connect credence in such a thing with you is—is—" and Van Buster, otherwise known as Damon, paused for lack of an expletive, and finally exploded in "Preposterous!"

"But I do believe in it, and in my faith I am not alone, for on my side I can array the greatest lights of every age from the days of Chaldean necromancy down to the cold, scientific 'to day.' Pause and reflect, O Damon and Pythias, too, for I can see the skeptical twinkle in your eye. Remember that in every time, in every land, and in every people, there have been and there are many who did believe in the soul's return after death. Can you, with this great mass of evidence staring you in the face, say that it is all the creation of diseased brains and abnormal imaginations?" And as Damon and Pythias both affirmed his accusation, he concluded with a pious hope that some day they would be forced to change their minds by a proof very unpleasantly applied.

"Come, come, Pythias! What have you to say in our mutual defense? Show our credulous friend the firm foundation on which we stand. Bring all your mighty logic to bear, and sophistry, too, for it is a very bad case.

The (Oakland) *High School Aegis.* 10 (October 21, 1895):1-4.

Show him that this psychic force is but the creation of man's too fertile imagination; prove to him that these earth-bound spirits, astral forms and disembodied entities are but chimeras!"

"Ah, Damon," he lazily drawled, "I care not to waste my stupendous knowledge and laborious research on such petty subjects. If I were challenged into controversy on the land, tariff or finance question, I fain would reply; but this seems too much like the nursery babble on the bogie man. Earth-bound spirits forsooth! All I can say to dear George is that he is an ass, and until he can introduce me to some astral form, I dismiss the subject."

In no wise put out by the sarcasm of his friends, George said: "I feel like singing that old doggerel—

'Just go down to Derby town,
And see the same as I.'

For I have seen many, and what I consider authentic, proofs of the existence and activity of this force. I know that all argument is useless when I have opposed to me, two such master minds; yet so far have they sank into intellectual stagnation, that they know not, and know not that they know not.

"We all view the world through colored glasses; but their glasses are so very, very green, that one almost feels—"

"And you must confess that yours are rather smoky," interrupted Damon. "But come, George, we'll not quarrel over such a subject. You know the position I always assume when dealing with the unknown. I neither affirm nor deny, and I can but say that plausibility, if not possibility, is with your belief. In justice to you, to myself and to the world, all I can say is that I do not know, but would like to know. And I coincide with Pythias in asking you to bring us personally in contact with these disembodied souls."

"There's the old Birchall mansion," drawled Pythias; "perhaps we can gain an introduction there. They say it's haunted."

"The very place!" cried Damon. "Do you think the 'ghost' that walks the gloomy corridors at midnight's dread hour, etc., would condescend to become visible for the edification of two such miserable, unbelieving mortals as we are? Here's a grand opportunity—it's only ten, and we can be there by eleven. Pythias and I will arm ourselves with a couple of dozen candles, half a dozen ounces of Durham, and *Trilby* to read aloud turn about,—the last to affect and prepare our imaginations. What say you, Pythias, to the lark?"

12

"I am always agreeable," he replied. "I've got the time to spare now from my grind. I'm through with the ex'es, you know. But I move to amend by striking out *Trilby* and inserting chess. Also that we bring a bunch of fire-crackers to let off when the ghost makes his appearance. It might be a Chinese devil, you know. And of course you'll accompany us, George? No? Then you had better find a companion and keep guard outside in case of accidents, and to see that we do not run away."

"That's easily arranged," answered George. "I can get Fred. He will just be going out now to hunt cats."

"Hunt cats!" from Damon and Pythias.

"Yes, hunt cats. You see, he's deep in Gray's *Anatomy* now, and is hard run for subjects. Why, he even did away with his sister's big Maltese, and so proud was he when he had articulated it, that he had the cheek to show it to her, telling her it was the skeleton of a rabbit."

"The brute!"

"The cat?"

"No, Fred. How poor Dora must have mourned for her lost tabby."

"He ought to be thrashed."

"No, dissected, then articulated and presented to his bereaved relatives as a missing link. They would no more recognize him than did Dora her cat."

"If cats had souls I would be afraid to venture out at night if I were he. Have they got souls, George?"

"I don't know; but don't let's waste any more time, if we intend carrying this project out. We must all meet by eleven sharp, in front of the house."

They agreed. So paying their reckoning, they left the restaurant— George to hunt up Fred, and Damon and Pythias to invest their spare cash in candles, fire-crackers and Durham.

By eleven, the four friends had assembled in front of the Birchall mansion. They were all high spirited, and when they came to part, George addressed them as follows:

"O Damon, the agnostic, and Pythias, the skeptic, heed well my last words. Ye venture within a place purported by the vulgar to be haunted. The truth of this as yet remains to be proven; but remember that this power, which you will have to contend with, will not be resisted as those earthly forces of which you have knowledge. It is mysterious, imponderable and powerful; it is invisible, yet oftentimes visible; and it can exert itself in innumerable ways. Opening locked doors, putting out lights, dropping bricks, and strange sounds, cries, curses and moans, are but the lower demonstrations of this phenomena. Also, as we have in this life men

13

inclined to good and evil, so have we, in the life to come, spirits, both good and bad. Woe betide you if you are thrown in contact with evil spirits. You may be lifted up bodily and dashed to the floor or against the walls like a football; you may see grewsome sights even beyond the conception of mortal; and so great a terror may be brought upon you, that your minds may lose their balance and leave you gibbering idiots or violently insane. And again, these evil spirits have the power to deprive you of one, two or all your senses, if they so wish. They can burst your ear-drums; sear your eyes; destroy your voice; sadly impair your sense of taste and smell, and paralyze the body in any or every nerve. And even as in the days of Christ, they may make their habitation within your bodies, and you will be tormented with evil spirits, and then—the asylum and padded cell stares you in the face. I have no advice to give you in dealing with this mysterious subject, for I am ignorant; but my parting words are, 'keep cool; may you prosper in your undertaking, and beware!' "

They then separated—Damon and Pythias in quest of ghosts, and George and Fred in quest of cats.

The first couple strode up to the front door; but finding it locked, and that the spirits did not respond after they had duly exercised the great, old fashioned knocker, they tried the windows on the long portico. These were also locked. After quite a scramble, they scaled the portico and found a second story window open. As soon as they gained an entrance they lighted a couple of candles and proceeded to explore.

Everything was old fashioned, dusty and musty; they had expected this. Commencing on the third floor, they thoroughly overhauled everything—opening the closets, pulling aside the rotten tapestries, looking for trap doors and even sounding the walls. These actions, however, are accounted for by the fact that both had recently read *Emile Gaborieau.* Emulating Monsieur Lecoq, they even descended to the basement; but this was such a complex affair that they gave it up in despair.

Returning to the second floor with a couple of stools and a box they had found, they proceeded to make themselves comfortable in the cleanest room they could find. Though half a dozen candles illuminated the apartment, it still seemed dreary and desolate, and dampened their high spirits "to just the pitch," as Damon said, "for a good game of chess."

By the time an hour and a half had elapsed, they concluded their first game, and a magnificent game it had been. Pythias opened his watch and remarked, "Half past twelve and no ghost."

"The reason is the room is so smoky that the poor ghosts can't become visible," replied Damon. "Throw open the window and let some of it out."

14

This task accomplished, they arranged the board for another game. Just as Damon stretched forth his hand to advance the white king's pawn, he suddenly stopped with a startled expression on his face, as also did Pythias. Silently, and with questioning look, they glanced at each other, and their mutual, yet incomprehensible consternation, was apparent.

Again did he essay to advance the pawn, and again did he stop, and again did they gaze, startled, into each other's faces. The silence seemed so palpable that it pressed against them like a leaden weight. The tension on their nerves was terrible, and each strove to break it, but in vain. Then they thought of the warning George had given them. Was it possible? Could it be true? Had they been deprived of the power of speech by this conscious, psychic force, which neither believed in? As in a nightmare, they longed to cry out; to break the horrible, paralyzing influence. Pythias was deathly pale, while the perspiration formed in great drops on Damon's forehead, and trickling down the bridge of his nose, fell in a minute cataract upon his clean, white tie and glossy shirt front.

For an age it seemed to them, but not more than a couple of minutes they sat staring agonized at each other. At last their intuition warned them that affairs were approaching a crisis. They knew the strain could not last much longer.

Suddenly, weird and shrill, there rose on the still night air, and was wafted in through the open window, the cry of a cat; then there was a scramble as over a fence, the sound of rocks striking against boards, and the cat's triumphant cry was changed to a yowl of pain and terror which quickly turned to a choking gurgle, and they heard the enthusiastic voice of Fred cry, "Number one!"

As a diver rising from depths of ocean feels the wondrous pleasure when he drives the vitiated air from his lungs and breathes anew the essence of life, so felt they—but for a moment. The spell was not broken. Then their consternation returned, multiplied a thousand fold. Both felt a hysterical desire to laugh, so ludicrous appeared the situation. But by the mysterious power, even this was denied, and their faces were distorted in an idiotic gibber. This so horrified them, that they quickly brought their wills to bear, and their faces resumed the expression of bewilderment.

Simultaneously a light dawned upon them. They had the power of motion left. The movement of their lips had demonstrated this. They half rose, as though to flee, when the cowardice of it shamed them, and they resumed their seats. Pythias touched a bunch of firecrackers to the candle and threw them in the middle of the room.

The crackers sputtered and whizzed, snapped and banged, filling the room with a dense cloud of smoke, which hung over them like a pall,

15

weirdly oppressive in the terrifying silence that followed.

Then a strange sensation came over Damon. All fear of the supernatural seemed to leave him, being replaced by a wild, fierce, all absorbing desire to begin the game. In a vague sort of way, he realized that he was undergoing a reincarnation. He felt himself to be rapidly evolving into some one else, or some one else was rapidly evolving into him. His own personality disappeared and as in a dream, he found another and more powerful personality had been projected into, or had overcome—swallowed up his own. To himself he seemed to have become old and feeble, as he bent under a weight of years; yet, he felt the burden to be strangely light, as though upheld by the burning, enthusiastic excitement, which boiled and bubbled and thrilled within him. He felt as though his destiny lay in the board before him; as though his life, his soul, his all, hung in the balance of the game he was to play.

Then implacable hatred and horrid desire for revenge quickened to life within him. A thousand wrongs seemed to rise before him with vivid brightness; a thousand devils seemed urging him on to the consummation of his desire. How he hated that thing—that man who was Satan incarnate, who opposed him across the chessboard. He cast a defiant glance at him, and with the swiftness of a soaring eagle, his hatred increased as he looked on the treacherous, smiling face and into the half-veiled, deceitful eyes. It was not Pythias; he was gone—why and when he did not even wonder.

As these strange things had happened to Damon, so happened they to Pythias. He despised the opponent who faced him. He felt endowed with all the cunning and low trickery of the world. The other was within his power; he knew that and was glad, as he smiled into his face with exasperating elation. The exultation to overthrow, to cast him down, rose paramount. He also desired to begin.

The game commenced. Damon boldly opened by offering the gambit. Pythias responded, but played on the defensive. Damon's attack was brilliant and rapid; but he was met by combinations so bold and novel, that by the twenty-seventh move it was broken up and Pythias still retained the gambit pawn.

Exerting himself anew, Damon, by a most sound and enduring method of attack, so placed Pythias that he had either to lose his queen or suffer mate in four moves. But by a startling series of daring moves, Pythias extricated himself with the loss of two pawns and a knight.

Elated by success, Damon attacked wildly, but was repulsed by the more cautious play of his opponent, who, by creating a diversion on the right flank, and by delicate maneuvering recovered himself, and once more grappled his adversary on equal ground. And so the game, one of the

16

greatest the world had ever seen, proceeded. It was a mighty duel in which the participants forgot that the world still moved on, and when the first gray of dawn appeared at the window, it found Damon in a serious predicament.

He would be forced to double his rooks to avoid checkmate—he saw that. Then his opponent would check his queen under cover, and capture his red bishop. Checkmate would then be inevitable. Suddenly, however, a light broke upon the situation. A brilliant move was apparent to him. By a series of moves which he would inaugurate, he could force his adversary's queen and turn the tables.

Fate intervened. The shrill cry of a cat rose on the air and distracted his concentration. The contemplated move was lost to him, and the threatened mate so veiled the position to his reason, that he doubled his rooks, and inevitable mate in six moves confronted him.

His brain reeled; all the wrongs of a life-time hideously clamored for vengeance; all the deceits, the lies, the betrayals of his opponent, rose to his brain in startling brightness. He cursed the smiling fiend opposite him, and staggered to his feet. Murder ranged like a burning demon through his thoughts, and springing upon Pythias with an awful cry, he buried both hands in his throat. He threw him, back down, upon the chess board, and not with the rage of a fiend, but with a wonderfully sublime joy, choked him till his face grew black and agonized.

It would have gone very bad for Pythias had not a rush of feet been heard on the stairs, a couple of policemen dashed in, and with Fred and George, tore them apart.

Then Damon came, bewildered, to his senses, and helped to restore his chum.

* * * * *

"It was the old Birchall-Duinsmore murder, nearly enacted over again," said the sergeant, as they stood on the corner talking it over. "Duinsmore, his nephew, had been his life's curse. From boyhood he had always brought him trouble. As a man, he broke Birchall's heart a dozen different ways, and at last, by cunning, thievish financering, he robbed him of all he had, except the mansion. One night, he prevailed upon the old man to stake it on a game of chess. It was all that stood between him and the potter's field, and when he lost it, he became demented, and throttled his nephew across the very board on which had been played the decisive game."

"Good chess players?"

"It has been said that they were about the best the world has ever seen."

17

A THOUSAND DEATHS

The forty dollars Jack London received for this science fiction story from H. D. Umbstaetter of *The Black Cat* saved the starving young writer from taking a post office job and enabled him to continue writing. London, between January and May, 1899, had published four stories in the once-prestigious *Overland Monthly*, but his pay for these brilliant Klondike tales (such as "To the Man on the Trail," "The White Silence," and "The Son of the Wolf") was an almost criminal $5 to $7.50.

London was able to repay his debt to editor Umbstaetter by writing the introduction to the editor's 1911 collection *The Red Hot Dollar & Other Stories from the Black Cat.*

The story probably has significance beyond its experimental nature. The London scholar Edwin B. Erbentraut, in an article entitled " 'A Thousand Deaths': Hyperbolic Anger" (*Jack London Newsletter*, vol. 4, no. 3 (Sept.-Dec., 1971): 125-29), believes the story "must have been an indispensable relief valve for the pressurized psyche of an impassioned genius." Erbentraut sees an important relationship between the fictional father and son and Jack's attitude toward William Henry Chaney. (Significantly, in an exchange of correspondence in 1897 Chaney denied, in a dignified letter to London, any chance of being the writer's father.)

I had been in the water about an hour, and cold, exhausted, with a terrible cramp in my right calf, it seemed as though my hour had come. Fruitlessly struggling against the strong ebb tide, I had beheld the maddening procession of the water-front lights slip by; but now I gave up attempting to breast the stream and contented myself with the bitter thoughts of a wasted career, now drawing to a close.

It had been my luck to come of good, English stock, but of parents whose account with the bankers far exceeded their knowledge of child-nature and the rearing of children. While born with a silver spoon in

The Black Cat (Boston), 4 (May, 1899):33-42.

my mouth, the blessed atmosphere of the home circle was to me unknown. My father, a very learned man and a celebrated antiquarian, gave no thought to his family, being constantly lost in the abstractions of his study; while my mother, noted far more for her good looks than her good sense, sated herself with the adulation of the society in which she was perpetually plunged. I went through the regular school and college routine of a boy of the English bourgeois, and as the years brought me increasing strength and passions, my parents suddenly became aware that I was possessed of an immortal soul, and endeavored to draw the curb. But it was too late; I perpetrated the wildest and most audacious folly, and was disowned by my people, ostracized by the society I had so long outraged, and with the thousand pounds my father gave me, with the declaration that he would neither see me again nor give me more, I took a first-class passage to Australia.

Since then my life had been one long peregrination—from the Orient to the Occident, from the Arctic to the Antarctic—to find myself at last, an able seaman at thirty, in the full vigor of my manhood, drowning in San Francisco Bay because of a disastrously successful attempt to desert my ship.

My right leg was drawn up by the cramp, and I was suffering the keenest agony. A slight breeze stirred up a choppy sea, which washed into my mouth and down my throat, nor could I prevent it. Though I still contrived to keep afloat, it was merely mechanical, for I was rapidly becoming unconscious. I have a dim recollection of drifting past the sea-wall, and of catching a glimpse of an up-river steamer's starboard light; then everything became a blank.

* * * * *

I heard the low hum of insect life, and felt the balmy air of a spring morning fanning my cheek. Gradually it assumed a rhythmic flow, to whose soft pulsations my body seemed to respond. I floated on the gentle bosom of a summer's sea, rising and falling with dreamy pleasure on each crooning wave. But the pulsations grew stronger; the humming louder; the waves, larger, fiercer—I was dashed about on a stormy sea. A great agony fastened upon me. Brilliant, intermittent sparks of light flashed athwart my inner consciousness; in my ears there was the sound of many waters; then a sudden snapping of an intangible something, and I awoke.

The scene, of which I was protagonist, was a curious one. A glance sufficed to inform me that I lay on the cabin floor of some gentleman's yacht, in a most uncomfortable posture. On either side, grasping my arms and working them up and down like pump handles, were two peculiarly clad, dark-skinned creatures. Though conversant with most aboriginal

19

types, I could not conjecture their nationality. Some attachment had been fastened about my head, which connected my respiratory organs with the machine I shall next describe. My nostrils, however, had been closed, forcing me to breathe through the mouth. Foreshortened by the obliquity of my line of vision, I beheld two tubes, similar to small hosing but of different composition, which emerged from my mouth and went off at an acute angle from each other. The first came to an abrupt termination and lay on the floor beside me; the second traversed the floor in numerous coils, connecting with the apparatus I have promised to describe.

In the days before my life had become tangential, I had dabbled not a little in science, and, conversant with the appurtenances and general paraphernalia of the laboratory, I appreciated the machine I now beheld. It was composed chiefly of glass, the construction being of that crude sort which is employed for experimentative purposes. A vessel of water was surrounded by an air chamber, to which was fixed a vertical tube, surmounted by a globe. In the center of this was a vacuum gauge. The water in the tube moved upward and downward, creating alternate inhalations and exhalations, which were in turn communicated to me through the hose. With this, and the aid of the men who pumped my arms so vigorously, had the process of breathing been artifically carried on, my chest rising and falling and my lungs expanding and contracting, till nature could be persuaded to again take up her wonted labor.

As I opened my eyes the appliance about my head, nostrils and mouth was removed. Draining a stiff three fingers of brandy, I staggered to my feet to thank my preserver, and confronted—my father. But long years of fellowship with danger had taught me self-control, and I waited to see if he would recognize me. Not so; he saw in me no more than a runaway sailor and treated me accordingly.

Leaving me to the care of the blackies, he fell to revising the notes he had made on my resuscitation. As I ate of the handsome fare served up to me, confusion began on deck, and from the chanteys of the sailors and the rattling of blocks and tackles I surmised that we were getting under way. What a lark! Off on a cruise with my recluse father into the wide Pacific! Little did I realize, as I laughed to myself, which side the joke was to be on. Aye, had I known, I would have plunged overboard and welcomed the dirty fo'c'sle from which I had just escaped.

I was not allowed on deck till we had sunk the Farallones and the last pilot boat. I appreciated this forethought on the part of my father and made it a point to thank him heartily, in my bluff seaman's manner. I could not suspect that he had his own ends in view, in thus keeping my presence secret to all save the crew. He told me briefly of my rescue by his sailors, assuring me that the obligation was on his side, as my appearance had been most opportune. He had constructed the apparatus for the vindication of a theory concerning certain biological phenomena, and had been waiting for an opportunity to use it.

"You have proved it beyond all doubt," he said; then added with a sigh, "But only in the small matter of drowning."

But, to take a reef in my yarn—he offered me an advance of two pounds on my previous wages to sail with him, and this I considered handsome, for he really did not need me. Contrary to my expectations, I did not join the sailors' mess, for'ard, being assigned to a comfortable stateroom and eating at the captain's table. He had perceived that I was no common sailor, and I resolved to take this chance for reinstating myself in his good graces. I wove a fictitious past to account for my education and present position, and did my best to come in touch with him. I was not long in disclosing a predilection for scientific pursuits, nor he in appreciating my aptitude. I became his assistant, with a corresponding increase in wages, and before long, as he grew confidential and expounded his theories, I was as enthusiastic as himself.

The days flew quickly by, for I was deeply interested in my new studies, passing my waking hours in his well-stocked library, or listening to his plans and aiding him in his laboratory work. But we were forced to forgo many enticing experiments, a rolling ship not being exactly the proper place for delicate or intricate work. He promised me, however, many delightful hours in the magnificent laboratory for which we were bound. He had taken possession of an uncharted South Sea island, as he said, and turned it into a scientific paradise.

We had not been on the island long, before I discovered the horrible mare's nest I had fallen into. But before I describe the strange things which came to pass, I must briefly outline the causes which culminated in as startling an experience as ever fell to the lot of man.

Late in life, my father had abandoned the musty charms of antiquity and succumbed to the more fascinating ones embraced under the general head of biology. Having been thoroughly grounded during his youth in the fundamentals, he rapidly explored all the higher branches as far as the scientific world had gone, and found himself on the no man's land of the unknowable. It was his intention to pre-empt some of this unclaimed territory, and it was at this stage of his investigations that we had been thrown together. Having a good brain, though I say it myself, I had mastered his speculations and methods of reasoning, becoming almost as mad as himself. But I should not say this. The marvelous results we afterward obtained can only go to prove his sanity. I can but say that he

21

was the most abnormal specimen of cold-blooded cruelty I have ever seen.

After having penetrated the dual mysteries of physiology and psychology, his thought had led him to the verge of a great field, for which, the better to explore, he began studies in higher organic chemistry, pathology, toxicology and other sciences and sub-sciences rendered kindred as accessories to his speculative hypotheses. Starting from the proposition that the direct cause of the temporary and permanent arrest of vitality was due to the coagulation of certain elements and compounds in the protoplasm, he had isolated and subjected these various substances to innumerable experiments. Since the temporary arrest of vitality in an organism brought coma, and a permanent arrest death, he held that by artificial means this coagulation of the protoplasm could be retarded, prevented, and even overcome in the extreme states of solidification. Or, to do away with the technical nomenclature, he argued that death, when not violent and in which none of the organs had suffered injury, was merely suspended vitality; and that, in such instances, life could be induced to resume its functions by the use of proper methods. This, then, was his idea: To discover the method—and by practical experimentation prove the possibility—of renewing vitality in a structure from which life had seemingly fled. Of course, he recognized the futility of such endeavor after decomposition had set in; he must have organisms which but the moment, the hour, or the day before, had been quick with life. With me, in a crude way, he had proved this theory. I was really drowned, really dead, when picked from the water of San Francisco Bay—but the vital spark had been renewed by means of his aerotherapeutical apparatus, as he called it.

Now to his dark purpose concerning me. He first showed me how completely I was in his power. He had sent the yacht away for a year, retaining only his two blackies, who were utterly devoted to him. He then made an exhaustive review of his theory and outlined the method of proof he had adopted, concluding with the startling announcement that I was to be his subject.

I had faced death and weighed my chances in many a desperate venture, but never in one of this nature. I can swear I am no coward, yet this proposition of journeying back and forth across the borderland of death put the yellow fear upon me. I asked for time, which he granted, at the same time assuring me that but the one course was open—I must submit. Escape from the island was out of the question; escape by suicide was not to be entertained, though really preferable to what it seemed I must undergo; my only hope was to destroy my captors. But this latter was frustrated through the precautions taken by my father. I was

22

subjected to a constant surveillance, even in my sleep being guarded by one or the other of the blacks.

Having pleaded in vain, I announced and proved that I was his son. It was my last card, and I had placed all my hopes upon it. But he was inexorable; he was not a father but a scientific machine. I wonder yet how it ever came to pass that he married my mother or begat me, for there was not the slightest grain of emotion in his make-up. Reason was all in all to him, nor could he understand such things as love or sympathy in others, except as petty weaknesses which should be overcome. So he informed me that in the beginning he had given me life, and who had better right to take it away than he? Such, he said, was not his desire, however; he merely wished to borrow it occasionally, promising to return it punctually at the appointed time. Of course, there was a liability of mishaps, but I could do no more than take the chances, since the affairs of men were full of such.

The better to insure success, he wished me to be in the best possible condition, so I was dieted and trained like a great athlete before a decisive contest. What could I do? If I had to undergo the peril, it were best to be in good shape. In my intervals of relaxation he allowed me to assist in the arranging of the apparatus and in the various subsidiary experiments. The interest I took in all such operations can be imagined. I mastered the work as thoroughly as he, and often had the pleasure of seeing some of my suggestions or alterations put into effect. After such events I would smile grimly, conscious of officiating at my own funeral.

He began by inaugurating a series of experiments in toxicology. When all was ready, I was killed by a stiff dose of strychnine and allowed to lie dead for some twenty hours. During that period my body was dead, absolutely dead. All respiration and circulation ceased; but the frightful part of it was, that while the protoplasmic coagulation proceeded, I retained consciousness and was enabled to study it in all its ghastly details.

The apparatus to bring me back to life was an air-tight chamber, fitted to receive my body. The mechanism was simple—a few valves, a rotary shaft and crank, and an electric motor. When in operation, the interior atmosphere was alternately condensed and rarefied, thus communicating to my lungs an artificial respiration without the agency of the hosing previously used. Though my body was inert, and, for all I knew, in the first stages of decomposition, I was cognizant of everything that transpired. I knew when they placed me in the chamber, and though all my senses were quiescent, I was aware of hypodermic injections of a compound to react upon the coagulatory process. Then the chamber was closed and the machinery started. My anxiety was terrible; but the circulation became gradually restored, the different organs began to carry

23

.on their respective functions, and in an hour's time I was eating a hearty dinner.

It cannot be said that I participated in this series, nor in the subsequent ones, with much verve; but after two ineffectual attempts at escape, I began to take quite an interest. Besides, I was becoming accustomed. My father was beside himself at his success, and as the months rolled by his speculations took wilder and yet wilder flights. We ranged through the three great classes of poisons, the neurotics, the gaseous and the irritants, but carefully avoided some of the mineral irritants and passed the whole group of corrosives. During the poison regime I became quite accustomed to dying, and had but one mishap to shake my growing confidence. Scarifying a number of lesser blood vessels in my arm, he introduced a minute quantity of that most frightful of poisons, the arrow poison, or curare. I lost consciousness at the start, quickly followed by the cessation of respiration and circulation, and so far had the solidification of the protoplasm advanced, that he gave up all hope. But at the last moment he applied a discovery he had been working upon, receiving such encouragement as to redouble his efforts.

In a glass vacuum, similar but not exactly like a Crookes' tube, was placed a magnetic field. When penetrated by polarized light, it gave no phenomena of phosphorescence nor of rectilinear projection of atoms, but emitted non-luminous rays, similar to the X ray. While the X ray could reveal opaque objects hidden in dense mediums, this was possessed of far subtler penetration. By this he photographed my body, and found on the negative an infinite number of blurred shadows, due to the chemical and electric motions still going on. This was an infallible proof that the rigor mortis in which I lay was not genuine; that is, those mysterious forces, those delicate bonds which held my soul to my body, were still in action. The resultants of all other poisons were unapparent, save those of mercurial compounds, which usually left me languid for several days.

Another series of delightful experiments was with electricity. We verified Tesla's assertion that high currents were utterly harmless by passing 100,000 volts through my body. As this did not affect me, the current was reduced to 2,500, and I was quickly electrocuted. This time he ventured so far as to allow me to remain dead, or in a state of suspended vitality, for three days. It took four hours to bring me back.

Once, he superinduced lockjaw, but the agony of dying was so great that I positively refused to undergo similar experiments. The easiest deaths were by asphyxiation, such as drowning, strangling, and suffocation by gas; while those by morphine, opium, cocaine and chloroform, were not at all hard.

Another time, after being suffocated, he kept me in cold storage for three months, not permitting me to freeze or decay. This was without my knowledge, and I was in a great fright on discovering the lapse of time. I became afraid of what he might do with me when I lay dead, my alarm being increased by the predilection he was beginning to betray toward vivisection. The last time I was resurrected, I discovered that he had been tampering with my breast. Though he had carefully dressed and sewed the incisions up, they were so severe that I had to take to my bed for some time. It was during this convalescence that I evolved the plan by which I ultimately escaped.

While feigning unbounded enthusiasm in the work, I asked and received a vacation from my moribund occupation. During this period I devoted myself to laboratory work, while he was too deep in the vivisection of the many animals captured by the blacks to take notice of my work.

It was on these two propositions that I constructed my theory: First, electrolysis, or the decomposition of water into its constituent gases by means of electricity; and, second, by the hypothetical existence of a force, the converse of gravitation, which Astor has named "apergy." Terrestrial attraction, for instance, merely draws objects together but does not combine them; hence, apergy is merely repulsion. Now, atomic or molecular attraction not only draws objects together but integrates them; and it was the converse of this, or a disintegrative force, which I wished to not only discover and produce, but to direct at will. Thus the molecules of hydrogen and oxygen reacting on each other, separate and create new molecules, containing both elements and forming water. Electrolysis causes these molecules to split up and resume their original condition, producing the two gases separately. The force I wished to find must not only do this with two, but with all elements, no matter in what compounds they exist. If I could then entice my father within its radius, he would be instantly disintegrated and sent flying to the four quarters, a mass of isolated elements.

It must not be understood that this force, which I finally came to control, annihilated matter; it merely annihilated form. Nor, as I soon discovered, had it any effect on inorganic structure; but to all organic form it was absolutely fatal. This partiality puzzled me at first, though had I stopped to think deeper I would have seen through it. Since the number of atoms in organic molecules is far greater than in the most complex mineral molecules, organic compounds are characterized by their instability and the ease with which they are split up by physical forces and chemical reagents.

25

By two powerful batteries, connected with magnets constructed specially for this purpose, two tremendous forces were projected. Considered apart from each other, they were perfectly harmless; but they accomplished their purpose by focusing at an invisible point in mid-air. After practically demonstrating its success, besides narrowly escaping being blown into nothingness, I laid my trap. Concealing the magnets, so that their force made the whole space of my chamber doorway a field of death, and placing by my couch a button by which I could throw on the current from the storage batteries, I climbed into bed.

The blackies still guarded my sleeping quarters, one relieving the other at midnight. I turned on the current as soon as the first man arrived. Hardly had I begun to doze, when I was aroused by a sharp, metallic tinkle. There, on the mid-threshold, lay the collar of Dan, my father's St. Bernard. My keeper ran to pick it up. He disappeared like a gust of wind, his clothes falling to the floor in a heap. There was a slight whiff of ozone in the air, but since the principal gaseous components of his body were hydrogen, oxygen and nitrogen, which are equally colorless and odorless, there was no other manifestation of his departure. Yet when I shut off the current and removed the garments, I found a deposit of carbon in the form of animal charcoal; also other powders, the isolated, solid elements of his organism, such as sulphur, potassium and iron. Resetting the trap, I crawled back to bed. At midnight I got up and removed the remains of the second blacky, and then slept peacefully till morning.

I was awakened by the strident voice of my father, who was calling to me from across the laboratory. I laughed to myself. There had been no one to call him and he had overslept. I could hear him as he approached my room with the intention of rousing me, and so I sat up in bed, the better to observe his translation—perhaps apotheosis were a better term. He paused a moment at the threshold, then took the fatal step. Puff! It was like the wind sighing among the pines. He was gone. His clothes fell in a fantastic heap on the floor. Besides ozone, I noticed the faint, garlic-like odor of phosphorus. A little pile of elementary solids lay among his garments. That was all. The wide world lay before me. My captors were not.

THE REJUVENATION
OF MAJOR RATHBONE

With his twentieth published short story, London was now on the threshold of fame. In two months his immortal "An Odyssey of the North" would be published in the *Atlantic Monthly;* in six months his first book, a collection of Klondike tales, *The Son of the Wolf*, would be issued by Houghton Mifflin.

"Alchemy was a magnificent dream, fascinating, impossible; but before it passed away there sprang from its loins a more marvelous child, none other than chemistry. More marvelous, because it substituted fact for fancy, and immensely widened man's realm of achievement. It has turned probability into possibility, and from the ideal it has fashioned the real. Do you follow me?"

Dover absently hunted for a match, at the same time regarding me with a heavy seriousness which instantly called to my mind Old Doc Frawley, our clinical lecturer of but a few years previous. I nodded assent, and he, having appropriately wreathed himself in smoke, went on with his discourse.

"Alchemy has taught us many things, while not a few of its visions have been realized by us in these latter days. The Elixir of Life was absurd, perpetual youth a rank negation of the very principle of life. But—"

Dover here paused with exasperating solemnity.

* * *

"But prolongation of life is too common an incident nowadays for any one to question. Not so very long ago, a 'generation' represented thirty-three years, the average duration of human existence. To-day, because of the rapid strides of medicine, sanitation, distribution, and so

Conkey's Home Journal, 6 (November, 1899):5-6, 29.

forth, a 'generation' is reckoned at thirty-four years. By the time of our great-grandchildren, it may have increased to forty years. *Quien sabe?* And again, we ourselves may see it actually doubled."

"Ah!" he cried, observing my start. "You see what I am driving at?"

"Yes," I replied. "But—"

"Never mind the 'buts,' " he burst in autocratically. "You ossified conservatives have always hung back at the coat-tails of science—"

"And as often saved it from breaking its neck," I retaliated.

"Just hold your horses a minute, and let me go on. What is life? Schopenhauer has defined it as the affirmation of the will to live, which is a philosophical absurdity, by the way, but with which we have no concern. Now, what is death? Simply the wearing out, the exhaustion, the breaking down, of the cells, tissues, nerves, bones and muscles of the human organism. Surgeons find great difficulty in knitting the broken bones of elderly people. Why? Because the bone, weakened, approaching the stage of dissolution, is no longer able to cast off the mineral deposits thrust in upon it by the natural functions of the body. And how easily such a bone is fractured! Yet, were it possible to remove the large deposits of phosphate, carbonate of soda, and so forth, the bone would regain the spring and rebound which it possessed in its youth.

"Merely apply this process, in varying measures, to the rest of the anatomy, and you have what? Simply the retardation of the system's break-up, the circumvention of old age, the banishment of senility, and the recapture of giddy youth. If science has prolonged the life of the generation by one year, is it not equally possible that it may prolong that of the individual by many?"

To turn back the dial of life, to reverse the hour-glass of Time and run its golden sands anew—the audacity of it fascinated me. What was to prevent? If one year, why not twenty? Forty?

Pshaw! I was just beginning to smile at my credulity when Dover pulled open the drawer beside him and brought to view a metal-stoppered vial. I confess to a sharp pang of disappointment as I gazed upon the very ordinary liquid it contained—a heavy, almost colorless fluid, with none of the brilliant iridescence one would so naturally expect of such a magic compound. He shook it lovingly, almost caressingly; but there was no manifestation of its occult properties. Then he pressed open a black leather case and nodded suggestively at the hypodermic syringe on its velvet bed. The Brown-Sequard Elixir and Koch's experiments with lymph darted across my mind. I smiled with cheery doubtfulness; but he, divining my thought, made haste to say, "No, they were on the right road, but missed it."

28

THE REJUVENATION OF MAJOR RATHBONE

* * *

He opened an inner door of the laboratory and called "Hector! Come, old fellow, come on!"

Hector was a superannuated Newfoundland who had for years been utterly worthless for anything save lying around in people's way, and in this he was an admirable success. Conceive my astonishment when a heavy, burly animal rushed in like a whirlwind and upset things generally, till finally quelled by his master. Dover looked eloquently at me, without speaking.

"But that—that isn't Hector!" I cried, doubting against doubt.

He turned up the under side of the animal's ear, and I saw two hard-lipped slits, mementoes of his wild young fighting days, when his master and I were mere lads ourselves. I remembered the wounds perfectly.

* * *

"Sixteen years old and as lively as a puppy." Dover beamed triumphantly. "I've been experimenting on him for two months. Nobody knows as yet, but won't they open their eyes when Hector runs abroad again! The plain matter of fact is I've given new lease of life with the lymph injection—same lymph as that used by earlier investigators, only they failed to clarify their compounds while I have succeeded. What is it? An animal derivative to stay and remove the effects of senility by acting upon the stagnated life-cells of any animal organism. Take the anatomical changes in Hector here, produced by infusion of the lymph compound; in the main they may be characterized as the expulsion from the bones of mineral deposits and an infiltration of the muscular tissues. Of course there are minor considerations; but these I have also overcome, not, however, without the unfortunate demise of several of my earlier animal subjects. I could not bring myself to work on Hector till failure had been eliminated from the problem. And now—"

He rose to his feet and paced excitedly up and down. It was some time before he took up his uncompleted thought.

"And now I am prepared to administer this rejuvenator to humans. And I propose, first of all, to work on one who is very dear to me—"

"Not—not—?" I quavered.

"Yes, Uncle Max. That's why I have called in your assistance. I have found discovery capping discovery, till now the process of rejuvenation has become so accelerated that I am afraid of myself. Besides, Uncle Max is so very old that the greatest discretion is necessary. Such crucial transformations in the whole organism of an age-weakened body can only be brought about by the most drastic methods, and there is great need to be careful.

29

As I have said, I have grown afraid of myself, and need another mind to hold me in check. Do you understand? Will you help me?"

* * *

I have introduced the above conversation with my friend, Dover Wallingford, to show by what means I was led into one of the strangest scientific experiences of my life. Of the utterly unheard-of-things that followed, the village has not yet ceased to talk upon and wonder. And as the village is unacquainted with the real facts in the case, it has been stirred to its profoundest depths by the untoward happenings. The excitement created was tremendous; three camp-meetings ran simultaneously and with marvelous success; there has been much talk of signs and portents, and not a few otherwise normal members of the community have proclaimed the advent of the latter-day miracles, and even yet their ears are patiently alert for the Trump of Doom and their eyes lifted that they may witness the rolling up of the heavens as a scroll. As for Major Rathbone, otherwise Dover's Uncle Max, why he is looked upon by a certain portion of the village as a second Lazarus raised from the dead, as one who has almost seen God; while another portion of the village is equally set in its belief that he has entered into a league with Lucifer, and that some day he will disappear in a whirlwind of brimstone and hell-fire.

But be this as it may, I shall here state the facts as they really are. It is not my intention, however, to go into the details of the case, except as to the results regarding Major Rathbone. Several contingencies have arisen, which must be seen to before we electrify the sleepy old world with the working formula of our wonderful discovery.

Then we shall convene a synod of the nations, and the rejuvenation of mankind will be placed in the hands of competent boards of experts belonging to the several governments. And we here promise that it shall be as free as the air we breathe or the water we drink. Further, in view of our purely altruistic motives, we ask that our present secrecy be respected and not be made the object of invidious reflections by the world we intend befriending.

* * *

Now to work. I at once sent for my traps and took up my residence in one of the suites adjoining Dover's laboratory. Major Rathbone, dazzled by the glittering promise of youth, yielded readily to our solicitations. To the world at large, he was lying sick unto death; but in reality he was waxing heartier and stronger with every day spent upon him. For three months we devoted ourselves to the task—a task fraught with constant danger, yet so absorbing that we hardly noted the flight of time. The color returned to the Major's pallid skin, the muscles filled out, and the wrinkles

30

in part disappeared. He had been no mean athlete in his younger days, and having no organic weaknesses, his strength returned to him in a most miraculous manner. The snap and energy he gathered were surprising, and lusty youth so rioted in his blood that toward the last we were often hard put to restrain him. We who had started out to resuscitate a feeble old man, found upon our hands an impetuous young giant. The remarkable part of it was that his snow-white hair and beard remained unchanged. Try as we would, it resisted every effort. Further, the irascibility which had come with advancing years still remained. And this, allied with the natural stubbornness and truculency of his disposition, became a grievous burden to us.

Sometime in the early part of April, because of a red-tape tangle at the express office regarding a shipment of chemicals, both Dover and myself were forced to be away. We had given Michel, Dover's trusted man, the necessary instructions, so did not apprehend any trouble. But on our return he met us rather shame-facedly at the entrance to the grounds.

"He's gone!" he gasped. "He's gone!" he repeated again and again, in his distress. His right arm hung limp and nerveless at his side, and it required no little patience to finally come to an understanding.

"I told him it was the orders that he mustn't go out. But he bellered like a wild bull, and wanted to know whose orders. And when I told him, he said it was time I should know that he took orders from no man. And when I stood in his way he took me by the arm, so, and just squeezed tight. I'm afraid it's broken, sir. And then he called Hector and went off across the fields to the village."

"Oh, your arm's all right," Dover assured him after due examination. "Just crushed the biceps a little, be kind of stiff and sore for a couple of days, that's all." And then to me, "Come on; we've got to find him."

It was a simple matter to follow him to the village. As we came down the main street, a crowd before the postoffice attracted our attention, and though we arrived at the climax, we could easily divine what had gone before. A bulldog, belonging to a trio of mill-hands, had picked a quarrel with Hector; and as it had been impossible to balance the second puppyhood of Hector with a new set of teeth, it was patent that he had been at a miserable disadvantage in the fight that followed. It was evident that Major Rathbone had intervened in an endeavor to separate the animals, and that the roughs had resented this. Besides, he was such a harmless-looking old gentleman, with his snow-white hair and patriarchal aspect, that they anticipated having a little fun with him.

* * *

"Aw, g'wan," we could hear one of the burly fellows saying, at the

31

same time shoving the Major back as though he were a little boy.

He protested courteously that the dog was his; but they chose to regard him as a joke and refused to listen. The crowd was composed of a low breed of men, anyway, and they jammed in so closely to see the sport that we had hard work in cleaving a passage.

"Now, nibsy," commanded the mill-hand who had shoved Major Rathbone back, "don't yer think you'd better chase yerself home to yer mammy? This ain't no manner o' place fer leetle boys like you."

The Major was a fighter from the word go. And just then he let go. Before one could count three it was over; a swing under the first ruffian's ear, a half-jolt on the point of the second one's chin, and a shrewd block, with fake swing and swift uppercut on the jugular of the third, stretched the three brutes in the muck of the street. The crowd drew back hastily before this ancient prodigy, and we could hear more than one fervently abjuring his eyes.

As he arose from drawing the dogs apart, there was a cheery twinkle in the Major's eye which disconcerted us. We had approached him in the attitude of keepers recovering a patient; but his thorough sanity and perfect composure took us aback.

"Say," he said jovially, "there's a little place just round the corner here—best old rye—a-hem!" And he winked significantly as we linked arms like comrades and passed out through the petrified crowd.

From this moment our control was at an end. He always had been a masterful man, and from now on, he proceeded to demonstrate how capable he was of taking care of himself. His mysterious rejuvenation became, but would not remain, a nine days' wonder, for it grew and grew from day to day. Morning after morning he could be seen tramping home for breakfast across the dewy fields, with a fair-filled game bag and Dover's shotgun. In previous years he had been a devoted horseman. One afternoon we returned from a trip to the city to find half the village hanging over the paddock fence. On closer inspection we discovered the Major breaking in one of the colts which had hitherto defied the stablemen. It was an edifying spectacle— his gray locks and venerable beard the sport of the wind as he dashed round and round on the maddened animal's back. But conquer the brute he did, till a stable boy led it away, trembling and as abject as a kitten. Another time, taking what had now become his customary afternoon ride, his indomitable spirit was fired by a party of well-mounted young fellows, and he let out with his big black stallion till he gave them his dust all the way down the principal street of the drowsy town.

* * *

In short, he took up the reins of life where he had dropped them years before. He was a fiery conservative as regards politics, and the peculiarly distasteful state of affairs then prevailing enticed him again into the arena. A crisis was approaching between the mill-owners and their workingmen, and a turbulent class of "agitators" had drifted into our midst. Not only did the Major oppose them openly, but he thrashed several of the more offensive leaders, nipped the strike in its incipiency, and in a most exciting campaign swept into the mayoralty. The closeness of the count but served to accentuate how bitter had been the struggle. And in the meantime he presided at indignant mass-meetings, and had the whole community shouting "Cuba Libre!" and almost ready to march to her deliverance.

In truth, he rioted about the country like a young Nimrod, and administered the affairs of the town with the wisdom of a Solon. He snorted like an old war-horse at opposition, and woe to them that ventured to stand up against him. Success only stimulated him to greater activity; but, while such activity would have been commendable in a younger man, in one of his advanced years it seemed so inconsistent and inappropriate that his friends and relatives were shocked beyond measure. Dover and I could but hold our hands in helplessness and watch the antics of our hoary marvel.

* * *

His fame, or as we chose to call it, his notoriety spread till there was talk in the district of running him for Congress in the coming elections. Sensational space-writers filled columns of Sunday editions with garbled accounts of his doings and of his tremendous vitality. These "yellow-journal" interviewers would have driven us to distraction with their insistent clamor, had not the Major himself taken the matter in hand. For awhile it was his custom to occasionally throw an odd one out of the house before breakfast, and invariably, when he returned home in the evening, to attend similarly to the wants of three or four. A pest of curiosity-mongers and learned professors descended upon our quiet neighborhood. Spectacled gentlemen, usually bald-headed and always urbane, came singly, in pairs, in committees and delegations to note the facts and phenomena of this most remarkable of cases. Mystic enthusiasts, long-haired and wild-eyed, and devotees of countless occult systems haunted our front and back doors, and trampled upon the flowers till the gardener threatened to throw up his position in despair. And I veritably believe a saving of ten per cent on the coal bill could have been compassed by the burning up of unsolicited correspondence.

And to cap the whole business, when the United States declared war

33

against Spain, Major Rathbone at once resigned his mayorship and applied to the war department for a commission. In view of his civil war record and his present superb health, it was highly probable that his request would be granted.

"It seems that before we can foist this rejuvenator upon the world, we must also discover an antidote for it—a sort of emasculator to reduce the friskiness attendant upon the return to youth, you know."

We had sat down, though in seemingly hopeless despondency, to discuss the difficulty and to try and find some way out of it.

"You see," Dover went on, "after revivifying an aged person, that person passes wholly out of our power. We can impose no checks, nor in any way can we tone down whatever excess of youthful spontaneity we may have induced. I see, now, that great care must be exercised in the administration of our lymph—the greatest of care if we should wish to avoid all manner of absurdities in the conduct of the patient. But that isn't the question at issue. What are we to do with Uncle Max? I confess, beyond gaining delay through the War Office, that I am at the end of my tether."

For the nonce Dover was so helpless that I felt not a little elation in unfolding the plan I had been considering for some time.

"You spoke of antidotes," I began tentatively.

"Now, as we happen to know, there are antidotes and antidotes, and yet again are there antidotes, some as a remedy for this evil and some for that. Should a babe drink a pint of kerosene, what antidote would you suggest?"

* * *

Dover shook his head.

"And since there is no antidote for such an emergency, do we assume that the babe must die? Not at all. We administer an emetic. But of course, an emetic is out of the question in the present case. But again, say for one suffering from uxoriousness, or for an hypochondriac, what remedy should be applied? Certainly, neither of the two I have mentioned will do. Now, for a man, melancholy-mad, what would you prescribe?"

"Change," he replied, instantly. "Something else to withdraw him from himself and his morbid brooding to give him new interest in life, to supply him with a reason for existence."

"Very good," I continued, jubilantly. "You will notice that you have prescribed an antidote, it is true, but instead of a physical or medicinal one, it is intangible and abstract. Now, can you give me a similar remedy for excessive spirits or strength?"

Dover looked puzzled and waited for me to go on.

34

"Do you remember a certain strong man of the name of Samson? also Delilah, the fair Philistine? Have you ever noted the significance of 'Beauty and the beast?' Do you not know that the strength of the strong has been wilted, dynasties been raised or demolished, and countless nations plunged into or rescued from civil strife, all because of the love of woman?"

"There's your antidote," I added modestly, as an afterthought.

"Oh!" His eyes flashed hopefully for an instant, but dismay returned as he shook his head sadly and said, "But the eligibles? There are none."

"Do you recollect a certain romance of the Major's when he was quite a young man, long before the war?"

"You mean Miss Deborah Furbush, your Aunt Debby?"

"Yes; my Aunt Debby. They quarreled, you know. and never made up—"

"Nor spoke to each other since—"

* * *

"O yes, they have. Ever since his rejuvenation he has called there regularly to pay his respects and ask for her health. Sort of gloats over her, you see. She's been bedridden a year now; have to carry her up and down stairs, and nothing the matter except simple old age."

"If she's strong enough," Dover hazarded.

"Strong enough!" I cried. "I tell you, man, it's genuine senility— nothing in the world to guard against but a very slight valvular weakness of the heart. What d'ye say? Get a couple of months' delay on his commission, and start in on Aunt Debby at once. What say, old man? What say?"

Not only had I grown excited over this solution of our difficulty, but I had at last aroused his enthusiasm. Appreciating the need for haste, we at once gutted the laboratory of all essentials and took up our abode at my home, which, in turn, was just over the way from Aunt Debby's.

By this time we had the whole operation at the ends of our fingers, so were able to proceed with the utmost dispatch. But we were very sly about it, and Major Rathbone had not the slightest idea of what we were up to. A week from the time we began, the Furbush household was startled by Aunt Debby's rising to give her hand to the Major when he made his usual call. A fortnight later, from a coign of vantage in my windmill, we saw them strolling about the garden, and noted a certain new gallantry in the Major's carriage. And the rapidity with which Aunt Debby breasted the tide of Time was dizzying. She grew visibly younger, day by day, and the roses of youth returned to her cheek, giving her the most beautiful pink and pearl complexion imaginable.

35

* * *

Perhaps ten days after that, he drove up to the door and took her out driving. And how the village talked! Which was nothing to the way it gabbled, when, a month later, the Major's interest in the war abated and he declined his commission. And when the superannuated lovers walked bravely to the altar and then went off on their honeymoon, it seemed that all tongues wagged till they could wag no more.

As I have said, this lymph is a wonderful discovery.

EVEN UNTO DEATH

Aside from his lazy dependence on coincidence (remember the chance meeting of father and son in "A Thousand Deaths"), this story serves as an example for another London quirk: the reuse of plots. "Even Unto Death" is an early version of the longer treatment of this "weird tale," published in 1908 as "Flush of Gold."

It might have been due to mere coincidence, it might have been because there are undreamed of bonds between the quick and the dead, and it might have been that Bat Morganston felt a blind consciousness of the future when he turned suddenly to Frona Payne and asked, "Even unto death?"

Frona Payne was startled for the moment. Her shallow nature would not permit her to understand the strength of a strong man's love; such things had no place in her fickle standard. Yet she knew men well enough to repress her inclination to smile; so she looked up to him with her serious child's eyes, placing a hand on each brawny shoulder, and answered, "Even unto death, Bat, dear."

And as he crushed her to him, half-doubting, he passionately cried, "If it should happen so, even in death I shall claim you, and no mortal man shall come between!"

"How absurd," she thought as she freed herself and watched him untangling his dogs. And a handsome fellow he was, as he waded among the fierce brutes, pulling here and shoving there, cuffing right and left and dragging them over and under the frozen traces till the team stood clear. Nipped by the intense cold to a tender pink, his smooth-shaven face told a plain tale of strength and indomitability. His hair, falling about his

The San Francisco Evening Post Magazine, July 28, 1900, 4-5.

37

shoulders in thick masses of silky brown, was probably more responsible for winning the woman's fleeting affections than all the rest of him put together. Yet when men ran their eyes up and down his six feet two of brawn, they declared him a man, from his beaded moccasins to the crown of his wolf-skin cap. But then, they were men.

She kissed him once, twice, and yet a third time, in her shy trusting way; then he broke out the sled with the gee-pole, "mushed-up" the dogs as only a dog-driver can, and swung down the hill to the main river trail. The meridian sun, shouldering over the snowy summits to the south, turned the tiny frost particles to scintillating gems, and through this dazzling gossamer Bat Morganston disappeared on his journey down the Yukon to Forty Mile. Down there he was accounted a king, in virtue of the rich dirt which was his after the dreary years he had spent in the darkness of the Arctic Circle. Dawson had no claims upon him. He did not own a foot of gravel in the district, nor was he smitten with its inhabitants—the che-cha-quas that had rushed in like jackals and spoiled the good old times when men were men and every man a brother. In fact, the only reason for his presence, and a most unstable one at that, was Frona. He had harnessed his dogs and run up on the ice to renew the pledges of the previous summer, and to plead for an early date. Well, they were to be married in June, and he was returning to the management of his mines with a light heart. June!—the clean-up promised to be rich; he would sell out; and then, the States, Paris, the world! Of course he doubted—most men do when they leave a pretty woman behind—; but ere he had reached Forty Mile he no longer mistrusted, and by the time he froze his lungs on a moose-hunt and died a month later, he had attained a state of blissful optimism.

Frona waved him good-bye, and also with a light heart turned back to her father's cabin; but then, she had no doubts at all. They were to be married in June. That was all settled. And it was no unpleasant prospect. To tell the truth, she thought she would rather like it. Men thought a great deal of him, and it was a match not to be ashamed of. Besides, he was rich. People who should know said he could at any time clean up half a million, and if his American Creek interests turned out anywhere near as reported, he would be a second MacDonald. Now this meant a great deal, for MacDonald was the richest miner in the North, and the most conservative guessers varied by several millions in the appraisement of his wealth.

Now be it known that the sin Frona Payne committed was a sin of deed, not fact. There were no mail-teams between Forty Mile and Dawson and as Bat Morganston's mines were still a hundred miles into the frozen wilderness from Forty Mile, no news of his death came up the river. And since he had agreed to write only on the highly improbable contingency of a stray traveler passing his diggings, she thought nothing of his silence. To all intents, so far as she was concerned, he was alive. So the sin she committed was of a verity a sin of deed.

By no method may a woman's soul be analyzed, by no scales may a woman's motive be weighed; so no reason can be given for Frona Payne giving her heart and hand to Jack Crelin within three months of her farewell to Bat Morganston. True, Jack Crelin was a Circle City king, possessed of some of the choicest Birch Creek claims; but the men who had made the country did not rate him highly, and his only admirers were to be found among the sycophantic tenderfeet who generously helped him scatter his yellow dust. Perhaps it was the way he had about him, and perhaps it was the impulsive affinity of two shallow souls; but be it what it may, they agreed to marry each other in June, and to journey on down to Circle City and set up housekeeping after the primitive manner of the Northland.

The Yukon broke early, and soon after that important event the river steamer *Cassiar*, captained by her brother, was scheduled to sail. The *Cassiar* had the mingled honor and misfortune to be both the treasure ship and the hospital ship of the year. In her strong boxes she carried five millions of gold, in her staterooms ten score of crippled and diseased. And there were also Lower Country traders and kings, returning from their winter labors or pleasures at Dawson. Among these—a little anticipation of the event—were listed Mr. and Mrs. Jack Crelin. But when the sick and heart-weary lifted their voices to heaven at the cruel delay, and the gold-shippers waxed clamorous, the *Cassiar* was forced to sail before her time, and Mr. and Mrs. Jack Crelin were yet man and maid.

"Never mind, Frona," her brother said; "come aboard and I'll take charge of you. Father Mahan takes passage at Forty Mile, and you'll be snugly one before we say good-bye at Circle City."

Plimsol marks, boiler inspectors, and protesting boards of under-writers, not yet having penetrated the dismal dominions of the North, the *Cassiar* cast off her lines, with passengers, freight and chattels packed like badly assorted sardines. Wolf-dogs, whose work began and ceased with the snow, and who grew high-stomached with summer idleness, rioted over the steamer from stem to stern or killed each other on the slightest provocation. Stalwart Stick Indians of the Upper River regions lightened their heavy money pouches in brave endeavors to best the white man at his games of chance, or outraged their vitals with the whisky he sold at thirty dollars the bottle. There were squat Mongolian featured Malemute and Innuit wanderers from the Great Dalta two thousand miles away; not among the whites was the jangle of nationalities less pronounced. The nations of the world had sent their sons to the North, and the tongues they spoke were many. In short, the brother of Frona Payne commanded a floating Babel, commanded and guided it unerringly through an uncharted wilderness upon the breast of a howling flood—for the mighty Yukon had raised its sullen voice and roared its anger from mountain rim to mountain rim. Nine months of snow was passing between its banks in as many days, and the journey to the sea was long.

At Forty Mile more passengers and freight were crowded aboard. Among the pilgrims was Father Mahan, and in the baggage was an unpainted pine box, corresponding in size to the conventional last tenement of man. The rush of life has little heed for death, so this box was piled precariously upon a pyramid of freight on the *Cassiar*'s deck. But Bat Morganston, having lain till the moment of shipment in a comfortable ice-cave, did not care. Nobody cared. There were no mourners, save a huge wolf-dog, to whom the taste of his master's lash was still sweet. He crept aboard unnoticed, and ere the lines were cast off had taken up his accustomed vigil on the heap of freight by his master's side. He was such a vicious brute, and had such a fearful way of baring his fangs, that the other canine passengers gave him a wide berth, choosing to leave him alone with his dead.

The cabins were crowded with the sick, so the marriage began on the stifling deck. It was near midnight, but the sun, red-disked and somber, slanted its oblique rays from just above the northern sky line. Frona Payne and Jack Crelin stood side by side. Father Mahan began the service. From aft came the sound of scuffling among half a dozen drunken gamblers; but in the main the human cargo had crowded about the center of interest. And also the dogs.

Still, all would have been well had not a Labrador dog sought a coign of vantage among the freight. He had traveled countless journeys, was a veteran of a dozen famines and a thousand fights, and knew not fear. The truculent front of the dog which guarded the pine box interested him. He drew in, his naked fangs shining like jeweled ivory. They closed with snap and snarl, the carelessly piled freight tottering beneath them.

At this moment Father Mahan blessed the two which were now one, and Jack Crelin solemnly added, "Even unto death."

"Even unto death," Frona Payne repeated, and her mind leaped back to the other man who had spoken those words. For the instant she felt genuine sorrow and remorse for what she had done. And 'at that instant the two dogs shut their jaws in the death-grip, and the long pine box poised on the edge of its pyramid. Her husband jerked her from

40

beneath as it fell, end on. There was a crash and splintering; the cover fell away, and Bat Morganston, on his feet, erect, just as in life, with the sun glinting on his silky brown locks, swept forward.

It happened very quickly. Some say that his lips parted in a fearful smile, that he flung his arms about Frona Payne and held her till they fell together to the deck. This would seem impossible, seeing that the man was dead; but there are those who swear that these things were done. However, Frona Payne shrieked terribly as they drew her from beneath the body of her jilted lover, nor did her shrieking cease till land was made at Circle City.

And Bat Morganston's words were true, for to-day, if one should care to journey over to the hills which lie beyond Circle City, he will see, side by side, a cabin and a grave. In the one dwells Frona Payne; in the other Bat Morganston. They are waiting for each other till their fetters shall fall away and the Trump of Doom breaks the silence of the North.

A RELIC OF THE PLIOCENE

The origin of this story may have been a tall tale spun to London by one Peter "French Pete" de Ville, an ex-sourdough whom London met in San Francisco. According to Franklin Walker (in *Jack London and the Klondike*), de Ville was selling produce on Pacific Street when interviewed by London, then writing feature stories for the *San Francisco Examiner*. De Ville claimed to have spent thirty years wandering in the Far North and to have seen, among other things, fifty-foot bats, mastodons, and white men who were probably descendants of the lost Franklin expedition.

It appears that London based Thomas Stevens in "A Relic of the Pliocene" on a real-life Stevens whom he met in the Klondike in 1897, and on "French Pete" de Ville. (Stevens also appears in one other London tale—a nonfantasy titled "A Hyperborean Brew," published in 1901.)

In any case, London had some idea of a series of "tall tale" adventures in the North and left some notes to that effect. As it turned out, however, this story and some of the plotting in tales of the *Smoke Bellew* (1912) collection, were all London made from the idea.

I wash my hands of him at the start. I cannot father his tales, nor will I be responsible for them. I make these preliminary reservations, observe, as a guard upon my own integrity. I possess a certain definite position in a small way, also a wife; and for the good name of the community that honors my existence with its approval, and for the sake of her posterity and mine, I cannot take the chances I once did, nor foster probabilities with the careless improvidence of youth. So, I repeat, I wash my hands of him, this Nimrod, this mighty hunter, this homely, blue-eyed, freckle-faced Thomas Stevens.

Having been honest to myself, and to whatever prospective olive

Collier's Weekly, 26 (January 12, 1901):17, 20.

branches my wife may be pleased to tender me, I can now afford to be generous. I shall not criticize the tales told me by Thomas Stevens, and, further, I shall withhold my judgment. If it be asked why, I can only add that judgment I have none. Long have I pondered, weighed, and balanced, but never have my conclusions been twice the same—forsooth! because Thomas Stevens is a greater man than I. If he have told truths, well and good; if untruths, still well and good. For who can prove? or who disprove? I eliminate myself from the proposition, while those of little faith may do as I have done—go find the said Thomas Stevens, and discuss to his face the various matters which, if fortune serve, I shall relate. As to where he may be found? The directions are simple: anywhere between 53 north latitude and the Pole, on the one hand; and, on the other, the likeliest hunting grounds that lie between the east coast of Siberia and farthermost Labrador. That he is there, somewhere, within that clearly defined territory, I pledge the word of an honorable man whose expectations entail straight speaking and right living.

Thomas Stevens may have toyed prodigiously with truth, but when we first met (it were well to mark this point), he wandered into my camp when I thought myself a thousand miles beyond the outermost post of civilization. At the sight of his human face, the first in weary months, I could have sprung forward and folded him in my arms (and I am not by any means a demonstrative man); but to him his visit seemed the most casual thing under the sun. He just strolled into the light of my camp, passed the time of day after the custom of men on beaten trails, threw my snowshoes the one way and a couple of dogs the other, and so made room for himself by the fire. Said he'd just dropped in to borrow a pinch of soda and to see if I had any decent tobacco. He plucked forth an ancient pipe, loaded it with painstaking care, and, without as much as by your leave, whacked half the tobacco of my pouch into his. Yes, the stuff was fairly good. He sighed with the contentment of the just, and literally absorbed the smoke from the crisping yellow flakes, and it did my smoker's heart good to behold him.

Hunter? Trapper? Prospector? He shrugged his shoulders No; just sort of knocking round a bit. Had come up from the Great Slave some time since, and was thinking of traipsing over into the Yukon country. The Factor of Koshim had spoken about the discoveries on the Klondike, and he was of a mind to run over for a peep. I noticed that he spoke of the Klondike in the archaic vernacular, calling it the Reindeer River—a conceited custom that the Old Timers employ against the *che-cha-quas* and all tenderfeet in general. But he did it so naïvely and as such a matter of course, that there was no sting, and I forgave him. He also had it in view, he said, before he crossed the divide into the Yukon, to make a little run up Fort o' Good Hope way.

Now Fort o' Good Hope is a far journey to the north, over and beyond the Circle, in a place where the feet of few men have trod; and when a nondescript ragamuffin comes in out of the night, from nowhere in particular, to sit by one's fire and discourse on such in terms of "traipsing" and "a little run," it is fair time to rouse up and shake off the dream. Wherefore I looked about me; saw the fly, and, underneath, the pine boughs spread for the sleeping furs; saw the grub sacks, the camera, the frosty breaths of the dogs circling on the edge of the light; and, above, a great streamer of the aurora bridging the zenith from southeast to northwest. I shivered. There is a magic in the Northland night, that steals in on one like fevers from malarial marshes. You are clutched and downed before you are aware. Then I looked to the snowshoes, lying prone and crossed where he had flung them. Also I had an eye to my tobacco pouch. Half, at least, of its goodly store had vamoosed. That settled it. Fancy had not tricked me after all.

Crazed with suffering, I thought, looking steadfastly at the man—one of those wild stampeders, strayed far from his bearings and wandering like a lost soul through great vastnesses and unknown deeps. Oh, well, let his moods slip on, until, mayhap, he gathers his tangled wits together. Who knows?—the mere sound of a fellow-creature's voice may bring all straight again.

So I led him on in talk, and soon I marvelled, for he talked of game and the ways thereof. He had killed the Siberian wolf of westernmost Alaska, and the chamois in the secret Rockies. He averred he knew the haunts where the last buffalo still roamed; that he had hung on the flanks of the caribou when they ran by the hundred thousand, and slept in the Great Barrens on the musk-ox's winter trail.

And I shifted my judgment accordingly (the first revision, but by no account the last), and deemed him a monumental effigy of truth. Why it was I know not, but the spirit moved me to repeat a tale told to me by a man who had dwelt in the land too long to know better. It was of the great bear that hugs the steep slopes of St. Elias, never descending to the levels of the gentler inclines. Now God so constituted this creature for its hillside habitat that the legs of one side are all of a foot longer than those of the other. This is mighty convenient, as will be readily admitted. So I hunted this rare beast in my own name, told it in the first person, present tense, painted the requisite locale, gave it the necessary garnishings and touches of verisimilitude, and looked to see the man stunned by the recital.

44

Not he. Had he doubted, I could have forgiven him. Had he objected, denying the dangers of such a hunt by virtue of the animal's inability to turn about and go the other way—had he done this, I say, I could have taken him by the hand for the true sportsman that he was. Not he. He sniffed, looked on me, and sniffed again; then gave my tobacco due praise, thrust one foot into my lap, and bade me examine the gear. It was a *mucluc* of the Innuit pattern, sewed together with sinew threads, and devoid of beads or furbelows. But it was the skin itself that was remarkable. In that it was all of half an inch thick, it reminded me of walrus-hide; but there the resemblance ceased, for no walrus ever bore so marvellous a growth of hair. On the side and ankles this hair was well-nigh worn away, what of friction with underbrush and snow; but around the top and down the more sheltered back it was coarse, dirty black, and very thick. I parted it with difficulty and looked beneath for the fine fur that is common with northern animals, but found it in this case to be absent. This, however, was compensated for by the length. Indeed, the tufts that had survived wear and tear measured all of seven or eight inches.

I looked up into the man's face, and he pulled his foot down and asked, "Find hide like that on your St. Elias bear?"

I shook my head. "Nor on any other creature of land or sea," I answered candidly. The thickness of it, and the length of the hair, puzzled me.

"That," he said, and said without the slightest hint of impressiveness, "that came from a mammoth."

"Nonsense!" I exclaimed, for I could not forbear the protest of my unbelief. "The mammoth, my dear sir, long ago vanished from the earth. We know it once existed by the fossil remains that we have unearthed, and by a frozen carcass that the Siberian sun saw fit to melt from out the bosom of a glacier; but we also know that no living specimen exists. Our explorers—"

At this word he broke in impatiently. "Your explorers? Pish! A weakly breed. Let us hear no more of them. But tell me, O man, what you may know of the mammoth and his ways."

Beyond contradiction, this was leading to a yarn; so I baited my hook by ransacking my memory for whatever data I possessed on the subject in hand. To begin with, I emphasized that the animal was prehistoric, and marshalled all my facts in support of this. I mentioned the Siberian sand bars that abounded with ancient mammoth bones; spoke of the large quantities of fossil ivory purchased from the Innuits by the Alaska Commercial Company; and acknowledged having myself mined six-and eight-foot tusks from the pay gravel of the Klondike creeks. "All

45

fossils," I concluded, "found in the midst of debris deposited through countless ages."

"I remember when I was a kid," Thomas Stevens sniffed (he had a most confounded way of sniffing), "that I saw a petrified watermelon. Hence, though mistaken persons sometimes delude themselves into thinking that they are really raising or eating them, there are no such things as extant watermelons."

"But the question of food," I objected, ignoring his point, which was puerile and without bearing. "The soil must bring forth vegetable life in lavish abundance to support so monstrous creations. Nowhere in the North is the soil so prolific. Ergo, the mammoth cannot exist."

"I pardon your ignorance concerning many matters of this Northland, for you are a young man and have travelled little; but, at the same time, I am inclined to agree with you on one thing. The mammoth no longer exists. How do I know? I killed the last one with my own right arm."

Thus spake Nimrod, the Mighty Hunter. I threw a stick of firewood at the dogs and bade them quit their unholy howling, and waited. Undoubtedly this liar of singular felicity would open his mouth and requite me for my St. Elias bear.

"It was this way," he at last began, after the appropriate silence had intervened. "I was in camp one day—"

"Where?" I interrupted.

He waved his hand vaguely in the direction of the northeast, where stretched a terra incognita into which vastness few men have strayed and fewer emerged. "I was in camp one day with Klooch. Klooch was as handsome a little *kamooks* as ever whined betwixt the traces or shoved nose into a camp kettle. Her father was a full-blood Malemute from Russian Pastilik on Bering Sea, and I bred her, and with understanding, out of a clean-legged bitch of the Hudson Bay stock. I tell you, O man, she was a corker combination. And now, on this day I have in mind, she was brought to pup through a pure wild wolf of the woods—gray, and long of limb, with big lungs and no end of staying powers. Say! Was there ever the like? It was a new breed of dog I had started, and I could look forward to big things.

"As I have said, she was brought neatly to pup, and safely delivered. I was squatting on my hams over the litter—seven sturdy, blind little beggars—when from behind came a bray of trumpets and crash of brass. There was a rush, like the wind-squall that kicks the heels of the rain, and I was midway to my feet when knocked flat on my face. At the same instant I heard Klooch sigh, very much as a man does when you've planted your fist in his belly. You can stake your sack I lay quiet, but I twisted my

46

head around and saw a huge bulk swaying above me. Then the blue sky flashed into view and I got to my feet. A hairy mountain of flesh was just disappearing in the underbrush on the edge of the open. I caught a rear-end glimpse, with a stiff tail, as big in girth as my body, standing out straight behind. The next second only a trememdous hole remained in the thicket, though I could still hear the sounds as of a tornado dying quickly away, underbrush ripping and tearing, and trees snapping and crashing.

"I cast about for my rifle. It had been lying on the ground with the muzzle against a log; but now the stock was smashed, the barrel out of line, and the working-gear in a thousand bits. Then I looked for the slut, and—and what do you suppose?"

I shook my head.

"May my soul burn in a thousand hells if there was anything left of her! Klooch, the seven sturdy, blind little beggars—gone, all gone. Where she had stretched was a slimy, bloody depression in the soft earth, all of a yard in diameter, and around the edges a few scattered hairs."

I measured three feet on the snow, threw about it a circle, and glanced at Nimrod.

"The beast was thirty long and twenty high," he answered, " and its tusks scaled over six times three feet. I couldn't believe, myself, at the time, for all that it had just happened. But if my senses had played me, there was the broken gun and the hole in the brush. And there was—or, rather, there was not—Klooch and the pups. O man, it makes me hot all over now when I think of it. Klooch! Another Eve! The mother of a new race! And a rampaging, ranting, old bull mammoth, like a second flood, wiping them, root and branch, off the face of the earth! Do you wonder that the blood-soaked earth cried out to high God? Or that I grabbed the hand-axe and took the trail?"

"The hand-axe?" I exclaimed, startled out of myself by the picture. "The hand-axe, and a big bull mammoth, thirty feet long, twenty feet—"

Nimrod joined me in my merriment, chuckling gleefully. "Wouldn't it kill you?" he cried. "Wasn't it a beaver's dream? Many's the time I've laughed about it since, but at the time it was no laughing matter, I was that danged mad, what of the gun and Klooch. Think of it, O man! A brand-new, unclassified, uncopyrighted breed, and wiped out before ever it opened its eyes or took out its intention papers! Well, so be it. Life's full of disappointments, and rightly so. Meat is best after a famine, and a bed soft after a hard trail.

"As I was saying, I took out after the beast with the hand-axe, and hung to its heels down the valley; but when he circled back toward the head, I was left winded at the lower end. Speaking of grub, I might as well stop long enough to explain a couple of points. Up thereabouts, in the midst of the mountains, is an almighty curious formation. There is no end of little valleys, each like the other much as peas in a pod, and all neatly tucked away with straight, rocky walls rising on all sides. And at the lower ends are always small openings where the drainage or glaciers must have broken out. The only way in is through these mouths, and they are all small, and some smaller than others. As to grub—you've slushed around on the rain-soaked islands of the Alaskan coast down Sitka way, most likely, seeing as you're a traveller. And you know how stuff grows there—big, and juicy, and jungly. Well, that's the way it was with those valleys. Thick, rich soil, with ferns and grasses and such things in patches higher than your head. Rain three days out of four during the summer months; and food in them for a thousand mammoths, to say nothing of small game for man.

"But to get back. Down at the lower end of the valley I got winded and gave over. I began to speculate, for when my wind left me my dander got hotter and hotter, and I knew I'd never know peace of mind till I dined on roasted mammoth-foot. And I knew, also, that that stood for *skookum mamook puka-puk*—excuse Chinook, I mean there was a big fight coming. Now the mouth of my valley was very narrow, and the walls steep. High up on one side was one of those big pivot rocks, or balancing rocks, as some call them, weighing all of a couple of hundred tons. Just the thing. I hit back for camp, keeping an eye open so the bull couldn't slip past, and got my ammunition. It wasn't worth anything with the rifle smashed; so I opened the shells, planted the powder under the rock, and touched it off with slow fuse. Wasn't much of a charge, but the old boulder tilted up lazily and dropped down into place, with just space enough to let the creek drain nicely. Now I had him."

"But how did you have him?" I queried. "Who ever heard of a man killing a mammoth with a hand-axe? And, for that matter, with anything else?"

"O man, have I not told you I was mad?" Nimrod replied, with a slight manifestation of sensitiveness. "Mad clean through, what of Klooch and the gun? Also, was I not a hunter? And was this not new and most unusual game? A hand-axe? Pish! I did not need it. Listen, and you shall hear of a hunt, such as might have happened in the youth of the world when caveman rounded up the kill with hand-axe of stone. Such would have served me as well. Now is it not a fact that man can outwalk the dog or horse? That he can wear them out with the intelligence of his endurance?"

I nodded.

"Well?"

48

The light broke in on me, and I bade him continue.

"My valley was perhaps five miles around. The mouth was closed. There was no way to get out. A timid beast was that bull mammoth, and I had him at my mercy. I got on his heels again, hollered like a fiend, pelted him with cobbles, and raced him around the valley three times before I knocked off for supper. Don't you see? A race-course! A man and a mammoth! A hippodrome, with sun, moon, and stars to referee!

"It took me two months to do it, but I did it. And that's no beaver dream. Round and round I ran him, me travelling on the inner circle, eating jerked meat and salmon berries on the run, and snatching winks of sleep between. Of course, he'd get desperate at times and turn. Then I'd head for soft ground where the creek spread out, and lay anathema upon him and his ancestry, and dare him to come on. But he was too wise to bog in a mud puddle. Once he pinned me in against the walls, and I crawled back into a deep crevice and waited. Whenever he felt for me with his trunk, I'd belt him with the hand-axe till he pulled out, shrieking fit to split my ear drums, he was that mad. He knew he had me and didn't have me, and it near drove him wild. But he was no man's fool. He knew he was safe as long as I stayed in the crevice, and he made up his mind to keep me there. And he was dead right, only he hadn't figured on the commissary. There was neither grub nor water around that spot, so on the face of it he couldn't keep up the siege. He'd stand before the opening for hours, keeping an eye on me and flapping mosquitoes away with his big blanket ears. Then the thirst would come on him and he'd ramp round and roar till the earth shook, calling me every name he could lay tongue to. This was to frighten me, of course; and when he thought I was sufficiently impressed, he'd back away softly and try to make a sneak for the creek. Sometimes I'd let him get almost there—only a couple of hundred yards away it was—when out I'd pop and back he'd come, lumbering along like the old landslide he was. After I'd done this a few times, and he'd figured it out, he changed his tactics. Grasped the time element, you see. Without a word of warning, away he'd go, tearing for the water like mad, scheming to get there and back before I ran away. Finally, after cursing me most horribly, he raised the siege and deliberately stalked off to the water hole.

"That was the only time he penned me,—three days of it,—but after that the hippodrome never stopped. Round, and round, and round, like a six days' go-as-I-please, for he never pleased. My clothes went to rags and tatters, but I never stopped to mend, till at last I ran naked as a son of earth, with nothing but the old hand-axe in one hand and a cobble in the other. In fact, I never stopped, save for peeps of sleep in the crannies and ledges of the cliffs. As for the bull, he got perceptibly thinner and thinner—must have lost several tons at least—and as nervous as a schoolmarm on the wrong side of matrimony. When I'd come up with him and yell, or lam him with a rock at long range, he'd jump like a skittish colt and tremble all over. Then he'd pull out on the run, tail and trunk waving stiff, head over one shoulder and wicked eyes blazing, and the way he'd swear at me was something dreadful. A most immoral beast he was, a murderer, and a blasphemer.

"But toward the end he quit all this, and fell to whimpering and crying like a baby. His spirit broke and he became a quivering jelly-mountain of misery. He'd get attacks of palpitation of the heart, and stagger around like a drunken man, and fall down and bark his shins. And then he'd cry, but always on the run. O man, the gods themselves would have wept with him, and you yourself or any other man. It was pitiful, and there was so much of it, but I only hardened my heart and hit up the pace. At last I wore him clean out, and he lay down, broken-winded, broken-hearted, hungry, and thirsty. When I found he wouldn't budge, I hamstrung him, and spent the better part of the day wading into him with the hand-axe, he a sniffing and sobbing till I worked in far enough to shut him off. Thirty feet long he was, and twenty high, and a man could sling a hammock between his tusks and sleep comfortably. Barring the fact that I had run most of the juices out of him, he was fair eating, and his four feet, alone, roasted whole, would have lasted a man a twelvemonth. I spent the winter there myself."

"And where is this valley?" I asked.

He waved his hand in the direction of the northeast, and said: "Your tobacco is very good. I carry a fair share of it in my pouch, but I shall carry the recollection of it until I die. In token of my appreciation, and in return for the moccasins on your own feet, I will present to you these *muclucs*. They commemorate Klooch and the seven blind little beggars. They are also souvenirs of an unparalleled event in history, namely, the destruction of the oldest breed of animal on earth, and the youngest. And their chief virtue lies in that they will never wear out."

Having effected the exchange, he knocked the ashes from his pipe, gripped my hand good night, and wandered off through the snow. Concerning this tale, for which I have already disclaimed responsibility, I would recommend those of little faith to make a visit to the

50

Smithsonian Institute. If they bring the requisite credentials and do not come in vacation time, they will undoubtedly gain an audience with Professor Dolvidson. The *muclucs* are in his possession, and he will verify, not the manner in which they were obtained, but the material of which they are composed. When he states that they are made from the skin of the mammoth, the scientific world accepts his verdict. What more would you have?

THE SHADOW AND THE FLASH

In the literature of fantasy, H. G. Wells's *The Invisible Man* (1897) is probably the most famous treatment of invisibility. London's story (perhaps inspired by Wells's novel) is markedly different and, some science fiction experts believe, superior to its probable progenitor.

While Wells concerns himself with his invisible man's reign of terror, London is more taken with the problems of *being* invisible and the "theories" of invisibility—i.e., that anything pure black and anything purely crystalline would be invisible to the human eye.

One modern London critic, Charles Walcutt, in his provocative monograph *Jack London* (University of Minnesota Press, 1966), cites this kind of story as an example that London "... increasingly moved too far away from the representative concerns of man into the realms of fantasy." But far from injuring his reputation, London's fantasies were generally of high quality, and this tale is very good indeed.

When I look back, I realize what a peculiar friendship it was. First, there was Lloyd Inwood, tall, slender, and finely knit, nervous and dark. And then Paul Tichlorne, tall, slender, and finely knit, nervous and blond. Each was the replica of the other in everything except color. Lloyd's eyes were black; Paul's were blue. Under stress of excitement, the blood coursed olive in the face of Lloyd, crimson in the face of Paul. But outside this matter of coloring they were as like as two peas. Both were high-strung, prone to excessive tension and endurance, and they lived at concert pitch.

But there was a trio involved in this remarkable friendship, and the third was short, and fat, and chunky, and lazy, and, loath to say, it was I. Paul and Lloyd seemed born to rivalry with each other, and I to be peacemaker between them. We grew up together, the three of us, and full often have I received the angry blows each intended for the other. They were always competing, striving to outdo each other, and when entered upon some such struggle there was no limit either to their endeavors or passions.

This intense spirit of rivalry obtained in their studies and their games. If Paul memorized one canto of *Marmion,* Lloyd memorized two cantos, Paul came back with three, and Lloyd again with four, till each knew the whole poem by heart. I remember an incident that occurred at the swimming hole—an incident tragically significant of the life-struggle between them. The boys had a game of diving to the bottom of a ten-foot pool and holding on by submerged roots to see who could stay under the longest. Paul and Lloyd allowed themselves to be bantered into making the descent together. When I saw their faces, set and determined, disappear in the water as they sank swiftly down, I felt a foreboding of something dreadful. The moments sped, the ripples died away, the face of the pool grew placid and untroubled, and neither black nor golden head broke surface in quest of air. We above grew anxious. The longest record of the longest-winded boy had been exceeded, and still there was no sign. Air bubbles trickled slowly upward, showing that the breath had been expelled from their lungs, and after that the bubbles ceased to trickle upward. Each second became interminable, and, unable longer to endure the suspense, I plunged into the water.

I found them down at the bottom, clutching tight to the roots, their heads not a foot apart, their eyes wide open, each glaring fixedly at the other. They were suffering frightful torment, writhing and twisting in the pangs of voluntary suffocation; for neither would let go and acknowledge himself beaten. I tried to break Paul's hold on the root, but he resisted me fiercely. Then I lost my breath and came to the surface, badly scared. I quickly explained the situation, and half a dozen of us went down and by main strength tore them loose. By the time we got them out, both were unconscious, and it was only after much barrel-rolling and rubbing and pounding that they finally came to their senses. They would have drowned there, had no one rescued them.

When Paul Tichlorne entered college, he let it be generally understood that he was going in for the social sciences. Lloyd Inwood, entering at the same time, elected to take the same course. But Paul had had it secretly in mind all the time to study the natural sciences, specializing on chemistry, and at the last moment he switched over. Though Lloyd had already arranged his year's work and attended the first lectures, he at once followed Paul's lead and went in for the natural sciences and especially for chemistry. Their rivalry soon became a noted thing throughout the university. Each was a spur to the other, and they went into chemistry deeper than did ever students before—so deep, in fact, that ere they took their sheepskins they could have stumped any chemistry or "cow college" professor in the institution, save "old" Moss, head of the department, and even him they puzzled and edified more than once. Lloyd's discovery of the "death bacillus" of the sea toad, and his experiments on it with potassium cyanide, sent his name and that of his university ringing round the world; nor was Paul a whit behind when he succeeded in producing laboratory colloids exhibiting amoeba-like activities, and when he cast new light upon the processes of fertilization through his startling experiments with simple sodium chlorides and magnesium solutions on low forms of marine life.

It was in their undergraduate days, however, in the midst of their profoundest plunges into the mysteries of organic chemistry, that Doris Van Benschoten entered into their lives. Lloyd met her first, but within twenty-four hours Paul saw to it that he also made her acquaintance. Of course, they fell in love with her, and she became the only thing in life worth living for. They wooed her with equal ardor and fire, and so intense became their struggle for her that half the student-body took to wagering wildly on the result. Even "old" Moss, one day, after an astounding demonstration in his private laboratory by Paul, was guilty to the extent of a month's salary of backing him to become the bridegroom of Doris Van Benschoten.

In the end she solved the problem in her own way, to everybody's satisfaction except Paul's and Lloyd's. Getting them together, she said that she really could not choose between them because she loved them both equally well; and that, unfortunately, since polyandry was not permitted in the United States she would be compelled to forgo the honor and happiness of marrying either of them. Each blamed the other for this lamentable outcome, and the bitterness between them grew more bitter.

But things came to a head soon enough. It was at my home, after they had taken their degrees and dropped out of the world's sight, that the beginning of the end came to pass. Both were men of means, with little inclination and no necessity for professional life. My friendship and their mutual animosity were the two things that linked them in any way together. While they were very often at my place, they made it a fastidious point to avoid each other on such visits, though it was inevitable, under the circumstances, that they should come upon each other occasionally.

On the day I have in recollection, Paul Tichlorne had been mooning all morning in my study over a current scientific review. This left me free to my own affairs, and I was out among my roses when Lloyd Inwood

54

arrived. Clipping and pruning and tacking the climbers on the porch, with my mouth full of nails, and Lloyd following me about and lending a hand now and again, we fell to discussing the mythical race of invisible people, that strange and vagrant people the traditions of which have come down to us. Lloyd warmed to the talk in his nervous, jerky fashion, and was soon interrogating the physical properties and possibilities of invisibility. A perfectly black object, he contended, would elude and defy the acutest vision.

"Color is a sensation," he was saying. "It has no objective reality. Without light, we can see neither colors nor objects themselves. All objects are black in the dark, and in the dark it is impossible to see them. If no light strikes upon them, then no light is flung back from them to the eye, and so we have no vision-evidence of their being."

"But we see black objects in daylight," I objected.

"Very true," he went on warmly. "And that is because they are not perfectly black. Were they perfectly black, absolutely black, as it were, we could not see them—ay, not in the blaze of a thousand suns could we see them! And so I say, with the right pigments, properly compounded, an absolutely black paint could be produced which would render invisible whatever it was applied to."

"It would be a remarkable discovery," I said non-committally, for the whole thing seemed too fantastic for aught but speculative purposes.

"Remarkable!" Lloyd slapped me on the shoulder. "I should say so. Why, old chap, to coat myself with such a paint would be to put the world at my feet. The secrets of kings and courts would be mine, the machinations of diplomats and politicians, the play of stock-gamblers, the plans of.trusts and corporations. I could keep my hand on the inner pulse of things and become the greatest power in the world. And I " He broke off shortly, then added, "Well, I have begun my experiments, and I don't mind telling you that I'm right in line for it."

A laugh from the doorway startled us. Paul Tichlorne was standing there, a smile of mockery on his lips.

"You forget, my dear Lloyd," he said.

"Forget what?"

"You forget," Paul went on—"ah, you forget the shadow."

I saw Lloyd's face drop, but he answered sneeringly, "I can carry a sunshade, you know." Then he turned suddenly and fiercely upon him. "Look here, Paul, you'll keep out of this if you know what's good for you."

A rupture seemed imminent, but Paul laughed good-naturedly. "I wouldn't lay fingers on your dirty pigments. Succeed beyond your most sanguine expectations, yet you will always fetch up against the shadow. You can't get away from it. Now I shall go on the very opposite tack. In the very nature of my proposition the shadow will be eliminated—"

"Transparency!" ejaculated Lloyd, instantly. "But it can't be achieved."

"Oh, no; of course not." And Paul shrugged his shoulders and strolled off down the brier-rose path.

This was the beginning of it. Both men attacked the problem with all the tremendous energy for which they were noted, and with a rancor and bitterness that made me tremble for the success of either. Each trusted me to the utmost, and in the long weeks of experimentation that followed I was made a party to both sides, listening to their theorizings and witnessing their demonstrations. Never, by word or sign, did I convey to either the slightest hint of the other's progress, and they respected me for the seal I put upon my lips.

Lloyd Inwood, after prolonged and unintermittent application, when the tension upon his mind and body became too great to bear, had a strange way of obtaining relief. He attended prize fights. It was at one of these brutal exhibitions, whither he had dragged me in order to tell his latest results, that his theory received striking confirmation.

"Do you see that red-whiskered man?" he asked, pointing across the ring to the fifth tier of seats on the opposite side. "And do you see the next man to him the one in the white hat? Well, there is quite a gap between them, is there not?"

"Certainly," I answered. "They are a seat apart. The gap is the unoccupied seat."

He leaned over to me and spoke seriously. "Between the red-whiskered man and the white-hatted man sits Ben Wasson. You have heard me speak of him. He is the cleverest pugilist of his weight in the country. He is also a Caribbean negro, full-blooded, and the blackest in the United States. He has on a black overcoat buttoned up. I saw him when he came in and took that seat. As soon as he sat down he disappeared. Watch closely; he may smile."

I was for crossing over to verify Lloyd's statement, but he restrained me. "Wait," he said.

I waited and watched, till the red-whiskered man turned his head as though addressing the unoccupied seat; and then, in that empty space, I saw the rolling whites of a pair of eyes and the white double-crescent of two rows of teeth, and for the instant I could make out a negro's face. But with the passing of the smile his visibility passed, and the chair seemed vacant as before.

"Were he perfectly black, you could sit alongside him and not see him," Lloyd said; and I confess the illustration was apt enough to make me well-nigh convinced.

I visited Lloyd's laboratory a number of times after that, and found him always deep in his search after the absolute black. His experiments covered all sorts of pigments, such as lamp-blacks, tars, carbonized vegetable matters, soots of oils and fats, and the various carbonized animal substances.

"White light is composed of the seven primary colors," he argued to me. "But it is itself, of itself, invisible. Only by being reflected from objects do it and the objects become visible. But only that portion of it that is reflected becomes visible. For instance, here is a blue tobacco-box. The white light strikes against it, and, with one exception, all its component colors—violet, indigo, green, yellow, orange, and red—are absorbed. The one exception is *blue*. It is not absorbed, but reflected. Wherefore the tobacco-box gives us a sensation of blueness. We do not see the other colors because they are absorbed. We see only the blue. For the same reason grass is *green*. The green waves of white light are thrown upon our eyes."

"When we paint our houses, we do not apply color to them," he said at another time. "What we do is to apply certain substances that have the property of absorbing from white light all the colors except those that we would have our houses appear. When a substance reflects all the colors to the eye, it seems to us white. When it absorbs all the colors, it is black. But, as I said before, we have as yet no perfect black. *All* the colors are not absorbed. The perfect black, guarding against high lights, will be utterly and absolutely invisible. Look at that, for example."

He pointed to the palette lying on his work-table. Different shades of black pigments were brushed on it. One, in particular, I could hardly see. It gave my eyes a blurring sensation, and I rubbed them and looked again.

"That," he said impressively, "is the blackest black you or any mortal man ever looked upon. But just you wait, and I'll have a black so black that no mortal man will be able to look upon it—*and see it!*"

On the other hand, I used to find Paul Tichlorne plunged as deeply into the study of light polarization, diffraction, and interference, single and double refraction, and all manner of strange organic compounds.

"Transparency: a state or quality of body which permits all rays of light to pass through," he defined for me. "That is what I am seeking. Lloyd blunders up against the shadow with his perfect opaqueness. But I escape it. A transparent body casts no shadow; neither does it reflect light-waves—that is, the perfectly transparent does not. So, avoiding high lights, not only will such a body cast no shadow, but, since it reflects no light, it will also be invisible."

We were standing by the window at another time. Paul was engaged in polishing a number of lenses, which were ranged along the sill. Suddenly, after a pause in the conversation, he said, "Oh! I've dropped a lens. Stick your head out, old man, and see where it went to."

Out I started to thrust my head, but a sharp blow on the forehead caused me to recoil. I rubbed my bruised brow and gazed with reproachful inquiry at Paul, who was laughing in gleeful, boyish fashion.

"Well?" he said.

"Well?" I echoed.

"Why don't you investigate?" he demanded. And investigate I did. Before thrusting out my head, my senses, automatically active, had told me there was nothing there, that nothing intervened between me and out-of-doors, that the aperture of the window opening was utterly empty. I stretched forth my hand and felt a hard object, smooth and cool and flat, which my touch, out of its experience, told me to be glass. I looked again, but could see positively nothing.

"White quartzose sand," Paul rattled off, "sodic carbonate, slaked lime, cullet, manganese peroxide—there you have it, the finest French plate glass, made by the great St. Gobain Company, who made the finest plate glass in the world, and this is the finest piece they ever made. It cost a king's ransom. But look at it! You can't see it. You don't know it's there till you run your head against it.

"Eh, old boy! That's merely an object-lesson—certain elements, in themselves opaque, yet so compounded as to give a resultant body which is transparent. But that is a matter of inorganic chemistry, you say. Very true. But I care to assert, standing here on my two feet, that in the organic I can duplicate whatever occurs in the inorganic.

"Here!" He held a test-tube between me and the light, and I noted the cloudy or muddy liquid it contained. He emptied the contents of another test-tube into it, and almost instantly it became clear and sparkling.

"Or here!" With quick, nervous movements among his array of test-tubes, he turned a white solution to a wine color, and a light yellow solution to a dark brown. He dropped a piece of litmus paper into an acid, when it changed instantly to red, and on floating it in an alkali it turned as quickly to blue.

"The litmus paper is still the litmus paper," he enunciated in the formal manner of the lecturer. "I have not changed it into something else.

Then what did I do? I merely changed the arrangement of its molecules. Where, at first, it absorbed all colors from the light but red, its molecular structure was so changed that it absorbed red and all colors except blue. And so it goes, *ad infinitum.* Now, what I purpose to do is this." He paused for a space. "I purpose to seek—ay, and to find—the proper reagents, which, acting upon the living organism, will bring about molecular changes analogous to those you have just witnessed. But these reagents, which I shall find, and for that matter, upon which I already have my hands, will not turn the living body to blue or red or black, but they will turn it to transparency. All light will pass through it. It will be invisible. It will cast no shadow."

A few weeks later I went hunting with Paul. He had been promising me for some time that I should have the pleasure of shooting over a wonderful dog—the most wonderful dog, in fact, that ever man shot over, so he averred, and continued to aver till my curiosity was aroused. But on the morning in question I was disappointed, for there was no dog in evidence.

"Don't see him about," Paul remarked unconcernedly, and we set off across the fields.

I could not imagine, at the time, what was ailing me, but I had a feeling of some impending and deadly illness. My nerves were all awry, and, from the astounding tricks they played me, my senses seemed to have run riot. Strange sounds disturbed me. At times I heard the swish-swish of grass being shoved aside, and once the patter of feet across a patch of stony ground.

"Did you hear anything, Paul?" I asked once.

But he shook his head, and thrust his feet steadily forward.

While climbing a fence, I heard the low, eager whine of a dog, apparently from within a couple of feet of me; but on looking about me I saw nothing.

I dropped to the ground, limp and trembling.

"Paul," I said, "we had better return to the house. I am afraid I am going to be sick."

"Nonsense, old man," he answered. "The sunshine has gone to your head like wine. You'll be all right. It's famous weather."

But, passing along a narrow path through a clump of cottonwoods, some object brushed against my legs and I stumbled and nearly fell. I looked with sudden anxiety at Paul.

"What's the matter?" he asked. "Tripping over your own feet?"

I kept my tongue between my teeth and plodded on, though sore perplexed and thoroughly satisfied that some acute and mysterious malady

59

had attacked my nerves. So far my eyes had escaped; but, when we got to the open fields again, even my vision went back on me. Strange flashes of vari-colored, rainbow light began to appear and disappear on the path before me. Still, I managed to keep myself in hand, till the vari-colored lights persisted for a space of fully twenty seconds, dancing and flashing in continuous play. Then I sat down, weak and shaky.

"It's all up with me," I gasped, covering my eyes with my hands. "It has attacked my eyes. Paul, take me home."

But Paul laughed long and loud. "What did I tell you?—the most wonderful dog, eh? Well, what do you think?"

He turned partly from me and began to whistle. I heard the patter of feet, the panting of a heated animal, and the unmistakable yelp of a dog. Then Paul stooped down and apparently fondled the empty air.

"Here! Give me your fist."

And he rubbed my hand over the cold nose and jowls of a dog. A dog it certainly was, with the shape and the smooth, short coat of a pointer.

Suffice to say, I speedily recovered my spirits and control. Paul put a collar about the animal's neck and tied his handkerchief to its tail. And then was vouchsafed us the remarkable sight of an empty collar and a waving handkerchief cavorting over the fields. It was something to see that collar and handkerchief pin a bevy of quail in a clump of locusts and remain rigid and immovable till we had flushed the birds.

Now and again the dog emitted the vari-colored light-flashes I have mentioned. The one thing, Paul explained, which he had not anticipated and which he doubted could be overcome.

"They're a large family," he said, "these sun dogs, wind dogs, rainbows, halos, and parhelia. They are produced by refraction of light from mineral and ice crystals, from mist, rain, spray, and no end of things; and I am afraid they are the penalty I must pay for transparency. I escaped Lloyd's shadow only to fetch up against the rainbow flash."

A couple of days later, before the entrance to Paul's laboratory, I encountered a terrible stench. So overpowering was it that it was easy to discover the source—a mass of putrescent matter on the doorstep which in general outlines resembled a dog.

Paul was startled when he investigated my find. It was his invisible dog, or rather, what had been his invisible dog, for it was now plainly visible. It had been playing about but a few minutes before in all health and strength. Closer examination revealed that the skull had been crushed by some heavy blow. While it was strange that the animal should have been killed, the inexplicable thing was that it should so quickly decay.

"The reagents I injected into its system were harmless," Paul explained. "Yet they were powerful, and it appears that when death comes they force practically instantaneous disintegration. Remarkable! Most remarkable! Well, the only thing is not to die. They do not harm so long as one lives. But I do wonder who smashed in that dog's head."

Light, however, was thrown upon this when a frightened housemaid brought the news that Gaffer Bedshaw had that very morning, not more than an hour back, gone violently insane, and was strapped down at home, in the huntsman's lodge, where he raved of a battle with a ferocious and gigantic beast that he had encountered in the Tichlorne pasture. He claimed that the thing, whatever it was, was invisible, that with his own eyes he had seen that it was invisible; wherefore his tearful wife and daughters shook their heads, and wherefore he but waxed the more violent, and the gardener and the coachman tightened the straps by another hole.

Nor, while Paul Tichlorne was thus successfully mastering the problem of invisibility, was Lloyd Inwood a whit behind. I went over in answer to a message of his to come and see how he was getting on. Now his laboratory occupied an isolated situation in the midst of his vast grounds. It was built in a pleasant little glade, surrounded on all sides by a dense forest growth, and was to be gained by way of a winding and erratic path. But I had travelled that path so often as to know every foot of it, and conceive my surprise when I came upon the glade and found no laboratory. The quaint shed structure with its red sandstone chimney was not. Nor did it look as if it ever had been. There were no signs of ruin, no debris, nothing.

I started to walk across what had once been its site. "This," I said to myself, "should be where the step went up to the door." Barely were the words out of my mouth when I stubbed my toe on some obstacle, pitched forward, and butted my head into something that *felt* very much like a door. I reached out my hand. It *was* a door. I found the knob and turned it. And at once, as the door swung inward on its hinges, the whole interior of the laboratory impinged upon my vision. Greeting Lloyd, I closed the door and backed up the path a few paces. I could see nothing of the building. Returning and opening the door, at once all the furniture and every detail of the interior were visible. It was indeed startling, the sudden transition from void to light and form and color.

"What do you think of it, eh?" Lloyd asked, wringing my hand. "I slapped a couple of coats of absolute black on the outside yesterday afternoon to see how it worked. How's your head? You bumped it pretty solidly, I imagine."

CURIOUS FRAGMENTS

"Never mind that," he interrupted my congratulations. "I've something better for you to do."

While he talked he began to strip, and when he stood naked before me he thrust a pot and brush into my hand and said, "Here, give me a coat of this."

It was an oily, shellac-like stuff, which spread quickly and easily over the skin and dried immediately.

"Merely preliminary and precautionary," he explained when I had finished; "but now for the real stuff."

I picked up another pot he indicated, and glanced inside, but could see nothing.

"It's empty," I said.

"Stick your finger in it."

I obeyed, and was aware of a sensation of cool moistness. On withdrawing my hand I glanced at the forefinger, the one I had immersed, but it had disappeared. I moved it, and knew from the alternate tension and relaxation of the muscles that I moved it, but it defied my sense of sight. To all appearances I had been shorn of a finger; nor could I get any visual impression of it till I extended it under the skylight and saw its shadow plainly blotted on the floor.

Lloyd chuckled. "Now spread it on, and keep your eyes open."

I dipped the brush into the seemingly empty pot, and gave him a long stroke across his chest. With the passage of the brush the living flesh disappeared from beneath. I covered his right leg, and he was a one-legged man defying all laws of gravitation. And so, stroke by stroke, member by member, I painted Lloyd Inwood into nothingness. It was a creepy experience, and I was glad when naught remained in sight but his burning black eyes, poised apparently unsupported in mid-air.

"I have a refined and harmless solution for them," he said. "A fine spray with an air-brush, and presto! I am not."

This deftly accomplished, he said, "Now I shall move about, and do you tell me what sensations you experience."

"In the first place, I cannot see you," I said, and I could hear his gleeful laugh from the midst of the emptiness. "Of course," I continued, "you cannot escape your shadow, but that was to be expected. When you pass between my eye and an object, the object disappears, but so unusual and incomprehensible is its disappearance that it seems to me as though my eyes had blurred. When you move rapidly, I experience a bewildering succession of blurs. The blurring sensation makes my eyes ache and my brain tired."

"Have you any other warnings of my presence?" he asked.

"No, and yes," I answered. "When you are near me I have feelings similar to those produced by dank warehouses, gloomy crypts, and deep mines. And as sailors feel the loom of the land on dark nights, so I think I feel the loom of your body. But it is all very vague and intangible."

Long we talked that last morning in his laboratory; and when I turned to go, he put his unseen hand in mine with nervous grip, and said, "Now I shall conquer the world!" And I could not dare to tell him of Paul Tichlorne's equal success.

At home I found a note from Paul, asking me to come up immediately, and it was high noon when I came spinning up the driveway on my wheel. Paul called me from the tennis court, and I dismounted and went over. But the court was empty. As I stood there, gaping open-mouthed, a tennis ball struck me on the arm, and as I turned about, another whizzed past my ear. For aught I could see of my assailant, they came whirling at me from out of space, and right well was I peppered with them. But when the balls already flung at me began to come back for a second whack, I realized the situation. Seizing a racquet and keeping my eyes open, I quickly saw a rainbow flash appearing and disappearing and darting over the ground. I took out after it, and when I laid the racquet upon it for a half-dozen stout blows, Paul's voice rang out:

"Enough! Enough! Oh! Ouch! Stop! Your're landing on my naked skin, you know! Ow! O-w-w! I'll be good! I'll be good! I only wanted you to see my metamorphosis," he said ruefully, and I imagined he was rubbing his hurts.

A few minutes later we were playing tennis—a handicap on my part, for I could have no knowledge of his position save when all the angles between himself, the sun, and me, were in proper conjunction. Then he flashed, and only then. But the flashes were more brilliant than the rainbow—purest blue, most delicate violet, brightest yellow, and all the intermediary shades, with the scintillant brilliancy of the diamond, dazzling, blinding, iridescent.

But in the midst of our play I felt a sudden cold chill, reminding me of deep mines and gloomy crypts, such a chill as I had experienced that very morning. The next moment, close to the net, I saw a ball rebound in mid-air and empty space, and at the same instant, a score of feet away, Paul Tichlorne emitted a rainbow flash. It could not be he from whom the ball had rebounded, and with sickening dread I realized that Lloyd Inwood had come upon the scene. To make sure, I looked for his shadow, and there it was, a

63

shapeless blotch the girth of his body (the sun was overhead), moving along the ground. I remembered his threat, and felt sure that all the long years of rivalry were about to culminate in uncanny battle.

I cried a warning to Paul, and heard a snarl as of a wild beast, and an answering snarl. I saw the dark blotch move swiftly across the court, and a brilliant burst of vari-colored light moving with equal swiftness to meet it; and then shadow and flash came together and there was the sound of unseen blows. The net went down before my frightened eyes. I sprang toward the fighters, crying:

"For God's sake!"

But their locked bodies smote against my knees, and I was overthrown.

"You keep out of this, old man!" I heard the voice of Lloyd Inwood from out of the emptiness. And then Paul's voice crying, "Yes, we've had enough of peacemaking!"

From the sound of their voices I knew they had separated. I could not locate Paul, and so approached the shadow that represented Lloyd. But from the other side came a stunning blow on the point of my jaw, and I heard Paul scream angrily, "Now will you keep away?"

Then they came together again, the impact of their blows, their groans and gasps, and the swift flashings and shadow-movings telling plainly of the deadliness of the struggle.

I shouted for help, and Gaffer Bedshaw came running into the court. I could see, as he approached, that he was looking at me strangely, but he collided with the combatants and was hurled headlong to the ground. With despairing shriek and a cry of "O Lord, I've got 'em!" he sprang to his feet and tore madly out of the court.

I could do nothing, so I sat up, fascinated and powerless, and watched the struggle. The noonday sun beat down with dazzling brightness on the naked tennis court. And it *was* naked. All I could see was the blotch of shadow and the rainbow flashes, the dust rising from the invisible feet, the earth tearing up from beneath the straining foot-grips, and the wire screen bulge once or twice as their bodies hurled against it. That was all, and after a time even that ceased. There were no more flashes, and the shadow had become long and stationary; and I remembered their set boyish faces when they clung to the roots in the deep coolness of the pool.

They found me an hour afterward. Some inkling of what had happened got to the servants and they quitted the Tichlorne service in a body. Gaffer Bedshaw never recovered from the second shock he received, and is confined in a madhouse, hopelessly incurable. The secrets of their marvellous discoveries died with Paul and Lloyd, both laboratories being destroyed by grief-stricken relatives. As for myself, I no longer care for chemical research, and science is a tabooed topic in my household. I have returned to my roses. Nature's colors are good enough for me.

THE ENEMY OF ALL THE WORLD

At the end of 1906, during hectic planning for the *Snark* voyage (it got under way the following April 23) which would take Jack and his wife Charmian to the South Seas for over two years, London toiled at his writing. He needed money. He completed *The Iron Heel* (1908) and the series of tramp stories which were published in 1907 in a book entitled *The Road;* and he wrote several short stories.

Four of those stories written in December, 1906, are to be found in this collection: "The Enemy of All the World," "The Unparalleled Invasion," "Goliah," and "A Curious Fragment." All four are set in the future—in London's future, that is—as are the footnotes in *The Iron Heel.*

It was Silas Bannerman who finally ran down that scientific wizard and arch-enemy of mankind, Emil Gluck. Gluck's confession, before he went to the electric chair, threw much light upon the series of mysterious events, many apparently unrelated, that so perturbed the world between the years 1933 and 1941. It was not until that remarkable document was made public that the world dreamed of there being any connection between the assassination of the King and Queen of Portugal and the murders of the New York City police officers. While the deeds of Emil Gluck were all that was abominable, we cannot but feel, to a certain extent, pity for the unfortunate, malformed, and maltreated genius. This side of his story has never been told before, and from his confession and from the great mass of evidence and the documents and records of the time we are able to construct a fairly accurate portrait of him, and to discern the factors and pressures that molded him into the human monster he became and that drove him onward and downward along the fearful path he trod.

The Red Book Magazine, 11 (October, 1908):817-27.

THE ENEMY OF ALL THE WORLD

Emil Gluck was born in Syracuse, New York, in 1895. His father, Josephus Gluck, was a special policeman and night watchman, who, in the year 1900, died suddenly of pneumonia. The mother, a pretty, fragile creature, who, before her marriage, had been a milliner, grieved herself to death over the loss of her husband. This sensitiveness of the mother was the heritage that in the boy became morbid and horrible.

In 1901, the boy, Emil, then six years of age, went to live with his aunt, Mrs. Ann Bartell. She was his mother's sister, but in her breast was no kindly feeling for the sensitive, shrinking boy. Ann Bartell was a vain, shallow, and heartless woman. Also, she was cursed with poverty and burdened with a husband who was a lazy, erratic ne'er-do-well. Young Emil Gluck was not wanted, and Ann Bartell could be trusted to impress this fact sufficiently upon him. As an illustration of the treatment he received in that early, formative period, the following instance is given.

When he had been living in the Bartell home a little more than a year, he broke his leg. He sustained the injury through playing on the forbidden roof—as all boys have done and will continue to do to the end of time. The leg was broken in two places between the knee and thigh. Emil, helped by his frightened playmates, managed to drag himself to the front sidewalk, where he fainted. The children of the neighborhood were afraid of the hard-featured shrew who presided over the Bartell house; but, summoning their resolution, they rang the bell and told Ann Bartell of the accident. She did not even look at the little lad who lay stricken on the sidewalk, but slammed the door and went back to her washtub. The time passed. A drizzle came on, and Emil Gluck, out of his faint, lay sobbing in the rain. The leg should have been set immediately. As it was, the inflammation rose rapidly and made a nasty case of it. At the end of two hours, the indignant women of the neighborhood protested to Ann Bartell. This time she came out and looked at the lad. Also she kicked him in the side as he lay helpless at her feet, and she hysterically disowned him. He was not her child, she said, and recommended that the ambulance be called to take him to the city receiving hospital. Then she went back into the house.

It was a woman, Elizabeth Shepstone, who came along, learned the situation, and had the boy placed on a shutter. It was she who called the doctor, and who, brushing aside Ann Bartell, had the boy carried into the house. When the doctor arrived, Ann Bartell promptly warned him that she would not pay him for his services. For two months the little Emil lay in bed, the first month on his back without once being turned over; and he lay neglected and alone, save for the occasional visits of the unremunerated and over-worked physician. He had no toys, nothing with

67

which to beguile the long and tedious hours. No kind word was spoken to him, no soothing hand laid upon his brow, no single touch or act of loving tenderness—naught but the reproaches and harshness of Ann Bartell, and the continually reiterated information that he was not wanted. And it can well be understood, in such environment, how there was generated in the lonely, neglected boy much of the bitterness and hostility for his kind that later was to express itself in deeds so frightful as to terrify the world.

It would seem strange that, from the hands of Ann Bartell, Emil Gluck should have received a college education; but the explanation is simple. Her ne'er-do-well husband, deserting her, made a strike in the Nevada gold-fields, and returned to her a many-times millionaire. Ann Bartell hated the boy, and immediately she sent him to the Farristown Academy, a hundred miles away. Shy and sensitive, a lonely and misunderstood little soul, he was more lonely than ever at Farristown. He never came home, at vacation and holidays, as the other boys did. Instead, he wandered about the deserted buildings and grounds, befriended and misunderstood by the servants and gardeners, reading much, it is remembered, spending his days in the fields or before the fireplace with his nose poked always in the pages of some book. It was at this time that he over-used his eyes and was compelled to take up the wearing of glasses, which same were so prominent in the photographs of him published in the newspapers in 1941.

He was a remarkable student. Application such as his would have taken him far; but he did not need application. A glance at a text meant mastery for him. The result was that he did an immense amount of collateral reading and acquired more in half a year than did the average student in half a dozen years. In 1909, barely fourteen years of age, he was ready—"more than ready," the head-master of the academy said—to enter Yale or Harvard. His juvenility prevented him from entering those universities, and so, in 1909, we find him a freshman at historic Bowdoin College, In 1913 he graduated with highest honors, and immediately afterward followed Professor Bradlough to Berkeley, California. The one friend that Emil Gluck discovered in all his life was Professor Bradlough. The latter's weak lungs had led him to exchange Maine for California, the removal being facilitated by the offer of a professorship in the State University. Throughout the year 1914, Emil Gluck resided in Berkeley and took special scientific courses. Toward the end of that year two deaths changed his prospects and his relations with life. The death of Professor Bradlough took from him the one friend he was ever to know, and the death of Ann Bartell left him penniless. Hating the unfortunate lad to the last, she cut him off with one hundred dollars.

The following year, at twenty years of age, Emil Gluck was enrolled as an instructor of chemistry in the University of California. Here the years passed quietly; he faithfully performed the drudgery that brought him his salary, and, a student always, he took half a dozen degrees. He was, among other things, a Doctor of Sociology, of Philosophy, and of Science, though he was known to the world, in later days, only as Professor Gluck.

He was twenty-seven years old when he first sprang into prominence in the newspapers through the publication of his book *Sex and Progress*. The book remains to-day a milestone in the history and philosophy of marriage. It is a heavy tome of over seven hundred pages, painfully careful and accurate, and startlingly original. It was a book for scientists, and not one calculated to make a stir. But Gluck, in the last chapter, using barely three lines for it, mentioned the hypothetical desirability of trial marriages. At once the newspapers seized these three lines, "played them up yellow," as the slang was in those days, and set the whole world laughing at Emil Gluck, the bespectacled young professor of twenty-seven. Photographers snapped him, he was besieged by reporters, women's clubs throughout the land passed resolutions condemning him and his immoral theories; and on the floor of the California Assembly, while discussing the state appropriation to the University, a motion demanding the expulsion of Gluck was made under threat of withholding the appropriation—of course none of his persecutors had read the book; the twisted newspaper version of only three lines of it was enough for them. Here began Emil Gluck's hatred for newspaper men. By them his serious and intrinsically valuable work of six years had been made a laughing stock and a notoriety. To his dying day, and to their everlasting regret, he never forgave them.

It was the newspapers that were responsible for the next disaster that befell him. For the five years following the publication of his book he had remained silent, and silence for a lonely man is not good. One can conjecture sympathetically the awful solitude of Emil Gluck in that populous university; for he was without friends and without sympathy. His only recourse was books, and he went on reading and studying enormously. But in 1927 he accepted an invitation to appear before the Human Interest Society of Emeryville. He did not trust himself to speak, and as we write we have before us a copy of his learned paper. It is sober, scholarly, and scientific, and, it must also be added, conservative. But in one place he dealt with, and I quote his words, "the industrial and social revolution that is taking place in society." A reporter, present, seized upon the word "revolution," divorced it from the text, and wrote a garbled account that made Emil Gluck appear an anarchist. At once, "Professor

Gluck, anarchist," flamed over the wires and was appropriately "featured" in all the newspapers in the land.

He had attempted to reply to the previous newspaper attack, but now he remained silent. Bitterness had already corroded his soul. The University faculty appealed to him to defend himself, but he sullenly declined, even refusing to enter in defence a copy of his paper to save himself from expulsion. He refused to resign, and was discharged from the University faculty. It must be added that political pressure had been put upon the University Regents and the President.

Persecuted, maligned, and misunderstood, the forlorn and lonely man made no attempt at retaliation. All his life he had been sinned against, and all his life he had sinned against no one. But his cup of bitterness was not yet full to overflowing. Having lost his position, and being without any income, he had to find work. His first place was at the Union Iron Works, in San Francisco, where he proved a most able draughtsman. It was here that he obtained his first-hand knowledge of battleships and their construction. But the reporters discovered him and featured him in his new vocation. He immediately resigned and found another place; but after the reporters had driven him away from half a dozen positions, he steeled himself to brazen out the newspaper persecution. This occurred when he started his electro-plating establishment in Oakland, on Telegraph Avenue. It was a small shop, employing three men and two boys. Gluck himself worked long hours. Night after night, as Policeman Carew testified on the stand, he did not leave the shop till one and two in the morning. It was during this period that he perfected the improved ignition device for gas engines, the royalties from which ultimately made him wealthy.

He started his electro-plating establishment early in the spring of 1928, and it was in the same year that he formed the disastrous love attachment for Irene Tackley. Now it is not to be imagined that an extraordinary creature such as Emil Gluck could be any other than an extraordinary lover. In addition to his genius, his loneliness, and his morbidness, it must be taken into consideration that he knew nothing about women. Whatever tides of desire flooded his being, he was unschooled in the conventional expression of them; while his excessive timidity was bound to make his love-making unusual. Irene Tackley was a rather pretty young woman, but shallow and light-headed. At the time she worked in a small candy store across the street from Gluck's shop. He used to come in and drink ice-cream sodas and lemon-squashes, and stare at her. It seems the girl did not care for him, and merely played with him. He was "queer," she said; and at another time she called him a crank when describing how he sat at the counter and peered at her through his spectacles, blushing and stammering when she took notice of him and often leaving the shop in precipitate confusion.

Gluck made her the most amazing presents—a silver tea service, a diamond ring, a set of furs, opera glasses, a ponderous "History of the World" in many volumes, and a motorcycle all silver-plated in his own shop. Enters now the girl's lover, putting his foot down, showing great anger, compelling her to return Gluck's strange assortment of presents. This man, William Sherbourne, was a gross and stolid creature, a heavy-jawed man of the working class who had become a successful building contractor in a small way. Gluck did not understand. He tried to get an explanation, attempting to speak with the girl when she went home from work in the evening. She complained to Sherbourne, and one night he gave Gluck a beating. It was a very severe beating, for it is on the records of the Red Cross Emergency Hospital that Gluck was treated there that night and was unable to leave the hospital for a week.

Still Gluck did not understand. He continued to seek an explanation from the girl. In fear of Sherbourne, he applied to the Chief of Police for permission to carry a revolver, which permission was refused, the newspapers as usual playing it up sensationally. Then came the murder of Irene Tackley, six days before her contemplated marriage with Sherbourne. It was on a Saturday night. She had worked late in the candy store, departing after eleven o'clock with her week's wages in her purse. She rode on a San Pablo Avenue surface car to Thirty-fourth Street, where she alighted and started to walk the three blocks to her home. That was the last seen of her alive. Next morning she was found, strangled, in a vacant lot.

Emil Gluck was immediately arrested. Nothing that he could do could save him. He was convicted, not merely on circumstantial evidence, but on evidence "cooked up" by the Oakland police. There is no discussion but that a large portion of the evidence was manufactured. The testimony of Captain Shehan was the sheerest perjury, it being proved long afterward that on the night in question he had not only not been in the vicinity of the murder, but that he had been out of the city in a resort on the San Leandro Road. The unfortunate Gluck received life imprisonment in San Quentin, while the newspapers and the public held that it was a miscarriage of justice—that the death penalty should have been visited upon him.

Gluck entered San Quentin prison on April 17, 1929. He was then thirty-four years of age. And for three years and a half, much of the time in solitary confinement, he was left to meditate upon the injustice of man. It was during that period that his bitterness corroded him and he became a hater of all his kind. Three other things he did during the same period; he wrote his famous treatise "Human Morals," his remarkable brochure "The Criminal Sane," and he worked out his awful and monstrous scheme of revenge. It was an episode that had occurred in his electro-plating establishment that suggested to him his unique weapon of revenge. As stated in his confession, he worked every detail out theoretically during his imprisonment, and was able, on his release, immediately to embark on his career of vengeance.

His release was sensational. Also it was miserably and criminally delayed by the soulless legal red tape then in vogue. On the night of February 1, 1932, Tim Haswell, a hold-up man, was shot during an attempted robbery by a citizen of Piedmont Heights. Tim Haswell lingered three days, during which time he not only confessed to the murder of Irene Tackley, but furnished conclusive proofs of the same. Bert Danniker, a convict dying of consumption in Folsom Prison, was implicated as accessory, and his confession followed. It is inconceivable to us of to-day—the bungling, dilatory processes of justice a generation ago. Emil Gluck was proved in February to be an innocent man, yet he was not released until the following October. For eight months, a greatly wronged man, he was compelled to undergo his unmerited punishment. This was not conducive to sweetness and light, and we can well imagine how he ate his soul with bitterness during those dreary eight months.

He came back to the world in the fall of 1932, as usual a "feature" topic in all the newspapers. The papers, instead of expressing heartfelt regret, continued their old sensational persecution. One paper did more—the *San Francisco Intelligencer*. John Hartwell, its editor, elaborated an ingenious theory that got around the confessions of the two criminals and went to show that Gluck was responsible, after all, for the murder of Irene Tackley. Hartwell died. And Sherbourne died, too, while Policeman Phillipps was shot in the leg and discharged from the Oakland police force.

The murder of Hartwell was long a mystery. He was alone in his editorial office at the time. The reports of the revolver were heard by the office boy, who rushed in to find Hartwell expiring in his chair. What puzzled the police was the fact, not merely that he had been shot with his own revolver, but that the revolver had been exploded in the drawer of his desk. The bullets had torn through the front of the drawer and entered his body. The police scouted the theory of suicide, murder was dismissed as absurd, and the blame was thrown upon the Eureka Smokeless Cartridge Company. Spontaneous explosion was the police explanation, and the chemists of the cartridge company were well bullied at the inquest. But

72

what the police did not know was that across the street, in the Mercer Building, Room 633, rented by Emil Gluck, had been occupied by Emil Gluck at the very moment Hartwell's revolver so mysteriously exploded.

At the time, no connection was made between Hartwell's death and the death of William Sherbourne. Sherbourne had continued to live in the home he had built for Irene Tackley, and one morning in January, 1933, he was found dead. Suicide was the verdict of the coroner's inquest, for he had been shot by his own revolver. The curious thing that happened that night was the shooting of Policeman Phillipps on the sidewalk in front of Sherbourne's house. The policeman crawled to a police telephone on the corner and rang up for an ambulance. He claimed that someone had shot him from behind in the leg. The leg in question was so badly shattered by three .38 caliber bullets that amputation was necessary. But when the police discovered that the damage had been done by his own revolver, a great laugh went up, and he was charged with having been drunk. In spite of his denial of having touched a drop, and of his persistent assertion that the revolver had been in his hip pocket and that he had not laid finger to it, he was discharged from the force. Emil Gluck's confession, six years later, cleared the unfortunate policeman of disgrace, and he is alive to-day and in good health, the recipient of a handsome pension from the city.

Emil Gluck, having disposed of his immediate enemies, now sought a wider field, though his enmity for newspaper men and for the police remained always active. The royalties on his ignition device for gasoline engines had mounted up while he lay in prison, and year by year the earning power of his invention increased. He was independent, able to travel wherever he willed over the earth and to glut his monstrous appetite for revenge. He had become a monomaniac and an anarchist—not a philosophic anarchist, merely, but a violent anarchist. Perhaps the word is misused, and he is better described as a nihilist, or an annihilist. It is known that he affiliated with none of the groups of terrorists. He operated wholly alone, but he created a thousand-fold more terror and achieved a thousand-fold more destruction than all the terrorist groups added together.

He signalized his departure from California by blowing up Fort Mason. In his confession he spoke of it as a little experiment—he was merely trying his hand. For eight years he wandered over the earth, a mysterious terror, destroying property to the tune of hundreds of millions of dollars, and destroying countless lives. One good result of his awful deeds was the destruction he wrought among the terrorists themselves. Every time he did anything the terrorists in the vicinity were gathered in by the police drag-net and many of them were executed. Seventeen were executed at Rome alone, following the assassination of the Italian King. Perhaps the most world-amazing achievement of his was the assassination of the King and Queen of Portugal. It was their wedding day. All possible precautions had been taken against the terrorists, and the way from the Cathedral, through Lisbon's streets, was double-banked with troops, while a squad of two hundred mounted troopers surrounded the carriage. Suddenly the amazing thing happened. The automatic rifles of the troopers began to go off, as well as the rifles, in the immediate vicinity, of the double-banked infantry. In the excitement the muzzles of the exploding rifles were turned in all directions. The slaughter was terrible—horses, troops, spectators, and the King and Queen, were riddled with bullets. To complicate the affair, in different parts of the crowd behind the foot-soldiers, two terrorists had bombs explode on their persons. These bombs they had intended to throw if they got the opportunity. But who was to know this? The frightful havoc wrought by the bursting bombs but added to the confusion; it was considered part of the general attack.

One puzzling thing that could not be explained away was the conduct of the troopers with their exploding rifles. It seemed impossible that they should be in the plot, yet there were the hundreds their flying bullets had slain, including the King and Queen. On the other hand, more baffling than ever, was the fact that seventy per cent of the troopers themselves had been killed or wounded. Some explained this on the ground that the loyal foot-soldiers, witnessing the attack on the royal carriage, had opened fire on the traitors. Yet not one bit of evidence to verify this could be drawn from the survivors, though many were put to the torture. They contended stubbornly that they had not discharged their rifles at all, but that their rifles had discharged themselves. They were laughed at by the chemists, who held that, while it was just barely probable that a single cartridge, charged with the new smokeless powder, might spontaneously explode, it was beyond all probability and possibility for all the cartridges in a given area, so charged, spontaneously to explode. And so, in the end, no explanation of the amazing occurrence was reached. The general opinion of the rest of the world was that the whole affair was a blind panic of the feverish Latins, precipitated, it was true, by the bursting of two terrorist bombs; and in this connection was recalled the laughable encounter of long years before between the Russian fleet and the English fishing boats.

And Emil Gluck chuckled and went his way. He knew. But how was the world to know? He had stumbled upon the secret in his old electro-plating shop on Telegraph Avenue in the city of Oakland. It happened, at that time, that a wireless telegraph station was established by the Thurston Power Company close to his shop. In a short time his electro-plating vat was put out of order. The vat-wiring had many bad joints, and, on investigation, Gluck discovered minute welds at the joints in the wiring. These, by lowering the resistance, had caused an excessive current to pass through the solution, "boiling" it and spoiling the work. But what had caused the welds? was the question in Gluck's mind. His reasoning was simple. Before the establishment of the wireless station, the vat had worked well. Not until after the establishment of the wireless station had the vat been ruined. Therefore the wireless station had been the cause. But how? He quickly answered the question. If an electric discharge was capable of operating a coherer across three thousand miles of ocean, then, certainly, the electric discharges from the wireless station four hundred feet away could produce coherer effects on the bad joints in the vat wiring.

Gluck thought no more about it at the time. He merely re-wired his vat and went on electro-plating. But afterwards, in prison, he remembered the incident, and like a flash there came into his mind the full significance of it. He saw in it the silent, secret weapon with which to revenge himself on the world. His great discovery, which died with him, was control over the direction and scope of the electric discharge. At the time, this was the unsolved problem of wireless telegraphy—as it still is to-day—but Emil Gluck, in his prison cell, mastered it. And, when he was released, he applied it. It was fairly simple, given the directing power that was his, to introduce a spark into the powder-magazines of a fort, a battleship, or a revolver. And not alone could he thus explode powder at a distance, but he could ignite conflagrations. The great Boston fire was started by him—quite by accident, however, as he stated in his confession, adding that it was a pleasing accident and that he had never had any reason to regret it.

It was Emil Gluck that caused the terrible German-American War, with the loss of 800,000 lives and the consumption of almost incalculable treasure. It will be remembered that in 1939, because of the Pickard incident, strained relations existed between the two countries. Germany, though aggrieved, was not anxious for war, and, as a peace token, sent the Crown Prince and seven battleships on a friendly visit to the United States. On the night of February 15 the seven warships lay at anchor in the Hudson opposite New York City. And on that night Emil Gluck, alone, with all his apparatus on board, was out in a launch. This launch, it was afterwards proved, was bought by him from the Ross, Turner Company, while much of the apparatus he used that night had been purchased from the Columbia Electric Works. But this was not known at the time. All that was known was that the seven battleships blew up, one after another, at regular, four-minute intervals. Ninety per cent of the crews and officers, along with the Crown Prince, perished. Many years before, the American battleship *Maine* was blown up in the harbor of Havana, and war with Spain had immediately followed—though there has always existed a reasonable doubt as to whether the explosion was due to conspiracy or accident. But accident could not explain the blowing up of the seven battleships on the Hudson at four-minute intervals. Germany believed that it had been done by a submarine, and immediately declared war. It was six months after Gluck's confession that she returned the Philippines and Hawaii to the United States.

In the meanwhile Emil Gluck, the malevolent wizard and arch-hater, travelled his whirlwind path of destruction. He left no traces. Scientifically thorough, he always cleaned up after himself. His method was to rent a room or a house, and secretly to install his apparatus—which apparatus, by the way, he so perfected and simplified that it occupied little space. After he had accomplished his purpose he carefully removed the apparatus. He bade fair to live out a long life of horrible crime.

The epidemic of shooting of New York City policemen was a remarkable affair. It became one of the horror mysteries of the time. In two short weeks over a hundred policemen were shot in the legs by their own revolvers. Inspector Jones did not solve the mystery, but it was his idea that finally outwitted Gluck. On his recommendation the policemen ceased carrying revolvers, and no more accidental shootings occurred.

It was in the early spring of 1940 that Gluck destroyed the Mare Island navy yard. From a room in Vallejo he sent his electric discharges across the Vallejo Straits to Mare Island. He first played his flashes on the battleship *Maryland*. She lay at the dock of one of the mine magazines. On her forward deck, on a huge temporary platform of timbers, were disposed over a hundred mines. These mines were for the defence of the Golden Gate. Any one of these mines was capable of destroying a dozen battleships, and there were over a hundred mines. The destruction was terrific, but it was only Gluck's overture. He played his flashes down the Mare Island shore, blowing up five torpedo boats, the torpedo station, and the great magazine at the eastern end of the island. Returning westward again, and scooping in occasional isolated magazines on the high ground back from the shore, he blew up three cruisers and the battleships *Oregon, Delaware, New Hampshire,* and *Florida*—the latter had just gone into dry-dock, and the magnificent dry-dock was destroyed along with her.

It was a frightful catastrophe, and a shiver of horror passed through

76

the land. But it was nothing to what was to follow. In the late fall of that year Emil Gluck made a clean sweep of the Atlantic seaboard from Maine to Florida. Nothing escaped. Forts, mines, coast defences of all sorts, torpedo stations, magazines—everything went up. Three months afterward, in mid-winter, he smote the north shore of the Mediterranean from Gibraltar to Greece in the same stupefying manner. A wail went up from the nations. It was clear that human agency was behind all this destruction, and it was equally clear, what of Emil Gluck's impartiality, that the destruction was not the work of any particular nation. One thing was patent, namely, that whoever was the human behind it all, that human was a menace to the world. No nation was safe. There was no defence against this unknown and all-powerful foe. Warfare was futile—nay, not merely futile but itself the very essence of the peril. For a twelve-month the manufacture of powder ceased, and all soldiers and sailors were withdrawn from all fortifications and war vessels. And even a world disarmament was seriously considered at the Convention of the Powers, held at The Hague at that time.

And then Silas Bannerman, a secret service agent of the United States, leaped into world-fame by arresting Emil Gluck. At first Bannerman was laughed at, but he had prepared his case well, and in a few weeks the most skeptical were convinced of Emil Gluck's guilt. The one thing, however, that Silas Bannerman never succeeded in explaining, even to his own satisfaction, was how first he came to connect Gluck with the atrocious crimes. It is true, Bannerman was in Vallejo, on secret government business, at the time of the destruction of Mare Island; and it is true that on the streets of Vallejo Emil Gluck was pointed out to him as a queer crank; but no impression was made at the time. It was not until afterward, when on a vacation in the Rocky Mountains and when reading the first published reports of the destruction along the Atlantic Coast, that suddenly Bannerman thought of Emil Gluck. And on the instant there flashed into his mind the connection between Gluck and the destruction. It was only an hypothesis, but it was sufficient. The great thing was the conception of the hypothesis, in itself an act of unconscious cerebration—a thing as unaccountable as the flashing, for instance, into Newton's mind of the principle of gravitation.

The rest was easy. Where was Gluck at the time of the destruction along the Atlantic seaboard? was the question that formed in Bannerman's mind. By his own request he was put upon the case. In no time he ascertained that Gluck had himself been up and down the Atlantic Coast in the late fall of 1940. Also he ascertained that Gluck had been in New York City during the epidemic of the shooting of police officers. Where was Gluck now?—was Bannerman's next query. And, as if in answer, came the wholesale destruction along the Mediterranean. Gluck had sailed for Europe a month before—Bannerman knew that. It was not necessary for Bannerman to go to Europe. By means of cable messages and the co-operation of the European secret services, he traced Gluck's course along the Mediterranean and found that in every instance it coincided with the blowing up of coast defences and ships. Also, he learned that Gluck had just sailed on the Green Star liner *Plutonic* for the United States.

The case was complete in Bannerman's mind, though in the interval of waiting he worked up the details. In this he was ably assisted by George Brown, an operator employed by the Wood's System of Wireless Telegraphy. When the *Plutonic* arrived off Sandy Hook she was boarded by Bannerman from a Government tug, and Emil Gluck was made prisoner. The trial and the confession followed. In the confession Gluck professed regret only for one thing, namely, that he had taken his time. As he said, had he dreamed that he was ever to be discovered he would have worked more rapidly and accomplished a thousand times the destruction he did. His secret died with him, though it is now known that the French Government managed to get access to him and offered him a billion francs for his invention wherewith he was able to direct and closely to confine electric discharges. "What?" was Gluck's reply—"to sell to you that which would enable you to enslave and maltreat suffering humanity?" And though the war departments of the nations have continued to experiment in their secret laboratories, they have so far failed to light upon the slightest trace of the secret. Emil Gluck was executed on December 4, 1941, and so died, at the age of forty-six, one of the world's most unfortunate geniuses, a man of tremendous intellect, but whose mighty powers, instead of making toward good, were so twisted and warped that he became the most amazing of criminals.

—Culled from Mr. A. G. Burnside's ".Eccentricities of Crime," by kind permission of the publishers, Messrs. Holiday and Whitsund.

A CURIOUS FRAGMENT

Like the story preceding which carries the notation at the end "Culled from Mr. A. G. Burnside's 'Eccentricities of Crime,' " this tale also derives (as do the two which follow) from an imaginary literary work. In the present case it is carried in one of the fifty volumes of *Historical Fragments and Sketches* (4427 A.D.).

"A Curious Fragment" is an interesting example of London's juxtaposition of fantasy and socialism. He did it in *The Iron Heel*, in "Goliah," in "The Strength of the Strong," and in numerous other instances.

As curious as the story itself is its original publication in *Town Topics*, a New York periodical which combined social gossip and extortion on a grand scale under the editorship of Colonel William d'Alton Mann, among the most picaresque rascals of the Gilded Age. By the time Jack London's contribution came along, however, Colonel Mann's fangs had been pulled and *Town Topics* was rocking along on journalism and fiction—a less profitable combination than gossip and blackmail, which had been Mann's specialties in the 1890s.

[The capitalist, or industrial oligarch, Roger Vanderwater, mentioned in the narrative, has been identified as the ninth in the line of the Vanderwaters that controlled for hundreds of years the cotton factories of the South. This Roger Vanderwater flourished in the last decades of the twenty-sixth century after Christ, which was the fifth century of the terrible industrial oligarchy that was reared upon the ruins of the early Republic.

From internal evidences we are convinced that the narrative which follows was not reduced to writing till the twenty-ninth century. Not only was it unlawful to write or print such matter during that period, but the

Town Topics, December 10, 1908, 45-47.

working-class was so illiterate that only in rare instances were its members able to read and write. This was the dark reign of the overman, in whose speech the great mass of the people were characterized as the "herd animals." All literacy was frowned upon and stamped out. From the statute-books of the times may be instanced that black law that made it a capital offense for any man, no matter of what class, to teach even the alphabet to a member of the working-class. Such stringent limitation of education to the ruling class was necessary if that class was to continue to rule.

One result of the foregoing was the development of the professional story-tellers. These story-tellers were paid by the oligarchy, and the tales they told were legendary, mythical, romantic, and harmless. But the spirit of freedom never quite died out, and agitators, under the guise of story-tellers, preached revolt to the slave class. That the following tale was banned by the oligarchs we have proof from the records of the criminal police court of Ashbury, wherein, on January 27, 2734, one John Tourney, found guilty of telling the tale in a boozing-ken of laborers, was sentenced to five years' penal servitude in the borax mines of the Arizona Desert.—Editor's note.]

Listen, my brothers, and I will tell you a tale of an arm. It was the arm of Tom Dixon, and Tom Dixon was a weaver of the first class in a factory of that hell-hound and master, Roger Vanderwater. This factory was called "Hell's Bottom" . . . by the slaves who toiled in it, and I guess they ought to know; and it was situated in Kingsbury, at the other end of the town from Vanderwater's summer palace. You do not know where Kingsbury is? There are many things, my brothers, that you do not know, and it is sad. It is because you do not know that you are slaves. When I have told you this tale, I should like to form a class among you for the learning of written and printed speech. Our masters read and write and possess many books, and it is because of that that they are our masters, and live in palaces, and do not work. When the toilers learn to read and write,—all of them,—they will grow strong; then they will use their strength to break their bonds, and there will be no more masters and no more slaves.

Kingsbury, my brothers, is in the old State of Alabama. For three hundred years the Vanderwaters have owned Kingsbury and its slave pens and factories, and slave pens and factories in many other places and States. You have heard of the Vanderwaters,—who has not?—but let me tell you things you do not know about them. The first Vanderwater was a slave, even as you and I. Have you got that? He was a slave, and that was over three hundred years ago. His father was a machinist in the slave pen of Alexander Burrell, and his mother was a washerwoman in the same slave pen. There is no doubt about this. I am telling you truth. It is history. It is printed, every word of it, in the history books of our masters, which you cannot read because your masters will not permit you to learn to read. You can understand why they will not permit you to learn to read, when there are such things in the books. They know, and they are very wise. If you did read such things, you might be wanting in respect to your masters, which would be a dangerous thing . . . to your masters. But I know, for I can read, and I am telling you what I have read with my own eyes in the history books of our masters.

The first Vanderwater's name was not Vanderwater; it was Vange—Bill Vange, the son of Yergis Vange, the machinist, and Laura Carnly, the washerwoman. Young Bill Vange was strong. He might have remained with the slaves and led them to freedom; instead, however, he served the masters and was well rewarded. He began his service, when yet a small child, as a spy in his home slave pen. He is known to have informed on his own father for seditious utterance. This is fact. I have read it with my own eyes in the records. He was too good a slave for the slave pen. Alexander Burrell took him out, while yet a child, and he was taught to read and write. He was taught many things, and he was entered in the secret service of the government. Of course, he no longer wore the slave dress, except for disguise at such times when he sought to penetrate the secrets and plots of the slaves. It was he, when but eighteen years of age, who brought that great hero and comrade, Ralph Jacobus, to trial and execution in the electric chair. Of course, you have all heard the sacred name of Ralph Jacobus, but it is news to you that he was brought to his death by the first Vanderwater, whose name was Vange. I know. I have read it in the books. There are many interesting things like that in the books.

And after Ralph Jacobus died his shameful death, Bill Vange's name began the many changes it was to undergo. He was known as "Sly Vange" far and wide. He rose high in the secret service, and he was rewarded in grand ways, but still he was not a member of the master class. The men were willing that he should become so; it was the women of the master class who refused to have Sly Vange one of them. Sly Vange gave good service to the masters. He had been a slave himself, and he knew the ways of the slaves. There was no fooling him. In those days the slaves were braver than now, and they were always trying for their freedom. And Sly Vange was everywhere, in all their schemes and plans, bringing their schemes and plans to naught and their leaders to the electric chair. It was

81

in 2255 that his name was next changed for him. It was in that year that the Great Mutiny took place. In that region west of the Rocky Mountains, seventeen millions of slaves strove bravely to overthrow their masters. Who knows, if Sly Vange had not lived, but that they would have succeeded? But Sly Vange was very much alive. The masters gave him supreme command of the situation. In eight months of fighting, one million and three hundred and fifty thousand slaves were killed. Vange, Bill Vange, Sly Vange, killed them, and he broke the Great Mutiny. And he was greatly rewarded, and so red were his hands with the blood of the slaves that thereafter he was called "Bloody Vange." You see, my brothers, what interesting things are to be found in the books when one can read them. And, take my word for it, there are many other things, even more interesting, in the books. And if you will but study with me, in a year's time you can read those books for yourselves—ay, in six months some of you will be able to read those books for yourselves.

Bloody Vange lived to a ripe old age, and always, to the last, was he received in the councils of the masters; but never was he made a master himself. He had first opened his eyes, you see, in a slave pen. But oh, he was well rewarded! He had a dozen palaces in which to live. He, who was no master, owned thousands of slaves. He had a great pleasure yacht upon the sea that was a floating palace, and he owned a whole island in the sea where toiled ten thousand slaves on his coffee plantations. But in his old age he was lonely, for he lived apart, hated by his brothers, the slaves, and looked down upon by those he had served and who refused to be his brothers. The masters looked down upon him because he had been born a slave. Enormously wealthy he died; but he died horribly, tormented by his conscience, regretting all he had done and the red stain on his name.

But with his children it was different. They had not been born in the slave pen, and by the special ruling of the Chief Oligarch of that time, John Morrison, they were elevated to the master class. And it was then that the name of Vange disappears from the page of history. It becomes Vanderwater, and Jason Vange, the son of Bloody Vange, becomes Jason Vanderwater, the founder of the Vanderwater line. But that was three hundred years ago, and the Vanderwaters of to-day forget their beginnings and imagine that somehow the clay of their bodies is different stuff from the clay in your body and mine and in the bodies of all slaves. And I ask you, Why should a slave become the master of another slave? And why should the son of a slave become the master of many slaves? I leave these questions for you to answer for yourselves, but do not forget that in the beginning the Vanderwaters were slaves.

And now, my brothers, I come back to the beginning of my tale to tell you of Tom Dixon's arm. Roger Vanderwater's factory in Kingsbury was rightly named "Hell's Bottom," but the men who toiled in it were men, as you shall see. Women toiled there, too, and children, little children. All that toiled there had the regular slave rights under the law, but only under the law, for they were deprived of many of their rights by the two overseers of Hell's Bottom, Joseph Clancy and Adolph Munster.

It is a long story, but I shall not tell all of it to you. I shall tell only about the arm. It happened that, according to the law, a portion of the starvation wage of the slaves was held back each month and put into a fund. This fund was for the purpose of helping such unfortunate fellow-workmen as happened to be injured by accidents or to be overtaken by sickness. As you know with yourselves, these funds are controlled by the overseers. It is the law, and so it was that the fund at Hell's Bottom was controlled by the two overseers of accursed memory.

Now, Clancy and Munster took this fund for their own use. When accidents happened to the workmen, their fellows, as was the custom, made grants from the fund; but the overseers refused to pay over the grants. What could the slaves do? They had their rights under the law, but they had no access to the law. Those that complained to the overseers were punished. You know yourselves what form such punishment takes—the fines for faulty work that is not faulty; the overcharging of accounts in the Company's store; the vile treatment of one's women and children; and the allotment to bad machines whereon, work as one will, he starves.

Once, the slaves of Hell's Bottom protested to Vanderwater. It was the time of the year when he spent several months in Kingsbury. One of the slaves could write; it chanced that his mother could write, and she had secretly taught him as her mother had secretly taught her. So this slave wrote a round robin, wherein was contained their grievances, and all the slaves signed by mark. And, with proper stamps upon the envelope, the round robin was mailed to Roger Vanderwater. And Roger Vanderwater did nothing, save to turn the round robin over to the two overseers. Clancy and Munster were angered. They turned the guards loose at night on the slave pen. The guards were armed with pick handles. It is said that next day only half of the slaves were able to work in Hell's Bottom. They were well beaten. The slave who could write was so badly beaten that he lived only three months. But before he died, he wrote once more, to what purpose you shall hear.

Four or five weeks afterward, Tom Dixon, a slave, had his arm torn off by a belt in Hell's Bottom. His fellow-workmen, as usual, made a grant to him from the fund, and Clancy and Munster, as usual, refused to pay it over from the fund. The slave who could write, and who even then was dying, wrote anew a recital of their grievances. And this document was thrust into the hand of the arm that had been torn from Tom Dixon's body.

Now it chanced that Roger Vanderwater was lying ill in his palace at the other end of Kingsbury—not the dire illness that strikes down you and me, brothers; just a bit of biliousness, mayhap, or no more than a bad headache because he had eaten too heartily or drunk too deeply. But it was enough for him, being tender and soft from careful rearing. Such men, packed in cotton wool all their lives, are exceeding tender and soft. Believe me, brothers, Roger Vanderwater felt as badly with his aching head, or *thought* he felt as badly, as Tom Dixon really felt with his arm torn out by the roots.

It happened that Roger Vanderwater was fond of scientific farming, and that on his farm, three miles outside of Kingsbury, he had managed to grow a new kind of strawberry. He was very proud of that new strawberry of his, and he would have been out to see and pick the first ripe ones, had it not been for his illness. Because of his illness he had ordered the old farm slave to bring in personally the first box of the berries. All this was learned from the gossip of a palace scullion, who slept each night in the slave pen. The overseer of the plantation should have brought in the berries, but he was on his back with a broken leg from trying to break a colt. The scullion brought the word in the night, and it was known that next day the berries would come in. And the men in the slave pen of Hell's Bottom, being men and not cowards, held a council.

The slave who could write, and who was sick and dying from the pick-handle beating, said he would carry Tom Dixon's arm; also, he said he must die anyway, and that it mattered nothing if he died a little sooner. So five slaves stole from the slave pen that night after the guards had made their last rounds. One of the slaves was the man who could write. They lay in the brush by the roadside until late in the morning, when the old farm slave came driving to town with the precious fruit for the master. What of the farm slave being old and rheumatic, and of the slave who could write being stiff and injured from his beating, they moved their bodies about when they walked, very much in the same fashion. The slave who could write put on the other's clothes, pulled the broad-brimmed hat over his eyes, climbed upon the seat of the wagon, and drove on to town. The old farm slave was kept tied all day in the bushes until evening, when the others loosed him and went back to the slave pen to take their punishment for having broken bounds.

In the meantime, Roger Vanderwater lay waiting for the berries in

84

his wonderful bedroom—such wonders and such comforts were there that they would have blinded the eyes of you and me who have never seen such things. The slave who could write said afterward that it was like a glimpse of Paradise. And why not? The labor and the lives of ten thousand slaves had gone to the making of that bedchamber, while they themselves slept in vile lairs like wild beasts. The slave who could write brought in the berries on a silver tray or platter—you see, Roger Vanderwater wanted to speak with him in person about the berries.

The slave who could write tottered his dying body across the wonderful room and knelt by the couch of Vanderwater, holding out before him the tray. Large, green leaves covered the top of the tray, and these the body-servant alongside whisked away so that Vanderwater could see. And Roger Vanderwater, propped upon his elbow, saw. He saw the fresh, wonderful fruit lying there like precious jewels, and in the midst of it the arm of Tom Dixon as it had been torn from his body, well-washed, of course, my brothers, and very white against the blood red fruit. And also he saw, clutched in the stiff, dead fingers, the petition of his slaves who toiled in Hell's Bottom.

"Take and read," said the slave who could write. And even as the master took the petition, the body-servant, who till then had been motionless with surprise, struck with his fist the kneeling slave upon the mouth. The slave was dying anyway, and was very weak, and did not mind. He made no sound, and, having fallen over on his side, he lay there quietly, bleeding from the blow on the mouth. The physician, who had run for the palace guards, came back with them, and the slave was dragged upright upon his feet. But as they dragged him up, his hand clutched Tom Dixon's arm from where it had fallen on the floor.

"He shall be flung alive to the hounds!" the body-servant was crying in great wrath. "He shall be flung alive to the hounds!"

But Roger Vanderwater, forgetting his headache, still leaning on his elbow, commanded silence, and went on reading the petition. And while he read, there was silence, all standing upright, the wrathful body-servant, the physician, the palace guards, and in their midst the slave, bleeding at the mouth and still holding Tom Dixon's arm. And when Roger Vanderwater had done, he turned upon the slave, saying:—

"If in this paper there be one lie, you shall be sorry that you were ever born."

And the slave said, "I have been sorry all my life that I was born."

Roger Vanderwater looked at him closely, and the slave said:—

"You have done your worst to me. I am dying now. In a week I shall be dead, so it does not matter if you kill me now."

"What do you with that?" the master asked, pointing to the arm; and the slave made answer:—

"I take it back to the pen to give it burial. Tom Dixon was my friend. We worked beside each other at our looms."

There is little more to my tale, brothers. The slave and the arm were sent back in a cart to the pen. Nor were any of the slaves punished for what they had done. Instead, Roger Vanderwater made investigation and punished the two overseers, Joseph Clancy and Adolph Munster. Their freeholds were taken from them. They were branded, each upon the forehead, their right hands were cut off, and they were turned loose upon the highway to wander and beg until they died. And the fund was managed rightfully thereafter for a time—for a time, only, my brothers; for after Roger Vanderwater came his son, Albert, who was a cruel master and half mad.

Brothers, that slave who carried the arm into the presence of the master was my father. He was a brave man. And even as his mother secretly taught him to read, so did he teach me. Because he died shortly after from the pick-handle beating, Roger Vanderwater took me out of the slave pen and tried to make various better things out of me. I might have become an overseer in Hell's Bottom, but I chose to become a story-teller, wandering over the land and getting close to my brothers, the slaves, everywhere. And I tell you stories like this, secretly, knowing that you will not betray me; for if you did, you know as well as I that my tongue will be torn out and that I shall tell stories no more. And my message is, brothers, that there is a good time coming, when all will be well in the world and there will be neither masters nor slaves. But first you must prepare for that good time by learning to read. There is power in the printed word. And here am I to teach you to read, and as well there are others to see that you get the books when I am gone along upon my way—the history books wherein you will learn about your masters, and learn to become strong even as they.

[Editor's Note.—From "Historical Fragments and Sketches," first published in fifty volumes in 4427, and now, after two hundred years, because of its accuracy and value, edited and republished by the National Committee on Historical Research.]

GOLIAH

This remarkable story was written, according to Martin Johnson (in
Through the South Seas with Jack London, 1913) in January, 1907, while
the *Snark* was under construction. "One day," Johnson wrote, "he
[London] read me the first part of it, in which he destroyed the Japanese
Navy. 'And today I destroy the American Navy,' he told me, gleefully.
'Oh, I haven't a bit of conscience when my imagination gets to working.' "

As socialistic writing, the story lacks much, according to Philip S.
Foner (in *Jack London: American Rebel,* 1964): "In 'Goliah' he described
the establishment of Socialism by dictatorship, assassination, and other
forms of violence. Here again London showed a lack of understanding of
the basic tenets of Socialism, which rejected all terrorist, anarchistic,
individualistic policies and worked for the broadest of peaceful mass
activity, condoning force only in those situations in which self-defense is
necessary and peaceful progress barred."

But whatever the case for London's (and Foner's) interpretation of
socialism and its tenets, "Goliah" is among the strongest of the author's
futuristic fantasies.

In 1924—to be precise, on the morning of January 3—the city of San
Francisco awoke to read in one of its daily papers a curious letter, which
had been received by Walter Bassett and which had evidently been written
by some crank. Walter Bassett was the greatest captain of industry west of
the Rockies, and was one of the small group that controlled the nation in
everything but name. As such, he was the recipient of lucubrations from
countless cranks; but this particular lucubration was so different from the
average ruck of similar letters that, instead of putting it into the
waste-basket, he had turned it over to a reporter. It was signed "Goliah,"

The Red Magazine (London), 2 (December 1908):115-29.

and the superscription gave his address as "Palgrave Island." The letter was as follows:—

"Mr. Walter Bassett,
   "Dear Sir:
   "I am inviting you, with nine of your fellow-captains of industry, to visit me here on my island for the purpose of considering plans for the reconstruction of society upon a more rational basis. Up to the present, social evolution has been a blind and aimless, blundering thing. The time has come for a change. Man has risen from the vitalized slime of the primeval sea to the mastery of matter; but he has not yet mastered society. Man is to-day as much the slave to his collective stupidity, as a hundred thousand generations ago he was a slave to matter.

   "There are two theoretical methods whereby man may become the master of society, and make of society an intelligent and efficacious device for the pursuit and capture of happiness and laughter. The first theory advances the proposition that no government can be wiser or better than the people that compose that government; that reform and development must spring from the individual; that in so far as the individuals become wiser and better, by that much will their government become wiser and better; in short, that the majority of individuals must become wiser and better before their government becomes wiser and better. The mob, the political convention, the abysmal brutality and stupid ignorance of all concourses of people, give the lie to this theory. In a mob the collective intelligence and mercy is that of the least intelligent and most brutal members that compose the mob. On the other hand, a thousand passengers will surrender themselves to the wisdom and discretion of the captain, when their ship is in a storm on the sea. In such matter, he is the wisest and most experienced among them.

   "The second theory advances the proposition that the majority of the people are not pioneers, that they are weighted down by the inertia of the established; that the government that is representative of them represents only their feebleness, and futility, and brutishness; that this blind thing called government is not the serf of their wills, but that they are the serfs of it; in short, speaking always of the great mass, that they do not make government, but that government makes them, and that government is and has been a stupid and awful monster, misbegotten of the glimmerings of intelligence that come from the inertia-crushed mass.

   "Personally, I incline to the second theory. Also, I am impatient. For a hundred thousand generations, from the first social groups of our savage forebears, government has remained a monster. To-day, the

88

inertia-crushed mass has less laughter in it than ever before. In spite of man's mastery of matter, human suffering and misery and degradation mar the fair world.

"Wherefore I have decided to step in and become captain of this world-ship for a while. I have the intelligence and the wide vision of the skilled expert. Also, I have the power. I shall be obeyed. The men of all the world shall perform my bidding and make governments so that they shall become laughter-producers. These modelled governments I have in mind shall not make the people happy, wise, and noble by decree; but they shall give opportunity for the people to become happy, wise, and noble.

"I have spoken. I have invited you, and nine of your fellow-captains, to confer with me. On March third the yacht *Energon* will sail from San Francisco. You are requested to be on board the night before. This is serious. The affairs of the world must be handled for a time by a strong hand. Mine is that strong hand. If you fail to obey my summons, you will die. Candidly, I do not expect that you will obey. But your death for failure to obey will cause obedience on the part of those I subsequently summon. You will have served a purpose. And please remember that I have no unscientific sentimentality about the value of human life. I carry always in the background of my consciousness the innumerable billions of lives that are to laugh and be happy in future aeons on the earth.

"Yours for the reconstruction of society,

"Goliah."

The publication of this letter did not cause even local amusement. Men might have smiled to themselves as they read it, but it was so palpably the handiwork of a crank that it did not merit discussion. Interest did not arouse till next morning. An Associated Press dispatch to the Eastern states, followed by interviews by eager-nosed reporters, had brought out the names of the other nine captains of industry who had received similar letters but who had not thought the matter of sufficient importance to be made public. But the interest aroused was mild, and it would have died out quickly had not Gabberton cartooned a chronic presidential aspirant as "Goliah." Then came the song that was sung hilariously from sea to sea, with the refrain, "Goliah will catch you if you don't watch out."

The weeks passed and the incident was forgotten. Walter Bassett had forgotten it likewise; but on the evening of February 22, he was called to the telephone by the Collector of the Port. "I just wanted to tell you," said the latter, "that the yacht *Energon* has arrived and gone to anchor in the stream off Pier Seven."

What happened that night Walter Bassett has never divulged. But it is known that he rode down in his auto to the water front, chartered one of Crowley's launches, and was put aboard the strange yacht. It is further known that when he returned to the shore, three hours later, he immediately dispatched a sheaf of telegrams to his nine fellow-captains of industry who had received letters from Goliah. These telegrams were similarly worded, and read: "The yacht *Energon* has arrived. There is something in this. I advise you to come."

Bassett was laughed at for his pains. It was a huge laugh that went up (for his telegrams had been made public), and the popular song on Goliah revived and became more popular than ever. Goliah and Bassett were cartooned and lampooned unmercifully, the former, as the Old Man of the Sea, riding on the latter's neck. The laugh tittered and rippled through clubs and social circles, was restrainedly merry in the editorial columns, and broke out in loud guffaws in the comic weeklies. There was a serious side as well, and Bassett's sanity was gravely questioned by many, and especially by his business associates.

Bassett had ever been a short-tempered man, and after he sent the second sheaf of telegrams to his brother captains, and had been laughed at again, he remained silent. In this second sheaf, he had said: "Come, I implore you. As you value your life, come." He arranged all his business affairs for an absence, and on the night of March 2 went on board the *Energon*. The latter, properly cleared, sailed next morning. And next morning the newsboys in every city and town were crying "Extra."

In the slang of the day, Goliah had delivered the goods. The nine captains of industry who had failed to accept his invitation were dead. A sort of violent disintegration of the tissues was the report of the various autopsies held on the bodies of the slain millionnaires; yet the surgeons and physicians (the most highly skilled in the land had participated) would not venture the opinion that the men had been slain. Much less would they venture the conclusion, "at the hands of parties unknown." It was all too mysterious. They were stunned. Their scientific credulity broke down. They had no warrant in the whole domain of science for believing that an anonymous person on Palgrave Island had murdered the poor gentlemen.

One thing was quickly learned, however; namely, that Palgrave Island was no myth. It was charted and well known to all navigators, lying on the line of 160 west longitude, right at its intersection by the tenth parallel north latitude, and only a few miles away from Diana Shoal. Like Midway and Fanning, Palgrave Island was isolated, volcanic and coral in formation. Furthermore, it was uninhabited. A survey ship, in 1887, had visited the place and reported the existence of several springs and of a

90

good harbor that was very dangerous of approach. And that was all that was known of the tiny speck of land that was soon to have focussed on it the awed attention of the world.

Goliah remained silent till March 24. On the morning of that day, the newspapers published his second letter, copies of which had been received by the ten chief politicians of the United States—ten leading men in the political world who were conventionally known as "statesmen." The letter, with the same superscription as before, was as follows:—

"Dear Sir:

"I have spoken in no uncertain tone. I must be obeyed. You may consider this an invitation or a summons; but if you still wish to tread this earth and laugh, you will be aboard the yacht *Energon*, in San Francisco harbor, not later than the evening of April 5. It is my wish and my will that you confer with me here on Palgrave Island in the matter of reconstructing society upon some rational basis.

"Do not misunderstand me, when I tell you that I am one with a theory. I want to see that theory work, and therefore I call upon your co-operation. In this theory of mine, lives are but pawns; I deal with quantities of lives. I am after laughter, and those that stand in the way of laughter must perish. The game is big. There are fifteen hundred million human lives to-day on the planet. What is your single life against them? It is as naught, in my theory. And remember that mine is the power. Remember that I am a scientist, and that one life, or one million of lives, mean nothing to me as arrayed against the countless billions of billions of the lives of the generations to come. It is for their laughter that I seek to reconstruct society now; and against them your own meager little life is a paltry thing indeed.

"Whoso has power can command his fellows. By virtue of that military device known as the phalanx, Alexander conquered his bit of the world. By virtue of that chemical device, gunpowder, Cortes with his several hundred cutthroats conquered the empire of the Montezumas. Now I am in possession of a device that is all my own. In the course of a century not more than half a dozen fundamental discoveries or inventions are made. I have made such an invention. The possession of it gives me the mastery of the world. I shall use this invention, not for commercial exploitation, but for the good of humanity. For that purpose I want help—willing agents, obedient hands; and I am strong enough to compel the service. I am taking the shortest way, though I am in no hurry. I shall not clutter my speed with haste.

"The incentive of material gain developed man from the savage to the semi-barbarian he is to-day. This incentive has been a useful device for the development of the human; but it has now fulfilled its function and is ready to be cast aside into the scrap-heap of rudimentary vestiges such as gills in the throat and belief in the divine right of kings. Of course you do not think so; but I do not see that that will prevent you from aiding me to fling the anachronism into the scrap-heap. For I tell you now that the time has come when mere food and shelter and similar sordid things shall be automatic, as free and easy and involuntary of access as the air. I shall make them automatic, what of my discovery and the power that discovery gives me. And with food and shelter automatic, the incentive of material gain passes away from the world forever. With food and shelter automatic, the higher incentives will universally obtain—the spiritual, aesthetic, and intellectual incentives that will tend to develop and make beautiful and noble body, mind, and spirit. Then all the world will be dominated by happiness and laughter. It will be the reign of universal laughter.

"Yours for that day,

"Goliah."

Still the world would not believe. The ten politicians were at Washington, so that they did not have the opportunity of being convinced that Bassett had had, and not one of them took the trouble to journey out to San Francisco to make the opportunity. As for Goliah, he was hailed by the newspapers as another Tom Lawson with a panacea; and there were specialists in mental disease who, by analysis of Goliah's letters, proved conclusively that he was a lunatic.

The yacht *Energon* arrived in the harbor of San Francisco on the afternoon of April 5, and Bassett came ashore. But the *Energon* did not sail next day, for not one of the ten summoned politicians had elected to make the journey to Palgrave Island. The newsboys, however, called "Extra" that day in all the cities. The ten politicians were dead. The yacht, lying peacefully at anchor in the harbor, became the center of excited interest. She was surrounded by a flotilla of launches and rowboats, and many tugs and steamboats ran excursions to her. While the rabble was firmly kept off, the proper authorities and even reporters were permitted to board her. The mayor of San Francisco and the chief of police reported that nothing suspicious was to be seen upon her, and the port authorities announced that her papers were correct and in order in every detail. Many photographs and columns of descriptive matter were run in the newspapers.

The crew was reported to be composed principally of Scandinavians,—fair-haired, blue-eyed Swedes, Norwegians afflicted with the temperamental melancholy of their race, stolid Russian Finns, and a slight sprinkling of Americans and English. It was noted that there was nothing mercurial and flyaway about them. They seemed weighty men oppressed by a sad and stolid bovine-sort of integrity. A sober seriousness and enormous certitude characterized all of them. They appeared men without nerves and without fear, as though upheld by some overwhelming power or carried in the hollow of some superhuman hand. The captain, a sad-eyed, strong-featured American, was cartooned in the papers as "Gloomy Gus" (the pessimistic hero of the comic supplement).

Some sea-captain recognized the *Energon* as the yacht *Scud,* once owned by Merrivale of the New York Yacht Club. With this clue it was soon ascertained that the *Scud* had disappeared several years before. The agent who sold her reported the purchaser to be merely another agent, a man he had seen neither before nor since. The yacht had been reconstructed at Duffey's Shipyard in New Jersey. The change in her name and registry occurred at that time and had been legally executed. Then the *Energon* had disappeared in the shroud of mystery.

In the meantime, Bassett was going crazy—at least his friends and business associates said so. He kept away from his vast business enterprises and said that he must hold his hands until the other masters of the world could join with him in the reconstruction of society—proof indubitable that Goliah's bee had entered his bonnet. To reporters he had little to say. He was not at liberty, he said, to relate what he had seen on Palgrave Island; but he could assure them that the matter was serious, the most serious thing that had ever happened. His final word was that the world was on the verge of a turnover, for good or ill he did not know, but, one way or the other, he was absolutely convinced that the turnover was coming. As for business, business could go hang. He had seen things, he had, and that was all there was to it.

There was a great telegraphing, during this period, between the local Federal officials and the state and war departments at Washington. A secret attempt was made late one afternoon to board the *Energon* and place the captain under arrest—the Attorney-General having given the opinion that the captain could be held for the murder of the ten "statesmen." The government launch was seen to leave Meigg's Wharf and steer for the *Energon,* and that was the last ever seen of the launch and the men on board of it. The government tried to keep the affair hushed up, but the cat was slipped out of the bag by the families of the missing men and the papers were filled with monstrous versions of the affair.

The government now proceeded to extreme measures. The battleship *Alaska* was ordered to capture the strange yacht, or, failing that, to sink her. These were secret instructions; but thousands of eyes, from the water front and from the shipping in the harbor, witnessed what happened that afternoon. The battleship got under way and steamed slowly toward the *Energon.* At half a mile distant the battleship blew up—simply blew up, that was all, her shattered frame sinking to the bottom of the bay, a riff-raff of wreckage and a few survivors strewing the surface. Among the survivors was a young lieutenant who had had charge of the wireless on board the *Alaska.* The reporters got hold of him first, and he talked. No sooner had the *Alaska* got under way, he said, than a message was received from the *Energon.* It was in the international code, and it was a warning to the *Alaska* to come no nearer than half a mile. He had sent the message, through the speaking tube, immediately to the captain. He did not know anything more, except that the *Energon* twice repeated the message and that five minutes afterward the explosion occurred. The captain of the *Alaska* had perished with his ship, and nothing more was to be learned.

The *Energon,* however, promptly hoisted anchor and cleared out to sea. A great clamor was raised by the papers; the government was charged with cowardice and vacillation in its dealings with a mere pleasure yacht and a lunatic who called himself "Goliah," and immediate and decisive action was demanded. Also, a great cry went up about the loss of life, especially the wanton killing of the ten "statesmen." Goliah promptly replied. In fact, so prompt was his reply that the experts in wireless telegraphy announced that, since it was impossible to send wireless messages so great a distance, Goliah was in their very midst and not on Palgrave Island. Goliah's letter was delivered to the Associated Press by a messenger boy who had been engaged on the street. The letter was as follows:—

"What are a few paltry lives? In your insane wars you destroy millions of lives and think nothing of it. In your fratricidal commercial struggle you kill countless babes, women, and men, and you triumphantly call the shambles 'individualism.' I call it anarchy. I am going to put a stop to your wholesale destruction of human beings. I want laughter, not slaughter. Those of you who stand in the way of laughter will get slaughter.

"Your government is trying to delude you into believing that the destruction of the *Alaska* was an accident. Know here and now that it was by my orders that the *Alaska* was destroyed. In a few short months, all battleships on all seas will be destroyed or flung to the scrap-heap, and all nations shall disarm; fortresses shall be dismantled, armies disbanded, and warfare shall cease from the earth. Mine is the power. I am the will of God.

94

GOLIAH

The whole world shall be in vassalage to me, but it shall be a vassalage of peace.

"I am

"Goliah."

"Blow Palgrave Island out of the water!" was the head-line retort of the newspapers. The government was of the same frame of mind, and the assembling of the fleets began. Walter Bassett broke out in ineffectual protest, but was swiftly silenced by the threat of a lunacy commission. Goliah remained silent. Against Palgrave Island five great fleets were hurled—the Asiatic Squadron, the South Pacific Squadron, the North Pacific Squadron, the Caribbean Squadron, and half of the North Atlantic Squadron, the two latter coming through the Panama Canal.

"I have the honor to report that we sighted Palgrave Island on the evening of April 29," ran the report of Captain Johnson, of the battleship *North Dakota* to the Secretary of the Navy. "The Asiatic Squadron was delayed and did not arrive until the morning of April 30. A council of the admirals was held, and it was decided to attack early next morning. The destroyer, *Swift VII*, crept in, unmolested, and reported no warlike preparations on the island. It noted several small merchant steamers in the harbor, and the existence of a small village in a hopelessly exposed position that could be swept by our fire.

"It had been decided that all the vessels should rush in, scattered, upon the island, opening fire at three miles, and continuing to the edge of the reef, there to retain loose formation and engage. Palgrave Island repeatedly warned us, by wireless, in the international code, to keep outside the ten-mile limit; but no heed was paid to the warnings.

"The *North Dakota* did not take part·in the movement of the morning of May 1. This was due to a slight accident of the preceding night that temporarily disabled our steering-gear. The morning of May 1 broke clear and calm. There was a slight breeze from the southwest that quickly died away. The *North Dakota* lay twelve miles off the island. At the signal the squadrons charged in upon the island, from all sides, at full speed. Our wireless receiver continued to tick off warnings from the island. The ten-mile limit was passed, and nothing happened. I watched through my glasses. At five miles nothing happened; at four miles nothing happened; at three miles, the *New York*, in the lead on our side of the island, opened fire. She fired only one shot. Then she blew up. The rest of the vessels never fired a shot. They began to blow up, everywhere, before our eyes. Several swerved about and started back, but they failed to escape. The

95

destroyer, *Dart XXX,* nearly made the ten-mile limit when she blew up. She was the last survivor. No harm came to the *North Dakota,* and that night, the steering-gear being repaired, I gave orders to sail for San Francisco."

To say that the United States was stunned is but to expose the inadequacy of language. The whole world was stunned. It confronted that blight of the human brain, the unprecedented. Human endeavor was a jest, a monstrous futility, when a lunatic on a lonely island, who owned a yacht and an exposed village, could destroy five of the proudest fleets of Christendom. And how had he done it? Nobody knew. The scientists lay down in the dust of the common road and wailed and gibbered. They did not know. Military experts committed suicide by scores. The mighty fabric of warfare they had fashioned was a gossamer veil rent asunder by a miserable lunatic. It was too much for their sanity. Mere human reason could not withstand the shock. As the savage is crushed by the sleight-of-hand of the witch-doctor, so was the world crushed by the magic of Goliah. How did he do it? It was the awful face of the Unknown upon which the world gazed and by which it was frightened out of the memory of its proudest achievements.

But all the world was not stunned. There was the invariable exception—the Island Empire of Japan. Drunken with the wine of success deep-quaffed, without superstition and without faith in aught but its own ascendant star, laughing at the wreckage of science and mad with pride of race, it went forth upon the way of war. America's fleets had been destroyed. From the battlements of heaven the multitudinous ancestral shades of Japan leaned down. The opportunity, God-given, had come. The Mikado was in truth a brother to the gods.

The war-monsters of Japan were loosed in mighty fleets. The Philippines were gathered in as a child gathers a nosegay. It took longer for the battleships to travel to Hawaii, to Panama, and to the Pacific Coast. The United States was panic-stricken, and there arose the powerful party of dishonorable peace. In the midst of the clamor the *Energon* arrived in San Francisco Bay and Goliah spoke once more. There was a little brush as the *Energon* came in, and a few explosions of magazines occurred along the war-tunnelled hills as the coast defences went to smash. Also, the blowing up of the submarine mines in the Golden Gate made a remarkably fine display. Goliah's message to the people of San Francisco, dated as usual from Palgrave Island, was published in the papers. It ran:—

"Peace? Peace be with you. You shall have peace. I have spoken to this purpose before. And give you me peace. Leave my yacht *Energon*

96

alone. Commit one overt act against her and not one stone in San Francisco shall stand upon another.

"To-morrow let all good citizens go out upon the hills that slope down to the sea. Go with music and laughter and garlands. Make festival for the new age that is dawning. Be like children upon your hills, and witness the passing of war. Do not miss the opportunity. It is your last chance to behold what henceforth you will be compelled to seek in museums of antiquities.

"I promise you a merry day,

"Goliah."

The madness of magic was in the air. With the people it was as if all their gods had crashed and the heavens still stood. Order and law had passed away from the universe; but the sun still shone, the wind still blew, the flowers still bloomed—that was the amazing thing about it. That water should continue to run downhill was a miracle. All the stabilities of the human mind and human achievement were crumbling. The one stable thing that remained was Goliah, a madman on an island. And so it was that the whole population of San Francisco went forth next day in colossal frolic upon the hills that overlooked the sea. Brass bands and banners went forth, brewery wagons and Sunday-school picnics—all the strange heterogeneous groupings of swarming metropolitan life.

On the sea-rim rose the smoke from the funnels of a hundred hostile vessels of war, all converging upon the helpless, undefended Golden Gate. And not all undefended, for out through the Golden Gate moved the *Energon,* a tiny toy of white, rolling like a straw in the stiff sea on the bar where a strong ebb-tide ran in the teeth of the summer sea-breeze. But the Japanese were cautious. Their thirty- and forty-thousand-ton battleships slowed down half a dozen miles offshore and maneuvered in ponderous evolutions, while tiny scout-boats (lean, six-funnelled destroyers) ran in, cutting blackly the flashing sea like so many sharks. But, compared with the *Energon,* they were leviathans. Compared with them, the *Energon* was as the sword of the archangel Michael, and they the forerunners of the hosts of hell.

But the flashing of the sword, the good people of San Francisco, gathered on her hills, never saw. Mysterious, invisible, it cleaved the air and smote the mightiest blows of combat the world had ever witnessed. The good people of San Francisco saw little and understood less. They saw only a million and a half of tons of brine-cleaving, thunder-flinging fabrics hurled skyward and smashed back in ruin to sink into the sea. It was all over in five minutes. Remained upon the wide expanse of sea only the

Energon, rolling white and toylike on the bar.

Goliah spoke to the Mikado and the Elder Statesmen. It was only an ordinary cable message, dispatched from San Francisco by the captain of the *Energon*, but it was of sufficient moment to cause the immediate withdrawal of Japan from the Philippines and of her surviving fleets from the sea. Japan the skeptical was converted. She had felt the weight of Goliah's arm. And meekly she obeyed when Goliah commanded her to dismantle her war vessels and to turn the metal into useful appliances for the arts of peace. In all the ports, navy-yards, machine-shops, and foundries of Japan tens of thousands of brown-skinned artisans converted the war-monsters into myriads of useful things, such as plowshares (Goliah insisted on plowshares), gasoline engines, bridge-trusses, telephone and telegraph wires, steel rails, locomotives, and rolling stock for railways. It was a world-penance for a world to see, and paltry indeed it made appear that earlier penance, barefooted in the snow, of an emperor to a pope for daring to squabble over temporal power.

Goliah's next summons was to the ten leading scientists of the United States. This time there was no hesitancy in obeying. The savants were ludicrously prompt, some of them waiting in San Francisco for weeks so as not to miss the scheduled sailing-date. They departed on the *Energon* on June 15; and while they were on the sea, on the way to Palgrave Island, Goliah performed another spectacular feat. Germany and France were preparing to fly at each other's throats. Goliah commanded peace. They ignored the command, tacitly agreeing to fight it out on land where it seemed safer for the belligerently inclined. Goliah set the date of June 19 for the cessation of hostile preparations. Both countries mobilized their armies on June 18, and hurled them at the common frontier. And on June 19, Goliah struck. All generals, war-secretaries, and jingo-leaders in the two countries died on that day; and that day two vast armies, undirected, like strayed sheep, walked over each other's frontiers and fraternized. But the great German war lord had escaped—it was learned, afterward, by hiding in the huge safe where were stored the secret archives of his empire. And when he emerged he was a very penitent war lord, and like the Mikado of Japan he was set to work beating his sword-blades into plowshares and pruning-hooks.

But in the escape of the German Emperor was discovered a great significance. The scientists of the world plucked up courage, got back their nerve. One thing was conclusively evident—Goliah's power was not magic. Law still reigned in the universe. Goliah's power had limitations, else had the German Emperor not escaped by secretly hiding in a steel safe. Many learned articles on the subject appeared in the magazines.

GOLIAH

The ten scientists arrived back from Palgrave Island on July 6. Heavy platoons of police protected them from the reporters. No, they had not seen Goliah, they said in the one official interview that was vouchsafed; but they had talked with him, and they had seen things. They were not permitted to state definitely all that they had seen and heard, but they could say that the world was about to be revolutionized. Goliah was in the possession of a tremendous discovery that placed all the world at his mercy, and it was a good thing for the world that Goliah was merciful. The ten scientists proceeded directly to Washington on a special train, where, for days, they were closeted with the heads of government, while the nation hung breathless on the outcome.

But the outcome was a long time in arriving. From Washington the President issued commands to the masters and leading figures of the nation. Everything was secret. Day by day deputations of bankers, railway lords, captains of industry, and Supreme Court justices arrived; and when they arrived they remained. The weeks dragged on, and then, on August 25, began the famous issuance of proclamations. Congress and the Senate co-operated with the President in this, while the Supreme Court justices gave their sanction and the money lords and the captains of industry agreed. War was declared upon the capitalist masters of the nation. Martial law was declared over the whole United States. The supreme power was vested in the President.

In one day, child-labor in the whole country was abolished. It was done by decree, and the United States was prepared with its army to enforce its decrees. In the same day all women factory workers were dismissed to their homes, and all the sweatshops were closed. "But we cannot make profits!" wailed the petty capitalists. "Fools!" was the retort of Goliah. "As if the meaning of life were profits! Give up your businesses and your profit-mongering." "But there is nobody to buy our business!" they wailed. "Buy and sell—is that all the meaning life has for you?" replied Goliah. "You have nothing to sell. Turn over your little cutthroating, anarchistic businesses to the government so that they may be rationally organized and operated." And the next day, by decree, the government began taking possession of all factories, shops, mines, ships, railroads, and producing lands.

The nationalization of the means of production and distribution went on apace. Here and there were skeptical capitalists of moment. They were made prisoners and haled to Palgrave Island, and when they returned they always acquiesced in what the government was doing. A little later the journey to Palgrave Island became unnecessary. When objection was made, the reply of the officials was:—"Goliah has spoken"—which was another way of saying, "He must be obeyed."

The captains of industry became heads of departments. It was found that civil engineers, for instance, worked just as well in government employ as, before, they had worked in private employ. It was found that men of high executive ability could not violate their nature. They could not escape exercising their executive ability, any more than a crab could escape crawling or a bird could escape flying. And so it was that all the splendid force of the men who had previously worked for themselves was now put to work for the good of society. The half-dozen great railway chiefs co-operated in the organizing of a national system of railways that was amazingly efficacious. Never again was there such a thing as a car shortage. These chiefs were not the Wall Street railway magnates, but they were the men who formerly had done the real work while in the employ of the Wall Street magnates.

Wall Street was dead. There was no more buying and selling and speculating. Nobody had anything to buy or sell. There was nothing in which to speculate. "Put the stock gamblers to work," said Goliah; "give those that are young, and that so desire, a chance to learn useful trades." "Put the drummers, and salesmen, and advertising agents, and real estate agents to work," said Goliah; and by hundreds of thousands the erstwhile useless middlemen and parasites went into useful occupations. The four hundred thousand idle gentlemen of the country who had lived upon incomes were likewise put to work. Then there were a lot of helpless men in high places who were cleared out, the remarkable thing about this being that they were cleared out by their own fellows. Of this class were the professional politicians, whose wisdom and power consisted of manipulating machine politics and of grafting. There was no longer any graft. Since there were no private interests to purchase special privileges, no bribes were offered to legislators, and legislators for the first time legislated for the people. The result was that men who were efficient, not in corruption, but in direction, found their way into the legislatures.

With this rational organization of society amazing results were brought about. The national day's work was eight hours, and yet production increased. In spite of the great permanent improvements and of the immense amount of energy consumed in systematizing the competitive chaos of society, production doubled and tripled upon itself. The standard of living increased, and still consumption could not keep up with production. The maximum working age was decreased to fifty years, to forty-nine years, and to forty-eight years. The minimum working age went up from sixteen years to eighteen years. The eight-hour day became a

100

seven-hour day, and in a few months the national working day was reduced to five hours.

In the meantime glimmerings were being caught, not of the identity of Goliah, but of how he had worked and prepared for his assuming control of the world. Little things leaked out, clues were followed up, apparently unrelated things were pieced together. Strange stories of blacks stolen from Africa were remembered, of Chinese and Japanese contract coolies who had mysteriously disappeared, of lonely South Sea Islands raided and their inhabitants carried away; stories of yachts and merchant steamers, mysteriously purchased, that had disappeared and the descriptions of which remotely tallied with the crafts that had carried the Orientals and Africans and islanders away. Where had Goliah got the sinews of war? was the question. And the surmised answer was: By exploiting these stolen laborers. It was they that lived in the exposed village on Palgrave Island. It was the product of their toil that had purchased the yachts and merchant steamers and enabled Goliah's agents to permeate society and carry out his will. And what was the product of their toil that had given Goliah the wealth necessary to realize his plan? Commercial radium, the newspapers proclaimed; and radiyte, and radiosole, and argatium, and argyte, and the mysterious golyte (that had proved so valuable in metallurgy). These were the new compounds, discovered in the first decade of the twentieth century, the commercial and scientific use of which had become so enormous in the second decade.

The line of fruit boats that ran from Hawaii to San Francisco was declared to be the property of Goliah. This was a surmise, for no other owner could be discovered, and the agents who handled the shipments of the fruit boats were only agents. Since no one else owned the fruit boats, then Goliah must own them. The point of which is: *that it leaked out that the major portion of the world's supply in these precious compounds was brought to San Francisco by those very fruit boats.* That the whole chain of surmise was correct was proved in later years when Goliah's slaves were liberated and honorably pensioned by the international government of the world. It was at that time that the seal of secrecy was lifted from the lips of his agents and higher emissaries, and those that chose revealed much of the mystery of Goliah's organization and methods. His destroying angels, however, remained forever dumb. Who the men were who went forth to the high places and killed at his bidding will be unknown to the end of time—for kill they did, by means of that very subtle and then-mysterious force that Goliah had discovered and named "Energon."

But at that time Energon, the little giant that was destined to do the work of the world, was unknown and undreamed of. Only Goliah knew, and he kept his secret well. Even his agents, who were armed with it, and who, in the case of the yacht *Energon,* destroyed a mighty fleet of warships by exploding their magazines, knew not what the subtle and potent force was, nor how it was manufactured. They knew only one of its many uses, and in that one use they had been instructed by Goliah. It is now well known that radium, and radiyte, and radiosole, and all the other compounds, were by-products of the manufacture of Energon by Goliah from the sunlight; but at that time nobody knew what Energon was, and Goliah continued to awe and rule the world.

One of the uses of Energon was in wireless telegraphy. It was by its means that Goliah was able to communicate with his agents all over the world. At that time the apparatus required by an agent was so clumsy that it could not be packed in anything less than a fair-sized steamer trunk. To-day, thanks to the improvements of Hendsoll, the perfected apparatus can be carried in a coat pocket.

It was in December, 1924, that Goliah sent out his famous "Christmas Letter," part of the text of which is here given:—

"So far, while I have kept the rest of the nations from each other's throats, I have devoted myself particularly to the United States. Now I have not given to the people of the United States a rational social organization. What I have done has been to compel them to make that organization themselves. There is more laughter in the United States these days, and there is more sense. Food and shelter are no longer obtained by the anarchistic methods of so-called individualism, but are now well nigh automatic. And the beauty of it is that the people of the United States have achieved all this for themselves. I did not achieve it for them. I repeat, they achieved it for themselves. All that I did was to put the fear of death in the hearts of the few that sat in the high places and obstructed the coming of rationality and laughter. The fear of death made those in the high places get out of the way, that was all, and gave the intelligence of man a chance to realize itself socially.

"In the year that is to come I shall devote myself to the rest of the world. I shall put the fear of death in the hearts of all that sit in the high places in all the nations. And they will do as they have done in the United States—get down out of the high places and give the intelligence of man a chance for social rationality. All the nations shall tread the path the United States is now on.

"And when all the nations are well along on that path, I shall have something else for them. But first they must travel that path for themselves. They must demonstrate that the intelligence of mankind

102

to-day, with the mechanical energy now at its disposal, is capable of organizing society so that food and shelter be made automatic, labor be reduced to a three-hour day, and joy and laughter be made universal. And when that is accomplished, not by me but by the intelligence of mankind, then I shall make a present to the world of a new mechanical energy. This is my discovery. This Energon is nothing more nor less than the cosmic energy that resides in the solar rays. When it is harnessed by mankind it will do the work of the world. There will be no more multitudes of miners slaving out their lives in the bowels of the earth, no more sooty firemen and greasy engineers. All may dress in white, if they so will. The work of life will have become play, and young and old will be the children of joy, and the business of living will become joy; and they will compete, one with another, in achieving ethical concepts and spiritual heights, in fashioning pictures and songs, and stories, in statecraft and beauty craft, in the sweat and the endeavor of the wrestler and the runner and the player of games—all will compete, not for sordid coin and base material reward, but for the joy that shall be theirs in the development and vigor of flesh and in the development and keenness of spirit. All will be joy-smiths, and their task shall be to beat out laughter from the ringing anvil of life.

"And now one word for the immediate future. On New Year's Day all nations shall disarm, all fortresses and war-ships shall be dismantled, and all armies shall be disbanded.

"Goliah."

On New Year's Day all the world disarmed. The millions of soldiers and sailors and workmen in the standing armies, in the navies, and in the countless arsenals, machine-shops, and factories for the manufacture of war machinery, were dismissed to their homes. These many millions of men, as well as their costly war machinery, had hitherto been supported on the back of labor. They now went into useful occupations, and the released labor giant heaved a mighty sigh of relief. The policing of the world was left to the peace officers and was purely social, whereas war had been distinctly anti-social.

Ninety per cent of the crimes against society had been crimes against private property. With the passing of private property, at least in the means of production, and with the organization of industry that gave every man a chance, the crimes against private property practically ceased. The police forces everywhere were reduced repeatedly and again and again. Nearly all occasional and habitual criminals ceased voluntarily from their depredations. There was no longer any need for them to commit crime. They merely changed with changing conditions. A smaller number of

103

criminals was put into hospitals and cured. And the remnant of the hopelessly criminal and degenerate was segregated. And the courts in all countries were likewise decreased in number again and again. Ninety-five per cent of all civil cases had been squabbles over property, conflicts of property-rights, lawsuits, contests of wills, breaches of contract, bankruptcies, etc. With the passing of private property, this ninety-five per cent of the cases that cluttered the courts also passed. The courts became shadows, attenuated ghosts, rudimentary vestiges of the anarchistic times that had preceded the coming of Goliah.

The year 1925 was a lively year in the world's history. Goliah ruled the world with a strong hand. Kings and emperors journeyed to Palgrave Island, saw the wonders of Energon, and went away, with the fear of death in their hearts, to abdicate thrones and crowns and hereditary licenses. When Goliah spoke to politicians (so-called "statesmen"), they obeyed . . . or died. He dictated universal reforms, dissolved refractory parliaments, and to the great conspiracy that was formed of mutinous money lords and captains of industry he sent his destroying angels. "The time is past for fooling," he told them. "You are anachronisms. You stand in the way of humanity. To the scrap-heap with you." To those that protested, and they were many, he said: "This is no time for logomachy. You can argue for centuries. It is what you have done in the past. I have no time for argument. Get out of the way."

With the exception of putting a stop to war, and of indicating the broad general plan, Goliah did nothing. By putting the fear of death into the hearts of those that sat in the high places and obstructed progress, Goliah made the opportunity for the unshackled intelligence of the best social thinkers of the world to exert itself. Goliah left all the multitudinous details of reconstruction to these social thinkers. He wanted them to prove that they were able to do it, and they proved it. It was due to their initiative that the white plague was stamped out from the world. It was due to them, and in spite of a deal of protesting from the sentimentalists, that all the extreme hereditary inefficients were segregated and denied marriage.

Goliah had nothing whatever to do with the instituting of the colleges of invention. This idea originated practically simultaneously in the minds of thousands of social thinkers. The time was ripe for the realization of the idea, and everywhere arose the splendid institutions of invention. For the first time the ingenuity of man was loosed upon the problem of simplifying life, instead of upon the making of money-earning devices. The affairs of life, such as house-cleaning, dish and window-washing, dust-removing, and scrubbing and clothes-washing, and all the endless sordid and necessary details, were simplified by invention until they became automatic. We of to-day cannot realize the barbarously filthy and slavish lives of those that lived prior to 1925.

The international government of the world was another idea that sprang simultaneously into the minds of thousands. The successful realization of this idea was a surprise to many, but as a surprise it was nothing to that received by the mildly protestant sociologists and biologists when irrefutable facts exploded the doctrine of Malthus. With leisure and joy in the world; with an immensely higher standard of living; and with the enormous spaciousness of opportunity for recreation, development, and pursuit of beauty and nobility and all the higher attributes, the birth-rate fell, and fell astoundingly. People ceased breeding like cattle. And better than that, it was immediately noticeable that a higher average of children was being born. The doctrine of Malthus was knocked into a cocked hat—or flung to the scrap-heap, as Goliah would have put it.

All that Goliah had predicted that the intelligence of mankind could accomplish with the mechanical energy at its disposal, came to pass. Human dissatisfaction practically disappeared. The elderly people were the great grumblers; but when they were honorably pensioned by society, as they passed the age limit for work, the great majority ceased grumbling. They found themselves better off in their idle old days under the new regime, enjoying vastly more pleasures and comforts than they had in their busy and toilsome youth under the old regime. The younger generation had easily adapted itself to the changed order, and the very young had never known anything else. The sum of human happiness had increased enormously. The world had become gay and sane. Even the old fogies of professors of sociology, who had opposed with might and main the coming of the new regime, made no complaint. They were a score of times better remunerated than in the old days, and they were not worked nearly so hard. Besides, they were busy revising sociology and writing new text-books on the subject. Here and there, it is true, there were atavisms, men who yearned for the flesh-pots and cannibal-feasts of the old alleged "individualism," creatures long of teeth and savage of claw who wanted to prey upon their fellow-men; but they were looked upon as diseased, and were treated in hospitals. A small remnant, however, proved incurable, and was confined in asylums and denied marriage. Thus there was no progeny to inherit their atavistic tendencies.

As the years went by, Goliah dropped out of the running of the world. There was nothing for him to run. The world was running itself, and doing it smoothly and beautifully. In 1937, Goliah made his

105

long-promised present of Energon to the world. He himself had devised a thousand ways in which the little giant should do the work of the world—all of which he made public at the same time. But instantly the colleges of invention seized upon Energon and utilized it in a hundred thousand additional ways. In fact, as Goliah confessed in his letter of March, 1938, the colleges of invention cleared up several puzzling features of Energon that had baffled him during the preceding years. With the introduction of the use of Energon the two-hour work-day was cut down almost to nothing. As Goliah had predicted, work indeed became play. And, so tremendous was man's productive capacity, due to Energon and the rational social utilization of it, that the humblest citizen enjoyed leisure and time and opportunity for an immensely greater abundance of living than had the most favored under the old anarchistic system.

Nobody had ever seen Goliah, and all peoples began to clamor for their savior to appear. While the world did not minimize his discovery of Energon, it was decided that greater than that was his wide social vision. He was a superman, a scientific superman; and the curiosity of the world to see him had become wellnigh unbearable. It was in 1941, after much hesitancy on his part, that he finally emerged from Palgrave Island. He arrived on June 6 in San Francisco, and for the first time, since his retirement to Palgrave Island, the world looked upon his face. And the world was disappointed. Its imagination had been touched. An heroic figure had been made out of Goliah. He was the man, or the demi-god, rather, who had turned the planet over. The deeds of Alexander, Caesar, Genghis Khan, and Napoleon were as the play of babes alongside his colossal achievements.

And ashore in San Francisco and through its streets stepped and rode a little old man, sixty-five years of age, well preserved, with a pink-and-white complexion and a bald spot on his head the size of an apple. He was short-sighted and wore spectacles. But when the spectacles were removed, his were quizzical blue eyes like a child's, filled with mild wonder at the world. Also his eyes had a way of twinkling, accompanied by a screwing up of the face, as if he laughed at the huge joke he had played upon the world, trapping it, in spite of itself, into happiness and laughter.

For a scientific superman and world tyrant, he had remarkable weaknesses. He loved sweets, and was inordinately fond of salted almonds and salted pecans, especially of the latter. He always carried a paper bag of them in his pocket, and he had a way of saying frequently that the chemism of his nature demanded such fare. Perhaps his most astonishing failing was cats. He had an ineradicable aversion to that domestic animal.

106

It will be remembered that he fainted dead away with sudden fright, while speaking in Brotherhood Palace, when the janitor's cat walked out upon the stage and brushed against his legs.

But no sooner had he revealed himself to the world than he was identified. Old-time friends had no difficulty in recognizing him as Percival Stultz, the German-American who, in 1898, had worked in the Union Iron Works, and who, for two years at that time, had been secretary of Branch 369 of the International Brotherhood of Machinists. It was in 1901, then twenty-five years of age, that he had taken special scientific courses at the University of California, at the same time supporting himself by soliciting what was then known as "life insurance." His records as a student are preserved in the university museum, and they are unenviable. He is remembered by the professors he sat under chiefly for his absent-mindedness. Undoubtedly, even then, he was catching glimpses of the wide visions that later were to be his.

His naming himself "Goliah" and shrouding himself in mystery was his little joke, he later explained. As Goliah, or any other thing like that, he said, he was able to touch the imagination of the world and turn it over; but as Percival Stultz, wearing side-whiskers and spectacles, and weighing one hundred and eighteen pounds, he would have been unable to turn over a pecan—"not even a salted pecan."

But the world quickly got over its disappointment in his personal appearance and antecedents. It knew him and revered him as the master-mind of the ages; and it loved him for himself, for his quizzical short-sighted eyes and the inimitable way in which he screwed up his face when he laughed; it loved him for his simplicity and comradeship and warm humanness, and for his fondness for salted pecans and his aversion to cats. And to-day, in the wonder-city of Asgard, rises in awful beauty that monument to him that dwarfs the pyramids and all the monstrous blood-stained monuments of antiquity. And on that monument, as all know, is inscribed in imperishable bronze the prophecy and the fulfillment: "ALL WILL BE JOY-SMITHS, AND THEIR TASK SHALL BE TO BEAT OUT LAUGHTER FROM THE RINGING ANVIL OF LIFE."

[Editorial Note:—*This remarkable production is the work of Harry Beckwith, a student in the Lowell High School of San Francisco, and it is here reproduced chiefly because of the youth of its author. Far be it from our policy to burden our readers with ancient history; and when it is known that Harry Beckwith was only* fifteen when the foregoing was written, our motive will be understood. "Goliah" won the Premier for high school composition in 2254, and last year Harry Beckwith took advantage of the privilege earned, by electing to spend six months in Asgard. The wealth of historical detail, the atmosphere of the times, and the mature style of the composition are especially noteworthy in one so young.]

THE UNPARALLELED
INVASION

Written at the end of 1906, this story projects events ahead to the
year of the American bicentennial (and incidentally the one hundredth
anniversary of London's own birth)—1976. Arthur Calder-Marshall has
written (in *The Bodley Head Jack London*) that the story "was a variation
on the theme of 'The Yellow Peril,' a common nightmare of the first
decade of this century." He adds, "It is amusing in its certainty that
towards the end of the twentieth century the conquest of the air would
have extended to the simplest types of airship. Yet it is remarkably
prophetic in its anticipation of the possibilities of bacteriological warfare."
    London felt, on the basis of his experiences as war correspondent in
the Russo-Japanese War (1904), that he knew what he was talking about.
When he returned from Manchuria, he wrote an essay entitled "The
Yellow Peril" (1904) and in it observed: "To-day, equipped with the finest
machines and systems of destruction the Caucasian mind had devised,
handling machines and systems with remarkable and deadly accuracy, this
rejuvenescent Japanese race has embarked on a course of conquest, the
goal of which no man knows." Prophetic indeed!

It was in the year 1976 that the trouble between the world and
China reached its culmination. It was because of this that the celebration
of the Second Centennial of American Liberty was deferred. Many other
plans of the nations of the earth were twisted and tangled and postponed
for the same reason. The world awoke rather abruptly to its danger; but
for over seventy years, unperceived, affairs had been shaping toward this
very end.
    The year 1904 logically marks the beginning of the development
that, seventy years later, was to bring consternation to the whole world.
The Japanese-Russian War took place in 1904, and the historians of the

McClure's Magazine, 35 (July, 1910):308-15.

time gravely noted it down that that event marked the entrance of Japan into the comity of nations. What it really did mark was the awakening of China. This awakening, long expected, had finally been given up. The Western nations had tried to arouse China, and they had failed. Out of their native optimism and race-egotism they had therefore concluded that the task was impossible, that China would never awaken.

What they had failed to take into account was this: *that between them and China was no common psychological speech.* Their thought-processes were radically dissimilar. There was no intimate vocabulary. The Western mind penetrated the Chinese mind but a short distance when it found itself in a fathomless maze. The Chinese mind penetrated the Western mind an equally short distance when it fetched up against a blank, incomprehensible wall. It was all a matter of language. There was no way to communicate Western ideas to the Chinese mind. China remained asleep. The material achievement and progress of the West was a closed book to her; nor could the West open the book. Back and deep down on the tie-ribs of consciousness, in the mind, say, of the English-speaking race, was a capacity to thrill to short, Saxon words; back and deep down on the tie-ribs of consciousness of the Chinese mind was a capacity to thrill to its own hieroglyphics; but the Chinese mind could not thrill to short, Saxon words; nor could the English-speaking mind thrill to hieroglyphics. The fabrics of their minds were woven from totally different stuffs. They were mental aliens. And so it was that Western material achievement and progress made no dent on the rounded sleep of China.

Came Japan and her victory over Russia in 1904. Now the Japanese race was the freak and paradox among Eastern peoples. In some strange way Japan was receptive to all the West had to offer. Japan swiftly assimilated the Western ideas, and digested them, and so capably applied them that she suddenly burst forth, full-panoplied, a world-power. There is no explaining this peculiar openness of Japan to the alien culture of the West. As well might be explained any biological sport in the animal kingdom.

Having decisively thrashed the great Russian Empire, Japan promptly set about dreaming a colossal dream of empire for herself. Korea she had made into a granary and a colony; treaty privileges and vulpine diplomacy gave her the monopoly of Manchuria. But Japan was not satisfied. She turned her eyes upon China. There lay a vast territory, and in that territory were the hugest deposits in the world of iron and coal—the backbone of industrial civilization. Given natural resources, the other great factor in industry is labor. In that territory was a population of 400,000,000 souls—one quarter of the then total population of the earth.

Furthermore, the Chinese were excellent workers, while their fatalistic philosophy (or religion) and their stolid nervous organization constituted them splendid soldiers—if they were properly managed. Needless to say, Japan was prepared to furnish that management.

But best of all, from the standpoint of Japan, the Chinese was a kindred race. The baffling enigma of the Chinese character to the West was no baffling enigma to the Japanese. The Japanese understood as we could never school ourselves or hope to understand. Their mental processes were the same. The Japanese thought with the same thought-symbols as did the Chinese, and they thought in the same peculiar grooves. Into the Chinese mind the Japanese went on where we were balked by the obstacle of incomprehension. They took the turning which we could not perceive, twisted around the obstacle, and were out of sight in the ramifications of the Chinese mind where we could not follow. They were brothers. Long ago one had borrowed the other's written language, and, untold generations before that, they had diverged from the common Mongol stock. There had been changes, differentiations brought about by diverse conditions and infusions of other blood; but down at the bottom of their beings, twisted into the fibers of them, was a heritage in common, a sameness in kind that time had not obliterated.

And so Japan took upon herself the management of China. In the years immediately following the war with Russia, her agents swarmed over the Chinese Empire. A thousand miles beyond the last mission station toiled her engineers and spies, clad as coolies, under the guise of itinerant merchants or proselyting Buddhist priests, noting down the horsepower of every waterfall, the likely sites for factories, the heights of mountains and passes, the strategic advantages and weaknesses, the wealth of the farming valleys, the number of bullocks in a district or the number of laborers that could be collected by forced levies. Never was there such a census, and it could have been taken by no other people than the dogged, patient, patriotic Japanese.

But in short time secrecy was thrown to the winds. Japan's officers reorganized the Chinese army; her drill sergeants made the medieval warriors over into twentieth-century soldiers, accustomed to all the modern machinery of war and with a higher average of marksmanship than the soldiers of any Western nation. The engineers of Japan deepened and widened the intricate system of canals, built factories and foundries, netted the empire with telegraphs and telephones, and inaugurated the era of railroad-building. It was these same protagonists of machine-civilization that discovered the great oil deposits of Chunsan, the iron mountains of Whang-Sing, the copper ranges of Chinchi, and they sank the gas wells of

111

Wow-Wee, that most marvelous reservoir of natural gas in all the world.

In China's councils of empire were the Japanese emissaries. In the ears of the statesmen whispered the Japanese statesmen. The political reconstruction of the Empire was due to them. They evicted the scholar class, which was violently reactionary, and put into office progressive officials. And in every town and city of the Empire newspapers were started. Of course, Japanese editors ran the policy of these papers, which policy they got direct from Tokio. It was these papers that educated and made progressive the great mass of the population.

China was at last awake. Where the West had failed, Japan succeeded. She had transmuted Western culture and achievement into terms that were intelligible to the Chinese understanding. Japan herself, when she so suddenly awakened, had astounded the world. But at the time she was only forty millions strong. China's awakening, what of her four hundred millions and the scientific advance of the world, was frightfully astounding. She was the colossus of the nations, and swiftly her voice was heard in no uncertain tones in the affairs and councils of the nations. Japan egged her on, and the proud Western peoples listened with respectful ears.

China's swift and remarkable rise was due, perhaps more than to anything else, to the superlative quality of her labor. The Chinese was the perfect type of industry. He had always been that. For sheer ability to work, no worker in the world could compare with him. Work was the breath of his nostrils. It was to him what wandering and fighting in far lands and spiritual adventure had been to other peoples. Liberty, to him, epitomized itself in access to the means of toil. To till the soil and labor interminably was all he asked of life and the powers that be. And the awakening of China had given its vast population not merely free and unlimited access to the means of toil, but access to the highest and most scientific machine-means of toil.

China rejuvenescent! It was but a step to China rampant. She discovered a new pride in herself and a will of her own. She began to chafe under the guidance of Japan, but she did not chafe long. On Japan's advice, in the beginning, she had expelled from the Empire all Western missionaries, engineers, drill sergeants, merchants, and teachers. She now began to expel the similar representatives of Japan. The latter's advisory statesmen were showered with honors and decorations, and sent home. The West had awakened Japan, and, as Japan had then requited the West, Japan was now requited by China. Japan was thanked for her kindly aid and flung out bag and baggage by her gigantic protégé. The Western nations chuckled. Japan's rainbow dream had gone glimmering. She grew

112

angry. China laughed at her. The blood and the swords of the Samurai would out, and Japan rashly went to war. This occurred in 1922, and in seven bloody months Manchuria, Korea, and Formosa were taken away from her and she was hurled back, bankrupt, to stifle in her tiny, crowded islands. Exit Japan from the world drama. Thereafter she devoted herself to art, and her task became to please the world greatly with her creations of wonder and beauty.

Contrary to expectation, China did not prove warlike. She had no Napoleonic dream, and was content to devote herself to the arts of peace. After a time of disquiet, the idea was accepted that China was to be feared, not in war, but in commerce. It will be seen that the real danger was not apprehended. China went on consummating her machine-civilization. Instead of a large standing army, she developed an immensely larger and splendidly efficient militia. Her navy was so small that it was the laughing stock of the world; nor did she attempt to strengthen her navy. The treaty ports of the world were never entered by her visiting battleships.

The real danger lay in the fecundity of her loins, and it was in 1970 that the first cry of alarm was raised. For some time all territories adjacent to China had been grumbling at Chinese immigration; but now it suddenly came home to the world that China's population was 500,000,000. She had increased by a hundred millions since her awakening. Burchaldter called to attention the fact that there were more Chinese in existence than white-skinned people. He performed a simple sum in arithmetic. He added together the populations of the United States, Canada, New Zealand, Australia, South Africa, England, France, Germany, Italy, Austria, European Russia, and all Scandinavia. The result was 495,000,000. And the population of China over-topped this tremendous total by 5,000,000. Burchaldter's figures went around the world, and the world shivered.

For many centuries China's population had been constant. Her territory had been saturated with population; that is to say, her territory, with the primitive method of production, had supported the maximum limit of population. But when she awoke and inaugurated the machine-civilization, her productive power had been enormously increased. Thus, on the same territory, she was able to support a far larger population. At once the birth rate began to rise and the death rate to fall. Before, when population pressed against the means of subsistence, the excess population had been swept away by famine. But now, thanks to the machine-civilization, China's means of subsistence had been enormously extended, and there were no famines; her population followed on the heels of the increase in the means of subsistence.

During this time of transition and development of power, China had entertained no dreams of conquest. The Chinese was not an imperial race. It was industrious, thrifty, and peace-loving. War was looked upon as an unpleasant but necessary task that at times must be performed. And so, while the Western races had squabbled and fought, and world-adventured against one another, China had calmly gone on working at her machines and growing. Now she was spilling over the boundaries of her Empire—that was all, just spilling over into the adjacent territories with all the certainty and terrifying slow momentum of a glacier.

Following upon the alarm raised by Burchaldter's figures, in 1970, France made a long-threatened stand. French Indo-China had been over-run, filled up, by Chinese immigrants. France called a halt. The Chinese wave flowed on. France assembled a force of a hundred thousand on the boundary between her unfortunate colony and China, and China sent down an army of militia-soldiers a million strong. Behind came the wives and sons and daughters and relatives, with their personal household luggage, in a second army. The French force was brushed aside like a fly. The Chinese militia-soldiers, along with their families, over five millions all told, coolly took possession of French Indo-China and settled down to stay for a few thousand years.

Outraged France was in arms. She hurled fleet after fleet against the coast of China, and nearly bankrupted herself by the effort. China had no navy. She withdrew like a turtle into her shell. For a year the French fleets blockaded the coast and bombarded exposed towns and villages. China did not mind. She did not depend upon the rest of the world for anything. She calmly kept out of range of the French guns and went on working. France wept and wailed, wrung her impotent hands and appealed to the dumfounded nations. Then she landed a punitive expedition to march to Peking. It was two hundred and fifty thousand strong, and it was the flower of France. It landed without opposition and marched into the interior. And that was the last ever seen of it. The line of communication was snapped on the second day. Not a survivor came back to tell what had happened. It had been swallowed up in China's cavernous maw, that was all.

In the five years that followed, China's expansion, in all land directions, went on apace. Siam was made part of the Empire, and, in spite of all that England could do, Burma and the Malay Peninsula were over-run; while all along the long south boundary of Siberia, Russia was pressed severely by China's advancing hordes. The process was simple. First came the Chinese immigration (or, rather, it was already there, having come there slowly and insidiously during the previous years). Next came the clash at arms and the brushing away of all opposition by a monster army of militia-soldiers, followed by their families and household baggage. And finally came their settling down as colonists in the conquered territory. Never was there so strange and effective a method of world conquest.

Napal and Bhutan were over-run, and the whole northern boundary of India pressed against by this fearful tide of life. To the west, Bokhara, and, even to the south and west, Afghanistan, were swallowed up. Persia, Turkestan, and all Central Asia felt the pressure of the flood. It was at this time that Burchaldter revised his figures. He had been mistaken. China's population must be seven hundred millions, eight hundred millions, nobody knew how many millions, but at any rate it would soon be a billion. There were two Chinese for every white-skinned human in the world, Burchaldter announced, and the world trembled. China's increase must have begun immediately, in 1904. It was remembered that since that date there had not been a single famine. At 5,000,000 a year increase, her total increase in the intervening seventy years must be 350,000,000. But who was to know? It might be more. Who was to know anything of this strange new menace of the twentieth century—China, old China, rejuvenescent, fruitful, and militant!

The Convention of 1975 was called at Philadelphia. All the Western nations, and some few of the Eastern, were represented. Nothing was accomplished. There was talk of all countries putting bounties on children to increase the birth rate, but it was laughed to scorn by the arithmeticians, who pointed out that China was too far in the lead in that direction. No feasible way of coping with China was suggested. China was appealed to and threatened by the United Powers, and that was all the Convention of Philadelphia came to; and the Convention and the Powers were laughed at by China. Li Tang Fwung, the power behind the Dragon Throne, deigned to reply.

"What does China care for the comity of nations?" said Li Tang Fwung. "We are the most ancient, honorable, and royal of races. We have our own destiny to accomplish. It is unpleasant that our destiny does not jibe with the destiny of the rest of the world, but what would you? You have talked windily about the royal races and the heritage of the earth, and we can only reply that that remains to be seen. You cannot invade us. Never mind about your navies. Don't shout. We know our navy is small. You see, we use it for police purposes. We do not care for the sea. Our strength is in our population, which will soon be a billion. Thanks to you, we are equipped with all modern war-machinery. Send your navies. We will not notice them. Send your punitive expeditions, but first remember

115

France. To land half a million soldiers on our shores would strain the resources of any of you. And our thousand millions would swallow them down in a mouthful. Send a million; send five million, and we will swallow them down just as readily. Pouf! A mere nothing, a meager morsel. Destroy, as you have threatened, you United States, the ten million coolies we have forced upon your shores—why, the amount scarcely equals half of our excess birth rate for a year."

So spoke Li Tang Fwung. The world was nonplussed, helpless, terrified. Truly had he spoken. There was no combating China's amazing birth rate. If her population was a billion, and was increasing twenty millions a year, in twenty-five years it would be a billion and a half—equal to the total population of the world in 1904. And nothing could be done. There was no way to dam up the over-spilling monstrous flood of life. War was futile. China laughed at a blockade of her coasts. She welcomed invasion. In her capacious maw was room for all the hosts of earth that could be hurled at her. And in the meantime her flood of yellow life poured out and on over Asia. China laughed and read in their magazines the learned lucubrations of the distracted Western scholars.

But there was one scholar China failed to reckon on—Jacobus Laningdale. Not that he was a scholar, except in the widest sense. Primarily, Jacobus Laningdale was a scientist, and, up to that time, a very obscure scientist, a professor employed in the laboratories of the Health Office of New York City. Jacobus Laningdale's head was very like any other head, but in that head was evolved an idea. Also, in that head was the wisdom to keep that idea secret. He did not write an article for the magazines. Instead, he asked for a vacation. On September 19, 1975, he arrived in Washington. It was evening, but he proceeded straight to the White House, for he had already arranged an audience with the President. He was closeted with President Moyer for three hours. What passed between them was not learned by the rest of the world until long after; in fact, at that time the world was not interested in Jacobus Laningdale. Next day the President called in his Cabinet. Jacobus Laningdale was present. The proceedings were kept secret. But that very afternoon Rufus Cowdery, Secretary of State, left Washington and early the following morning sailed for England. The secret that he carried began to spread, but it spread only among the heads of governments. Possibly half a dozen men in a nation were entrusted with the idea that had formed in Jacobus Laningdale's head. Following the spread of the secret, sprang up great activity in all the dock-years, arsenals, and navy-yards. The people of France and Austria became suspicious, but so sincere were their governments' calls for confidence that they acquiesced in the unknown project that was afoot.

116

This was the time of the Great Truce. All countries pledged themselves solemnly not to go to war with any other country. The first definite action was the gradual mobilization of the armies of Russia, Germany, Austria, Italy, Greece, and Turkey. Then began the eastward movement. All railroads into Asia were glutted with troop trains. China was the objective, that was all that was known. A little later began the great sea movement. Expeditions of warships were launched from all countries. Fleet followed fleet, and all proceeded to the coast of China. The nations cleaned out their navy-yards. They sent their revenue cutters and dispatch boats and lighthouse tenders, and they sent their last antiquated cruisers and battleships. Not content with this, they impressed the merchant marine. The statistics show that 58,640 merchant steamers, equipped with searchlights and rapid-fire guns, were dispatched by the various nations to China.

And China smiled and waited. On her land side, along her boundaries, were millions of the warriors of Europe. She mobilized five times as many millions of her militia and waited the invasion. On her sea coasts she did the same. But China was puzzled. After all this enormous preparation, there was no invasion. She could not understand. Along the great Siberian frontier all was quiet. Along her coasts the towns and villages were not even shelled. Never, in the history of the world, had there been so mighty a gathering of war fleets. The fleets of all the world were there, and day and night millions of tons of battleships plowed the brine of her coasts, and nothing happened. Nothing was attempted. Did they think to make her emerge from her shell? China smiled. Did they think to tire her out, or starve her out? China smiled again.

But on May 1, 1976, had the reader been in the imperial city of Peking, with its then population of eleven millions, he would have witnessed a curious sight. He would have seen the streets filled with the chattering yellow populace, every queued head tilted back, every slant eye turned skyward. And high up in the blue he would have beheld a tiny dot of black, which, because of its orderly evolutions, he would have identified as an airship. From this airship, as it curved its flight back and forth over the city, fell missiles—strange, harmless missiles, tubes of fragile glass that shattered into thousands of fragments on the streets and house-tops. But there was nothing deadly about these tubes of glass. Nothing happened. There were no explosions. It is true, several Chinese were killed by the tubes dropping on their heads from so enormous a height; but what were three Chinese against an excess birth rate of twenty millions? One tube struck perpendicularly in a fish pond in a garden and was not broken. It was dragged ashore by the master of the house. He did not dare to open it, but, accompanied by his friends, and surrounded by an ever-increasing crowd, he carried the mysterious tube to the magistrate of the district. The latter was a brave man. With all eyes upon him, he shattered the tube with a blow from his brass-bowled pipe. Nothing happened. Of those who were very near, one or two thought they saw some mosquitos fly out. That was all. The crowd set up a great laugh and dispersed.

As Peking was bombarded by glass tubes, so was all China. The tiny airships, dispatched from the warships, contained but two men each, and over all cities, towns, and villages they wheeled and curved, one man directing the ship, the other man throwing over the glass tubes.

Had the reader again been in Peking, six weeks later, he would have looked in vain for the eleven million inhabitants. Some few of them he would have found, a few hundred thousand, perhaps, their carcasses festering in the houses and in the deserted streets, and piled high on the abandoned death wagons. But for the rest he would have had to seek along the highways and byways of the Empire. And not all would he have found fleeing from plague-stricken Peking, for behind them, by hundreds of thousands of unburied corpses by the wayside, he could have marked their flight. And as it was with Peking, so was it with all the cities, towns, and villages of the Empire. The plague smote them all. Nor was it one plague, nor two plagues; it was a score of plagues. Every virulent form of infectious death stalked through the land. Too late the Chinese government apprehended the meaning of the colossal preparations, the marshalling of the world hosts, the flights of the tiny airships, and the rain of the tubes of glass. The proclamations of the government were vain. They could not stop the eleven million plague-stricken wretches, fleeing from the one city of Peking to spread disease through all the land. The physicians and health officers died at their posts; and death, the all-conqueror, rode over the decrees of the Emperor and Li Tang Fwung. It rode over them as well, for Li Tang Fwung died in the second week, and the Emperor, hidden away in the Summer Palace, died in the fourth week.

Had there been one plague, China might have coped with it. But from a score of plagues no creature was immune. The man who escaped smallpox went down before scarlet fever. The man who was immune to yellow fever was carried away by cholera; and if he were immune to that, too, the Black Death, which was the bubonic plague, swept him away. For it was these bacteria, and germs, and microbes, and bacilli, cultured in the laboratories of the West, that had come down upon China in the rain of glass.

All organization vanished. The government crumbled away. Decrees and proclamations were useless when the men who made them and signed

118

them one moment were dead the next. Nor could the maddened millions, spurred on to flight by death, pause to heed anything. They fled from the cities to infect the country, and wherever they fled they carried the plagues with them. The hot summer was on—Jacobus Laningdale had selected the time shrewdly—and the plague festered everywhere. Much is conjectured of what occurred, and much has been learned from the stories of the few survivors. The wretched creatures stormed across the Empire in many-millioned flight. The vast armies China had collected on her frontiers melted away. The farms were ravaged for food, and no more crops were planted, while the crops already in were left unattended and never came to harvest. The most remarkable thing, perhaps, was the flights. Many millions engaged in them, charging to the bounds of the Empire to be met and turned back by the gigantic armies of the West. The slaughter of the mad hosts on the boundaries was stupendous. Time and again the guarding line was drawn back twenty or thirty miles to escape the contagion of the multitudinous dead.

Once the plague broke through and seized upon the German and Austrian soldiers who were guarding the borders of Turkestan. Preparations had been made for such a happening, and though sixty thousand soldiers of Europe were carried off, the international corps of physicians isolated the contagion and dammed it back. It was during this struggle that it was suggested that a new plague-germ had originated, that in some way or other a sort of hybridization between plague-germs had taken place, producing a new and frightfully virulent germ. First suspected by Vomberg, who became infected with it and died, it was later isolated and studied by Stevens, Hazenfelt, Norman, and Landers.

Such was the unparalleled invasion of China. For that billion of people there was no hope. Pent in their vast and festering charnel house, all organization and cohesion lost, they could do naught but die. They could not escape. As they were flung back from their land frontiers, so were they flung back from the sea. Seventy-five thousand vessels patrolled the coasts. By day their smoking funnels dimmed the sea-rim, and by night their flashing searchlights plowed the dark and harrowed it for the tiniest escaping junk. The attempts of the immense fleets of junks were pitiful. Not one ever got by the guarding sea-hounds. Modern war-machinery held back the disorganized mass of China, while the plagues did the work.

But old War was made a thing of laughter. Naught remained to him but patrol duty. China had laughed at war, and war she was getting, but it was ultra-modern war, twentieth-century war, the war of the scientist and the laboratory, the war of Jacobus Laningdale. Hundred-ton guns were toys compared with the micro-organic projectiles hurled from the laboratories, the messengers of death, the destroying angels that stalked through the empire of a billion souls.

During all the summer and fall of 1976 China was an inferno. There was no eluding the microscopic projectiles that sought out the remotest hiding places. The hundreds of millions of dead remained unburied and the germs multiplied themselves, and, toward the last, millions died daily of starvation. Besides, starvation weakened the victims and destroyed their natural defenses against the plagues. Cannibalism, murder, and madness reigned. And so perished China.

Not until the following February, in the coldest weather, were the first expeditions made. These expeditions were small, composed of scientists and bodies of troops; but they entered China from every side. In spite of the most elaborate precautions against infection, numbers of soldiers and a few of the physicians were stricken. But the exploration went bravely on. They found China devastated, a howling wilderness through which wandered bands of wild dogs and desperate bandits who had survived. All survivors were put to death wherever found. And then began the great task, the sanitation of China. Five years and hundreds of millions of treasure were consumed, and then the world moved on—not in zones, as was the idea of Baron Albrecht, but heterogeneously, according to the democratic American program. It was a vast and happy intermingling of nationalities that settled down in China in 1982 and the years that followed—a tremendous and successful experiment in cross-fertilization. We know to-day the splendid mechanical, intellectual, and art output that followed.

It was in 1987, the Great Truce having been dissolved, that the ancient quarrel between France and Germany over Alsace and Lorraine recrudesced. The war-cloud grew dark and threatening in April, and on April 17 the Convention of Copenhagen was called. The representatives of the nations of the world being present, all nations solemnly pledged themselves never to use against one another the laboratory methods of warfare they had employed in the invasion of China.—*Excerpts from Walt Mervin's "Certain Essays in History."*

WHEN THE WORLD WAS YOUNG

On March 10, 1910, in Carmel, California, Sinclair Lewis recorded in his notebook a transaction that has become one of the curiosities of American letters. Wrote Lewis: "14 sh. st. pl. sold to Jack London—$70.00." (See Mark Schorer, *Sinclair Lewis: An American Life,* 1961.)

Among those fourteen short story plots which Lewis sold to London (there were at least two further sales later on) was one which Lewis had tentatively entitled "The Garden Terror," and it became "When the World Was Young" when London fleshed out the spare outline young Lewis provided.

An interesting other sidelight to this story is the remarkable similarity, at least in one memorable scene in the London tale, to one recurring in Edgar Rice Burroughs's celebrated Tarzan books. London's James Ward, in one of his atavistic nighttime foragings, encounters a grizzly bear, clubs the beast to death, then, leaping upon the dead animal, "in the white electric light, resting his club, he chanted a triumph in an unknown tongue."

In Tarzan's case the animal was usually a lion, but otherwise the similarities are remarkable, and Burroughs may have read this story when it appeared in the popular *Saturday Evening Post* just about fourteen months before he began work on the first Tarzan novel.

He was a very quiet, self-possessed sort of man, sitting a moment on top of the wall to sound the damp darkness for warnings of the dangers it might conceal. But the plummet of his hearing brought nothing to him save the moaning of wind through invisible trees and the rustling of leaves on swaying branches. A heavy fog drifted and drove before the wind, and though he could not see this fog, the wet of it blew upon his face, and the wall on which he sat was wet.

The Saturday Evening Post, 183 (September 10, 1910):16-17, 45-49.

Without noise he had climbed to the top of the wall from the outside, and without noise he dropped to the ground on the inside. From his pocket he drew an electric night-stick, but he did not use it. Dark as the way was, he was not anxious for light. Carrying the night-stick in his hand, his finger on the button, he advanced through the darkness. The ground was velvety and springy to his feet, being carpeted with dead pine-needles and leaves and mold which evidently had been undisturbed for years. Leaves and branches brushed against his body, but so dark was it that he could not avoid them. Soon he walked with his hand stretched out gropingly before him, and more than once the hand fetched up against the solid trunks of massive trees. All about him he knew were these trees; he sensed the loom of them everywhere; and he experienced a strange feeling of microscopic smallness in the midst of great bulks leaning toward him to crush him. Beyond, he knew, was the house, and he expected to find some trail or winding path that would lead easily to it.

Once, he found himself trapped. On every side he groped against trees and branches, or blundered into thickets of underbrush, until there seemed no way out. Then he turned on his light, circumspectly, directing its rays to the ground at his feet. Slowly and carefully he moved it about him, the white brightness showing in sharp detail all the obstacles to his progress. He saw an opening between huge-trunked trees, and advanced through it, putting out the light and treading on dry footing as yet protected from the drip of the fog by the dense foliage overhead. His sense of direction was good, and he knew he was going toward the house.

And then the thing happened—the thing unthinkable and unexpected. His descending foot came down upon something that was soft and alive, and that arose with a snort under the weight of his body. He sprang clear, and crouched for another spring, anywhere, tense and expectant, keyed for the onslaught of the unknown. He waited a moment, wondering what manner of animal it was that had arisen from under his foot and that now made no sound nor movement and that must be crouching and waiting just as tensely and expectantly as he. The strain became unbearable. Holding the night-stick before him, he pressed the button, saw, and screamed aloud in terror. He was prepared for anything from a frightened calf or fawn to a belligerent lion, but he was not prepared for what he saw. In that instant his tiny searchlight, sharp and white, had shown him what a thousand years would not enable him to forget—a man, huge and blond, yellow-haired and yellow-bearded, naked except for soft-tanned moccasins and what seemed a goat-skin about his middle. Arms and legs were bare, as were his shoulders and most of his chest. The skin was smooth and hairless, but browned by sun and wind, while under it heavy muscles were knotted like fat snakes.

Still, this alone, unexpected as it well was, was not what had made the man scream out. What had caused his terror was the unspeakable ferocity of the face, the wild-animal glare of the blue eyes scarcely dazzled by the light, the pine-needles matted and clinging in the beard and hair, and the whole formidable body crouched and in the act of springing at him. Practically in the instant he saw all this, and while his scream still rang, the thing leaped, he flung his night-stick full at it, and threw himself to the ground. He felt its feet and shins strike against his ribs, and he bounded up and away while the thing itself hurled onward in a heavy crashing fall into the underbrush.

As the noise of the fall ceased, the man stopped and on hands and knees waited. He could hear the thing moving about, searching for him, and he was afraid to advertise his location by attempting further flight. He knew that inevitably he would crackle the underbrush and be pursued. Once he drew out his revolver, then changed his mind. He had recovered his composure and hoped to get away without noise. Several times he heard the thing beating up the thickets for him, and there were moments when it, too, remained still and listened. This gave an idea to the man. One of his hands was resting on a chunk of dead wood. Carefully, first feeling about him in the darkness to know that the full swing of his arm was clear, he raised the chunk of wood and threw it. It was not a large piece, and it went far, landing noisily in a bush. He heard the thing bound into the bush, and at the same time himself crawled steadily away. And on hands and knees, slowly and cautiously, he crawled on, till his knees were wet on the soggy mold. When he listened he heard naught but the moaning wind and the drip-drip of the fog from the branches. Never abating his caution, he stood erect and went on to the stone wall, over which he climbed and dropped down to the road outside.

Feeling his way in a clump of bushes, he drew out a bicycle and prepared to mount. He was in the act of driving the gear around with his foot for the purpose of getting the opposite pedal in position, when he heard the thud of a heavy body that landed lightly and evidently on its feet. He did not wait for more, but ran, with hands on the handles of his bicycle, until he was able to vault astride the saddle, catch the pedals, and start a spurt. Behind he could hear the quick thud-thud of feet on the dust of the road, but he drew away from it and lost it.

Unfortunately, he had started away from the direction of town and was heading higher up into the hills. He knew that on this particular road there were no cross roads. The only way back was past that terror, and he could not steel himself to face it. At the end of half an hour, finding himself on an ever increasing grade, he dismounted. For still greater safety, leaving the wheel by the roadside, he climbed through a fence into what he decided was a hillside pasture, spread a newspaper on the ground, and sat down.

"Gosh!" he said aloud, mopping the sweat and fog from his face.

And "Gosh!" he said once again, while rolling a cigarette and as he pondered the problem of getting back.

But he made no attempt to go back. He was resolved not to face that road in the dark, and with head bowed on knees, he dozed, waiting for daylight.

How long afterward he did not know, he was awakened by the yapping bark of a young coyote. As he looked about and located it on the brow of the hill behind him, he noted the change that had come over the face of the night. The fog was gone; the stars and moon were out; even the wind had died down. It had transformed into a balmy California summer night. He tried to doze again, but the yap of the coyote disturbed him. Half asleep, he heard a wild and eery chant. Looking about him, he noticed that the coyote had ceased its noise and was running away along the crest of the hill, and behind it, in full pursuit, no longer chanting, ran the naked creature he had encountered in the garden. It was a young coyote, and it was being overtaken when the chase passed from view. The man trembled as with a chill as he started to his feet, clambered over the fence, and mounted his wheel. But it was his chance and he knew it. The terror was no longer between him and Mill Valley.

He sped at a breakneck rate down the hill, but in the turn at the bottom, in the deep shadows, he encountered a chuck-hole and pitched headlong over the handle bar.

"It's sure not my night," he muttered, as he examined the broken fork of the machine.

Shouldering the useless wheel, he trudged on. In time he came to the stone wall, and, half disbelieving his experience, he sought in the road for tracks, and found them—moccasin tracks, large ones, deep-bitten into the dust at the toes. It was while bending over them, examining, that again he heard the eery chant. He had seen the thing pursue the coyote, and he knew he had no chance on a straight run. He did not attempt it, contenting himself with hiding in the shadows on the off side of the road.

And again he saw the thing that was like a naked man, running swiftly and lightly and singing as it ran. Opposite him it paused, and his heart stood still. But instead of coming toward his hiding-place, it leaped into the air, caught the branch of a roadside tree, and swung swiftly upward, from limb to limb, like an ape. It swung across the wall, and a

124

dozen feet above the top, into the branches of another tree, and dropped out of sight to the ground. The man waited a few wondering minutes, then started on.

II

Dave Slotter leaned belligerently against the desk that barred the way to the private office of James Ward, senior partner of the firm of Ward, Knowles & Co. Dave was angry. Every one in the outer office had looked him over suspiciously, and the man who faced him was excessively suspicious.

"You just tell Mr. Ward it's important," he urged.

"I tell you he is dictating and cannot be disturbed," was the answer. "Come to-morrow."

"To-morrow will be too late. You just trot along and tell Mr. Ward it's a matter of life and death."

The secretary hesitated and Dave seized the advantage.

"You just tell him I was across the bay in Mill Valley last night, and that I want to put him wise to something."

"What name?" was the query.

"Never mind the name. He don't know me."

When Dave was shown into the private office, he was still in the belligerent frame of mind, but when he saw a large fair man whirl in a revolving chair from dictating to a stenographer to face him, Dave's demeanor abruptly changed. He did not know why it changed, and he was secretly angry with himself.

"You are Mr. Ward?" Dave asked with a fatuousness that still further irritated him. He had never intended it at all.

"Yes," came the answer. "And who are you?"

"Harry Bancroft," Dave lied. "You don't know me, and my name don't matter."

"You sent in word that you were in Mill Valley last night?"

"You live there, don't you?" Dave countered, looking suspiciously at the stenographer.

"Yes. What do you mean to see me about? I am very busy."

"I'd like to see you alone, sir."

Mr. Ward gave him a quick, penetrating look, hesitated, then made up his mind.

"That will do for a few minutes, Miss Potter."

The girl arose, gathered her notes together, and passed out. Dave looked at Mr. James Ward wonderingly, until that gentleman broke his

125

train of inchoate thought.

"Well?"

"I was over in Mill Valley last night," Dave began confusedly.

"I've heard that before. What do you want?"

And Dave proceeded in the face of a growing conviction that was unbelievable.

"I was at your house, or in the grounds, I mean."

"What were you doing there?"

"I came to break in," Dave answered in all frankness. "I heard you lived all alone with a Chinaman for cook, and it looked good to me. Only I didn't break in. Something happened that prevented. That's why I'm here. I come to warn you. I found a wild man loose in your grounds—a regular devil. He could pull a guy like me to pieces. He gave me the run of my life. He don't wear any clothes to speak of, he climbs trees like a monkey, and he runs like a deer. I saw him chasing a coyote, and the last I saw of it, by God, he was gaining on it."

Dave paused and looked for the effect that would follow his words. But no effect came. James Ward was quietly curious, and that was all.

"Very remarkable, very remarkable," he murmured. "A wild man, you say. Why have you come to tell me?"

"To warn you of your danger. I'm something of a hard proposition myself, but I don't believe in killing people . . . that is, unnecessarily. I realized that you was in danger. I thought I'd warn you. Honest, that's the game. Of course, if you wanted to give me anything for my trouble, I'd take it. That was in my mind, too. But I don't care whether you give me anything or not. I've warned you anyway, and done my duty."

Mr. Ward meditated and drummed on the surface of his desk. Dave noticed they were large, powerful hands, withal well cared for despite their dark sunburn. Also, he noted what had already caught his eye before—a tiny strip of flesh-colored courtplaster on the forehead over one eye. And still the thought that forced itself into his mind was unbelievable.

Mr. Ward took a wallet from his inside coat pocket, drew out a greenback, and passed it to Dave, who noted as he pocketed it that it was for twenty dollars.

"Thank you," said Mr. Ward, indicating that the interview was at an end. "I shall have the matter investigated. A wild man running loose *is* dangerous."

But so quiet a man was Mr. Ward, that Dave's courage returned. Besides, a new theory had suggested itself. The wild man was evidently Mr. Ward's brother, a lunatic privately confined. Dave had heard of such things. Perhaps Mr. Ward wanted it kept quiet. That was why he had given

126

him the twenty dollars.

"Say," Dave began, "now I come to think of it that wild man looked a lot like you—"

That was as far as Dave got, for at that moment he witnessed a transformation and found himself gazing into the same unspeakably ferocious blue eyes of the night before, at the same clutching talon-like hands, and at the same formidable bulk in the act of springing upon him. But this time Dave had no night-stick to throw, and he was caught by the biceps of both arms in a grip so terrific that it made him groan with pain. He saw the large white teeth exposed, for all the world as a dog's about to bite. Mr. Ward's beard brushed his face as the teeth went in for the grip on his throat. But the bite was not given. Instead, Dave felt the other's body stiffen as with an iron restraint, and then he was flung aside, without effort but with such force that only the wall stopped his momentum and dropped him gasping to the floor.

"What do you mean by coming here and trying to blackmail me?" Mr. Ward was snarling at him. "Here, give me back that money."

Dave passed the bill back without a word.

"I thought you came here with good intentions. I know you now. Let me see and hear no more of you, or I'll put you in prison where you belong. Do you understand?"

"Yes, sir," Dave gasped.

"Then go."

And Dave went, without further word, both his biceps aching intolerably from the bruise of that tremendous grip. As his hand rested on the door knob, he was stopped.

"You were lucky," Mr. Ward was saying, and Dave noted that his face and eyes were cruel and gloating and proud. "You were lucky. Had I wanted, I could have torn your muscles out of your arms and thrown them in the waste basket there."

"Yes, sir," said Dave; and absolute conviction vibrated in his voice.

He opened the door and passed out. The secretary looked at him interrogatively.

"Gosh!" was all Dave vouchsafed, and with this utterance passed out of the offices and the story.

III

James G. Ward was forty years of age, a successful business man, and very unhappy. For forty years he had vainly tried to solve a problem that was really himself and that with increasing years became more and more a

127

woeful affliction. In himself he was two men, and, chronologically speaking, these men were several thousand years or so apart. He had studied the question of dual personality probably more profoundly than any half dozen of the leading specialists in that intricate and mysterious psychological field. In himself he was a different case from any that had been recorded. Even the most fanciful flights of the fiction-writers had not quite hit upon him. He was not a Dr. Jekyll and Mr. Hyde, nor was he like the unfortunate young man in Kipling's "Greatest Story in the World." His two personalities were so mixed that they were practically aware of themselves and of each other all the time.

His one self was that of a man whose rearing and education were modern and who had lived through the latter part of the nineteenth century and well into the first decade of the twentieth. His other self he had located as a savage and a barbarian living under the primitive conditions of several thousand years before. But which self was he, and which was the other, he could never tell. For he was both selves, and both selves all the time. Very rarely indeed did it happen that one self did not know what the other was doing. Another thing was that he had no visions nor memories of the past in which that early self had lived. That early self lived in the present; but while it lived in the present, it was under the compulsion to live the way of life that must have been in that distant past.

In his childhood he had been a problem to his father and mother, and to the family doctors, though never had they come within a thousand miles of hitting upon the clue to his erratic conduct. Thus, they could not understand his excessive somnolence in the forenoon, nor his excessive activity at night. When they found him wandering along the hallways at night, or climbing over giddy roofs, or running in the hills, they decided he was a somnambulist. In reality he was wide-eyed awake and merely under the night-roaming compulsion of his early self. Questioned by an obtuse medico, he once told the truth and suffered the ignominy of having the revelation contemptuously labeled and dismissed as "dreams."

The point was, that as twilight and evening came on he became wakeful. The four walls of a room were an irk and a restraint. He heard a thousand voices whispering to him through the darkness. The night called to him, for he was, for that period of the twenty-four hours, essentially a night-prowler. But nobody understood, and never again did he attempt to explain. They classified him as a sleep-walker and took precautions accordingly—precautions that very often were futile. As his childhood advanced, he grew more cunning, so that the major portion of all his nights were spent in the open at realizing his other self. As a result, he slept in the forenoons. Morning studies and schools were impossible, and it was discovered that only in the afternoons, under private teachers, could he be taught anything. Thus was his modern self educated and developed.

But a problem, as a child, he ever remained. He was known as a little demon, of insensate cruelty and viciousness. The family medicos privately adjudged him a mental monstrosity and a degenerate. Such few boy companions as he had, hailed him as a wonder, though they were all afraid of him. He could outclimb, outswim, outrun, outdevil any of them; while none dared fight with him. He was too terribly strong, too madly furious.

When nine years of age he ran away to the hills, where he flourished, night-prowling, for seven weeks before he was discovered and brought home. The marvel was how he had managed to subsist and keep in condition during that time. They did not know, and he never told them, of the rabbits he had killed, of the quail, young and old, he had captured and devoured, of the farmers' chicken-roosts he had raided, nor of the cave-lair he had made and carpeted with dry leaves and grasses and in which he had slept in warmth and comfort through the forenoons of many days.

At college he was notorious for his sleepiness and stupidity during the morning lectures and for his brilliance in the afternoon. By collateral reading and by borrowing the notebooks of his fellow students he managed to scrape through the detestable morning courses, while his afternoon courses were triumphs. In football he proved a giant and a terror, and, in almost every form of track athletics, save for strange Berserker rages that were sometimes displayed, he could be depended upon to win. But his fellows were afraid to box with him, and he signalized his last wrestling bout by sinking his teeth into the shoulder of his opponent.

After college, his father, in despair, sent him among the cow-punchers of a Wyoming ranch. Three months later the doughty cowmen confessed he was too much for them and telegraphed his father to come and take the wild man away. Also, when the father arrived to take him away, the cowmen allowed that they would vastly prefer chumming with howling cannibals, gibbering lunatics, cavorting gorillas, grizzly bears, and man-eating tigers than with this particular young college product with hair parted in the middle.

There was one exception to the lack of memory of the life of his early self, and that was language. By some quirk of atavism, a certain portion of that early self's language had come down to him as a racial memory. In moments of happiness, exaltation, or battle, he was prone to burst out in wild barbaric songs or chants. It was by this means that he located in time and space that strayed half of him who should have been dead and dust for thousands of years. He sang, once, and deliberately,

129

several of the ancient chants in the presence of Professor Wertz, who gave courses in old Saxon and who was a philologist of repute and passion. At the first one, the professor pricked up his ears and demanded to know what mongrel tongue or hog-German it was. When the second chant was rendered, the professor was highly excited. James Ward then concluded the performance by giving a song that always irresistibly rushed to his lips when he was engaged in fierce struggling or fighting. Then it was that Professor Wertz proclaimed it no hog-German, but early German, or early Teuton, of a date that must far precede anything that had ever been discovered and handed down by the scholars. So early was it that it was beyond him; yet it was filled with haunting reminiscences of word-forms he knew and which his trained intuition told him were true and real. He demanded the source of the songs, and asked to borrow the precious book that contained them. Also, he demanded to know why young Ward had always posed as being profoundly ignorant of the German language. And Ward could neither explain his ignorance nor lend the book. Whereupon after pleadings and entreaties that extended through weeks, Professor Wertz took a dislike to the young man, believed him a liar, and classified him as a man of monstrous selfishness for not giving him a glimpse of this wonderful screed that was older than the oldest any philologist had ever known or dreamed.

But little good did it do this much-mixed young man to know that half of him was late American and the other half early Teuton. Nevertheless, the late American in him was no weakling, and he (if he were a he and had a shred of existence outside of these two) compelled an adjustment or compromise between his one self that was a night-prowling savage that kept his other self sleepy of mornings, and that other self that was cultured and refined and that wanted to be normal and live and love and prosecute business like other people. The afternoons and early evenings he gave to the one, the nights to the other; the forenoons and parts of the nights were devoted to sleep for the twain. But in the mornings he slept in bed like a civilized man. In the night time he slept like a wild animal, as he had slept the night Dave Slotter stepped on him in the woods.

Persuading his father to advance the capital, he went into business, and keen and successful business he made of it, devoting his afternoons whole-souled to it, while his partner devoted the mornings. The early evenings he spent socially, but, as the hour grew to nine or ten, an irresistible restlessness overcame him and he disappeared from the haunts of men until the next afternoon. Friends and acquaintances thought that he spent much of his time in sport. And they were right, though they never would have dreamed of the nature of the sport, even if they had seen him running coyotes in night-chases over the hills of Mill Valley. Neither were the schooner captains believed when they reported seeing, on cold winter mornings, a man swimming in the tide-rips of Raccoon Straits or in the swift currents between Goat Island and Angel Island miles from shore.

In the bungalow at Mill Valley he lived alone, save for Lee Sing, the Chinese cook and factotum, who knew much about the strangeness of his master, who was paid well for saying nothing, and who never did say anything. After the satisfaction of his nights, a morning's sleep, and a breakfast of Lee Sing's, James Ward crossed the bay to San Francisco on a midday ferryboat and went to the club and on to his office, as normal and conventional a man of business as could be found in the city. But as the evening lengthened, the night called to him. There came a quickening of all his perceptions and a restlessness. His hearing was suddenly acute; the myriad night-noises told him a luring and familiar story; and, if alone, he would begin to pace up and down the narrow room like any caged animal from the wild.

Once, he ventured to fall in love. He never permitted himself that diversion again. He was afraid. And for many a day the young lady, scared at least out of a portion of her young ladyhood, bore on her arms and shoulders and wrists divers black-and-blue bruises—tokens of caresses which he had bestowed in all fond gentleness but too late at night. There was the mistake. Had he ventured love-making in the afternoon, all would have been well, for it would have been as the quiet gentleman that he would have made love—but at night it was the uncouth, wife-stealing savage of the dark German forests. Out of his wisdom, he decided that afternoon love-making could be prosecuted successfully; but out of the same wisdom he was convinced that marriage would prove a ghastly failure. He found it appalling to imagine being married and encountering his wife after dark.

So he had eschewed all love-making, regulated his dual life, cleaned up a million in business, fought shy of match-making mamas and bright- and eager-eyed young ladies of various ages, met Lilian Gersdale and made it a rigid observance never to see her later than eight o'clock in the evening, run of nights after his coyotes, and slept in forest lairs—and through it all had kept his secret save for Lee Sing . . . and now, Dave Slotter. It was the latter's discovery of both his selves that frightened him. In spite of the counter fright he had given the burglar, the latter might talk. And even if he did not, sooner or later he would be found out by some one else.

Thus it was that James Ward made a fresh and heroic effort to control the Teutonic barbarian that was half of him. So well did he make it a point to see Lilian in the afternoons and early evenings, that the time came when she accepted him for better or worse, and when he prayed privily and fervently that it was not for worse. During this period no prize-fighter ever trained more harshly and faithfully for a contest than he trained to subdue the wild savage in him. Among other things, he strove to exhaust himself during the day, so that sleep would render him deaf to the call of the night. He took a vacation from the office and went on long hunting trips, following deer through the most inaccessible and rugged country he could find—and always in the daytime. Night found him indoors and tired. At home he installed a score of exercise machines, and where other men might go through a particular movement ten times, he went hundreds. Also, as a compromise, he built a sleeping porch on the second story. Here he at least breathed the blessed night air. Double screens prevented him from escaping into the woods, and each night Lee Sing locked him in and each morning let him out.

The time came, in the month of August, when he engaged additional servants to assist Lee Sing and dared a house party in his Mill Valley bungalow. Lilian, her mother and brother, and half a dozen mutual friends, were the guests. For two days and nights all went well. And on the third night, playing bridge till eleven o'clock, he had reason to be proud of himself. His restlessness he successfully hid, but as luck would have it, Lilian Gersdale was his opponent on his right. She was a frail, delicate flower of a woman, and in his night-mood her very frailty incensed him. Not that he loved her less, but that he felt almost irresistibly impelled to reach out and paw and maul her. Especially was this true when she was engaged in playing a winning hand against him.

He had one of the deer-hounds brought in, and, when it seemed he must fly to pieces with the tension, a caressing hand laid on the animal brought him relief. These contacts with the hairy coat gave him instant easement and enabled him to play out the evening. Nor did anyone guess the terrible struggle their host was making, the while he laughed so carelessly and played so keenly and deliberately.

When they separated for the night, he saw to it that he parted from Lilian in the presence of the others. Once on his sleeping porch, and safely locked in, he doubled and tripled and even quadrupled his exercises until, exhausted, he lay down on the couch to woo sleep and to ponder two problems that especially troubled him. One was this matter of exercise. It was a paradox. The more he exercised in this excessive fashion, the stronger he became. While it was true that he thus tired out his night-running Teutonic self, it seemed that he was merely setting back the

132

fatal day when his strength would be too much for him and overpower him, and then it would be a strength more terrible than he had yet known. The other problem was that of his marriage and of the stratagems he must employ in order to avoid his wife after dark. And thus fruitlessly pondering, he fell asleep.

Now, where the huge grizzly bear came from that night was long a mystery, while the people of the Springs Brothers' Circus, showing at Sausalito, searched long and vainly for "Big Ben, the Biggest Grizzly in Captivity." But Big Ben escaped, and, out of the mazes of half a thousand bungalows and country estates, selected the grounds of James J. Ward for visitation. The first Mr. Ward knew was when he found himself on his feet, quivering and tense, a surge of battle in his breast and on his lips the old war-chant. From without came a wild baying and bellowing of the hounds. And sharp as a knife-thrust through the pandemonium came the agony of a stricken dog—his dog, he knew.

Not stopping for slippers, pajama-clad, he burst through the door Lee Sing had so carefully locked, and sped down the stairs and out into the night. As his naked feet struck the graveled driveway, he stopped abruptly, reached under the steps to a hiding-place he knew well, and pulled forth a huge knotty club—his old companion on many a mad night adventure on the hills. The frantic hullabaloo of the dogs was coming nearer, and, swinging the club, he sprang straight into the thickets to meet it.

The aroused household assembled on the wide veranda. Somebody turned on the electric lights, but they could see nothing but one another's frightened faces. Beyond the brightly illuminated driveway the trees formed a wall of impenetrable blackness. Yet somewhere in that blackness a terrible struggle was going on. There was an infernal outcry of animals, a great snarling and growling, the sound of blows being struck, and a smashing and crashing of underbrush by heavy bodies.

The tide of battle swept out from among the trees and upon the driveway just beneath the onlookers. Then they saw. Mrs. Gersdale cried out and clung fainting to her son. Lilian, clutching the railing so spasmodically that a bruising hurt was left in her finger-ends for days, gazed horror-stricken at a yellow-haired, wild-eyed giant whom she recognized as the man who was to be her husband. He was swinging a great club, and fighting furiously and calmly with a shaggy monster that was bigger than any bear she had ever seen. One rip of the beast's claws had dragged away Ward's pajama-coat and streaked his flesh with blood.

While most of Lilian Gersdale's fright was for the man beloved, there was a large portion of it due to the man himself. Never had she dreamed so

133

formidable and magnificent a savage lurked under the starched shirt and conventional garb of her betrothed. And never had she had any conception of how a man battled. Such a battle was certainly not modern; nor was she there beholding a modern man, though she did not know it. For this was not Mr. James J. Ward, the San Francisco business man, but one unnamed and unknown, a crude, rude savage creature who, by some freak of chance, lived again after thrice a thousand years.

The hounds, ever maintaining their mad uproar, circled about the fight, or dashed in and out, distracting the bear. When the animal turned to meet such flanking assaults, the man leaped in and the club came down. Angered afresh by every such blow, the bear would rush, and the man, leaping and skipping, avoiding the dogs, went backwards or circled to one side or the other. Whereupon the dogs, taking advantage of the opening, would again spring in and draw the animal's wrath to them.

The end came suddenly. Whirling, the grizzly caught a hound with a wide sweeping cuff that sent the brute, its ribs caved in and its back broken, hurtling twenty feet. Then the human brute went mad. A foaming rage flecked the lips that parted with a wild inarticulate cry, as it sprang in, swung the club mightily in both hands, and brought it down full on the head of the uprearing grizzly. Not even the skull of a grizzly could withstand the crushing force of such a blow, and the animal went down to meet the worrying of the hounds. And through their scurrying leaped the man, squarely upon the body, where, in the white electric light, resting on his club, he chanted a triumph in an unknown tongue—a song so ancient that Professor Wertz would have given ten years of his life for it.

His guests rushed to possess him and acclaim him, but James Ward, suddenly looking out of the eyes of the early Teuton, saw the fair frail Twentieth Century girl he loved, and felt something snap in his brain. He staggered weakly toward her, dropped the club, and nearly fell. Something had gone wrong with him. Inside his brain was an intolerable agony. It seemed as if the soul of him were flying asunder. Following the excited gaze of the others, he glanced back and saw the carcass of the bear. The sight filled him with fear. He uttered a cry and would have fled, had they not restrained him and led him into the bungalow.

* * *

James J. Ward is still at the head of the firm of Ward, Knowles & Co. But he no longer lives in the country; nor does he run of nights after the coyotes under the moon. The early Teuton in him died the night of the Mill Valley fight with the bear. James J. Ward is now wholly James J.

Ward, and he shares no part of his being with any vagabond anachronism from the younger world. And so wholly is James J. Ward modern, that he knows in all its bitter fullness the curse of civilized fear. He is now afraid of the dark, and night in the forest is to him a thing of abysmal terror. His city house is of the spick and span order, and he evinces a great interest in burglar-proof devices. His home is a tangle of electric wires, and after bed-time a guest can scarcely breathe without setting off an alarm. Also, he has invented a combination keyless door-lock that travelers may carry in their vest pockets and apply immediately and successfully under all circumstances. But his wife does not deem him a coward. She knows better. And, like any hero, he is content to rest on his laurels. His bravery is never questioned by those of his friends who are aware of the Mill Valley episode.

THE STRENGTH OF THE STRONG

Besides being, as the historian Philip Foner says, "among the finest parables in American literature, ranking with Edward Bellamy's 'Parable of the Water Tank,' " this story is also an example of the protohuman or prehistoric fantasy tale, a disarmingly simple narration by Long Beard who tells his grandchildren of the rise and fall of their tribe. The grandfather narration would be used by London yet again in a story set in the future, *The Scarlet Plague,* included in this collection.

Foner says (in *Jack London: American Rebel,* 1964) that "London made effective use of the past to build his indictment of capitalism, and his simplicity of plot and style as well as his story-telling ability made 'The Strength of the Strong' an ideal propaganda piece."

After its appearance in *Hampton's,* the story was reprinted by the Chicago publisher Charles H. Kerr Co. as a pamphlet which became, in Foner's words, "one of the classics of socialist literature."

In a letter to *Cosmopolitan* on August 30, 1909, London gave this rationale for writing the story (Shepard and Hendricks, *Letters from Jack London,* pp. 287-88): "If you will remember, some time ago, Kipling made an attack on Socialism in the form of a parable or short story, entitled 'Melissa,' in which he exploited his Jingoism and showed that a co-operation of individuals strong enough to overcome war meant the degeneration of said individuals. I have written my 'Strength of the Strong' as a reply to his attack."

Parables don't lie, but liars will parable.
                                        —Lip-King.

Old Long Beard paused in his narrative, licked his greasy fingers, and wiped them on his naked sides where his one piece of ragged bearskin failed to cover him. Crouched around him, on their hams, were three young men, his grandsons, Deer-Runner, Yellow-Head, and Afraid-of-the-Dark. In appearance they were much the same. Skins of wild animals partly covered them. They were lean and meager of build, narrow-hipped and crooked-legged, and at the same time deep-chested, with heavy arms and enormous hands. There was much hair on their chests and shoulders, and on the outsides of their arms and legs. Their heads were matted with uncut hair, long locks of which often strayed before their eyes, beady and black and glittering like the eyes of birds. They were narrow between the eyes and broad between the cheeks, while their lower jaws were projecting and massive.

It was a night of clear starlight, and below them, stretching away remotely, lay range on range of forest-covered hills. In the distance the heavens were red from the glow of a volcano. At their backs yawned the black mouth of a cave, out of which, from time to time, blew draughty gusts of wind. Immediately in front of them blazed a fire. At one side, partly devoured, lay the carcass of a bear, with about it, at a respectable distance, several large dogs, shaggy and wolf-like. Beside each man lay his bow and arrows and a huge club. In the cave-mouth a number of rude spears leaned against the rock.

"So that was how we moved from the cave to the tree," old Long Beard spoke up.

They laughed boisterously, like big children, at recollection of a previous story his words called up. Long Beard laughed, too, the five-inch bodkin of bone, thrust midway through the cartilage of his nose, leaping and dancing and adding to his ferocious appearance. He did not exactly say the words recorded, but he made animal-like sounds with his mouth that meant the same thing.

"And that is the first I remember of the Sea Valley," Long Beard went on. "We were a very foolish crowd. We did not know the secret of strength. For, behold, each family lived by itself, and took care of itself. There were thirty families, but we got no strength from one another. We were in fear of each other all the time. No one ever paid visits. In the top of our tree we built a grass house, and on the platform outside was a pile of rocks, which were for the heads of any that might chance to try to visit us. Also, we had our spears and arrows. We never walked under the trees of the other families, either. My brother did, once, under old Boo-oogh's tree, and he got his head broken and that was the end of him.

"Old Boo-oogh was very strong. It was said he could pull a grown man's head right off. I never heard of him doing it, because no man would give him a chance. Father wouldn't. One day, when father was down on the beach, Boo-oogh took after mother. She couldn't run fast, for the day before she had got her leg clawed by a bear when she was up on the mountain gathering berries. So Boo-oogh caught her and carried her up into his tree. Father never got her back. He was afraid. Old Boo-oogh made faces at him.

"But father did not mind. Strong-Arm was another strong man. He was one of the best fishermen. But one day, climbing after sea-gull eggs, he had a fall from the cliff. He was never strong after that. He coughed a great deal, and his shoulders drew near to each other. So father took Strong-Arm's wife. When he came around and coughed under our tree, father laughed at him and threw rocks at him. It was our way in those days. We did not know how to add strength together and become strong."

"Would a brother take a brother's wife?" Deer-Runner demanded.

"Yes, if he had gone to live in another tree by himself."

"But we do not do such things now," Afraid-of-the-Dark objected.

"It is because I have taught your fathers better." Long Beard thrust his hairy paw into the bear meat and drew out a handful of suet, which he sucked with a meditative air. Again he wiped his hands on his naked sides and went on. "What I am telling you happened in the long ago, before we knew any better."

"You must have been fools not to know better," was Deer-Runner's comment, Yellow-Head grunting approval.

"So we were, but we became bigger fools, as you shall see. Still, we did learn better, and this was the way of it. We Fish-Eaters had not learned to add our strength until our strength was the strength of all of us. But the Meat-Eaters, who lived across the divide in the Big Valley, stood together, hunted together, fished together, and fought together. One day they came into our valley. Each family of us got into its own cave and tree. There were only ten Meat-Eaters, but they fought together, and we fought each family by itself."

Long Beard counted long and perplexedly on his fingers.

"There were sixty men of us," was what he managed to say with fingers and lips combined. "And we were very strong, only we did not know it. So we watched the ten men attack Boo-oogh's tree. He made a good fight, but he had no chance. We looked on. When some of the Meat-Easters tried to climb the tree, Boo-oogh had to show himself in order to drop stones on their heads, whereupon the other Meat-Eaters, who were waiting for that very thing, shot him full of arrows. And that was the end of Boo-oogh.

"Next, the Meat-Eaters got One-Eye and his family in his cave. They built a fire in the mouth and smoked him out, like we smoked out the bear there to-day. Then they went after Six-Fingers, up his tree, and, while they

138

were killing him and his grown son, the rest of us ran away. They caught some of our women, and killed two old men who could not run fast and several children. The women they carried away with them to the Big Valley.

"After that the rest of us crept back, and, somehow, perhaps because we were in fear and felt the need for one another, we talked the thing over. It was our first council—our first real council. And in that council we formed our first tribe. For we had learned the lesson. Of the ten Meat-Eaters, each man had had the strength of ten, for the ten had fought as one man. They had added their strength together. But of the thirty families and the sixty men of us, we had had the strength of but one man, for each had fought alone.

"It was a great talk we had, and it was hard talk, for we did not have the words then as now with which to talk. The Bug made some of the words long afterward, and so did others of us make words from time to time. But in the end we agreed to add our strength together and to be as one man when the Meat-Eaters came over the divide to steal our women. And that was the tribe.

"We set two men on the divide, one for the day and one for the night, to watch if the Meat-Eaters came. These were the eyes of the tribe. Then, also, day and night, there were to be ten men awake with their clubs and spears and arrows in their hands, ready to fight. Before, when a man went after fish, or clams, or gull-eggs, he carried his weapons with him, and half the time he was getting food and half the time watching for fear some other man would get him. Now that was all changed. The men went out without their weapons and spent all their time getting food. Likewise, when the women went into the mountains after roots and berries, five of the ten men went with them to guard them. While all the time, day and night, the eyes of the tribe watched from the top of the divide.

"But troubles came. As usual, it was about the women. Men without wives wanted other men's wives, and there was much fighting between men, and now and again one got his head smashed or a spear through his body. While one of the watchers was on top of the divide, another man stole his wife, and he came down to fight. Then the other watcher was in fear that someone would take his wife, and he came down likewise. Also, there was trouble among the ten men who carried always their weapons, and they fought five against five, till some ran away down the coast and the others ran after them.

"So it was that the tribe was left without eyes or guards. We had not the strength of sixty. We had no strength at all. So we held a council and made our first laws. I was but a cub at the time, but I remember. We said

139

that, in order to be strong, we must not fight one another, and we made a law that when a man killed another, him would the tribe kill. We made another law that whoso stole another man's wife him would the tribe kill. We said that whatever man had too great strength, and by that strength hurt his brothers in the tribe, him would we kill that his strength might hurt no more. For, if we let his strength hurt, the brothers would become afraid and the tribe would fall apart, and we would be as weak as when the Meat-Eaters first came upon us and killed Boo-oogh.

"Knuckle-Bone was a strong man, a very strong man, and he knew not law. He knew only his own strength, and in the fullness thereof he went forth and took the wife of Three-Clams. Three-Clams tried to fight, but Knuckle-Bone clubbed out his brains. Yet had Knuckle-Bone forgotten that all the men of us had added our strength to keep the law among us, and him we killed, at the foot of his tree, and hung his body on a branch as a warning that the law was stronger than any man. For we were the law, all of us, and no man was greater than the law.

"Then there were other troubles, for know, O Deer-Runner, and Yellow-Head, and Afraid-of-the-Dark, that it is not easy to make a tribe. There were many things, little things, that it was a great trouble to call all the men together to have a council about. We were having councils morning, noon, and night, and in the middle of the night. We could find little time to go out and get food, what of the councils, for there was always some little thing to be settled, such as naming two new watchers to take the place of the old ones on the hill, or naming how much food should fall to the share of the men who kept their weapons always in their hands and got no food for themselves.

"We stood in need of a chief man to do these things, who would be the voice of the council, and who would account to the council for the things he did. So we named Fith-Fith the chief man. He was a strong man, too, and very cunning, and when he was angry he made noises just like that, *fith-fith*, like a wildcat.

"The ten men who guarded the tribe were set to work making a wall of stones across the narrow part of the valley. The women and large children helped, as did other men, until the wall was strong. After that, all the families came down out of their caves and trees and built grass houses behind the shelter of the wall. These houses were large and much better than the caves and trees, and everybody had a better time of it because the men had added their strength together and become a tribe. Because of the wall and the guards and the watchers, there was more time to hunt and fish and pick roots and berries; there was more food, and better food, and no one went hungry. And Three-Legs, so named because his legs had been

140

smashed when a boy and who walked with a stick—Three-Legs got the seed of the wild corn and planted it in the ground in the valley near his house. Also, he tried planting fat roots and other things he found in the mountain valleys.

"Because of the safety in the Sea Valley, which was because of the wall and the watchers and the guards, and because there was food in plenty for all without having to fight for it, many families came in from the coast valleys on both sides and from the high back mountains where they had lived more like wild animals than men. And it was not long before the Sea Valley filled up, and in it were countless families. But, before this happened, the land, which had been free to all and belonged to all, was divided up. Three-Legs began it when he planted corn. But most of us did not care about the land. We thought the marking of the boundaries with fences of stone was a foolishness. We had plenty to eat, and what more did we want? I remember that my father and I built stone fences for Three-Legs and were given corn in return.

"So only a few got all the land, and Three-Legs got most of it. Also, others that had taken land gave it to the few that held on, being paid in return with corn and fat roots, and bearskins, and fishes which the farmers got from the fishermen in exchange for corn. And, the first thing we knew, all the land was gone.

"It was about this time that Fith-Fith died and Dog-Tooth, his son, was made chief. He demanded to be made chief anyway, because his father had been chief before him. Also, he looked upon himself as a greater chief than his father. He was a good chief at first, and worked hard, so that the council had less and less to do. Then arose a new voice in the Sea Valley. It was Twisted-Lip. We had never thought much of him, until he began to talk with the spirits of the dead. Later we called him Big-Fat, because he ate over-much, and did no work, and grew round and large. One day Big-Fat told us that the secrets of the dead were his, and that he was the voice of God. He became great friends with Dog-Tooth, who commanded that we build Big-Fat a grass house. And Big-Fat put taboos all around this house and kept God inside.

"More and more Dog-Tooth became greater than the council, and when the council grumbled and said it would name a new chief, Big-Fat spoke with the voice of God and said no. Also, Three-Legs and the others who held the land stood behind Dog-Tooth. Moreover, the strongest man in the council was Sea-Lion, and him the land-owners gave land to secretly, along with many bearskins and baskets of corn. So Sea-Lion said that Big-Fat's voice was truly the voice of God and must be obeyed. And soon

141

afterward Sea-Lion was named the voice of Dog-Tooth and did most of his talking for him.

"Then there was Little-Belly, a little man, so thin in the middle that he looked as if he had never had enough to eat. Inside the mouth of the river, after the sand-bar had combed the strength of the breakers, he built a big fish-trap. No man had ever seen or dreamed a fish-trap before. He worked weeks on it, with his son and his wife, while the rest of us laughed at their labors. But, when it was done, the first day he caught more fish in it than could the whole tribe in a week, whereat there was great rejoicing. There was only one other place in the river for a fish-trap, but, when my father and I and a dozen other men started to make a very large trap, the guards came from the big grass-house we had built for Dog-Tooth. And the guards poked us with their spears and told us begone, because Little-Belly was going to build a trap there himself on the word of Sea-Lion, who was the voice of Dog-Tooth.

"There was much grumbling, and my father called a council. But, when he rose to speak, him the Sea-Lion thrust through the throat with a spear and he died. And Dog-Tooth and Little-Belly, and Three-Legs and all that held land said it was good. And Big-Fat said it was the will of God. And after that all men were afraid to stand up in the council, and there was no more council.

"Another man, Pig-Jaw, began to keep goats. He had heard about it among the Meat-Eaters, and it was not long before he had many flocks. Other men, who had no land and no fish-traps, and who else would have gone hungry, were glad to work for Pig-Jaw, caring for his goats, guarding them from wild dogs and tigers, and driving them to the feeding pastures in the mountains. In return, Pig-Jaw gave them goat-meat to eat and goat-skins to wear, and sometimes they traded the goat-meat for fish and corn and fat roots.

It was in this time that money came to be. Sea-Lion was the man who first thought of it, and he talked it over with Dog-Tooth and Big-Fat. You see, these three were the ones that got a share of everything in the Sea Valley. One basket out of every three of corn was theirs, one fish out of every three, one goat out of every three. In return, they fed the guards and the watchers, and kept the rest for themselves. Sometimes, when a big haul of fish was made, they did not know what to do with all their share. So Sea-Lion set the women to making money out of shell—little round pieces, with a hole in each one, and all made smooth and fine. These were strung on strings, and the strings were called money.

"Each string was of the value of thirty fish, or forty fish, but the women, who made a string a day, were given two fish each. The fish came out of the shares of Dog-Tooth, Big-Fat, and Sea-Lion, which they three did not eat. So all the money belonged to them. Then they told Three-Legs and the other land owners that they would take their share of corn and roots in money, Little-Belly that they would take their share of fish in money, then Pig-Jaw that they would take their share of goats and cheese in money. Thus, a man who had nothing, worked for one who had, and was paid in money. With this money he bought corn, and fish, and meat, and cheese. And Three-Legs and all owners of things paid Dog-Tooth and Sea-Lion and Big-Fat their share in money. And they paid the guards and watchers in money, and the guards and watchers bought their food with the money. And, because money was cheap, Dog-Tooth made many more men into guards. And, because money was cheap to make, a number of men began to make money out of shell themselves. But the guards stuck spears in them and shot them full of arrows, because they were trying to break up the tribe. It was bad to break up the tribe, for then the Meat-Eaters would come over the divide and kill them all.

"Big-Fat was the voice of God, but he took Broken-Rib and made him into a priest, so that he became the voice of Big-Fat and did most of his talking for him. And both had other men to be servants to them. So, also, did Little-Belly and Three-Legs and Pig-Jaw have other men to lie in the sun about their grass houses and carry messages for them and give commands. And more and more were men taken away from work, so that those that were left worked harder than ever before. It seemed that men desired to do no work and strove to seek out other ways whereby men should work for them. Crooked-Eyes found such a way. He made the first fire-brew out of corn. And thereafter he worked no more, for he talked secretly with Dog-Tooth and Big-Fat and the other masters, and it was agreed that he should be the only one to make fire-brew. But Crooked-Eyes did no work himself. Men made the brew for him, and he paid them in money. Then he sold the fire-brew for money, and all men bought: And many strings of money did he give Dog-Tooth and Sea-Lion and all of them.

"Big-Fat and Broken-Rib stood by Dog-Tooth when he took his second wife, and his third wife. They said Dog-Tooth was different from other men and second only to God that Big-Fat kept in his taboo house, and Dog-Tooth said so, too, and wanted to know who were they to grumble about how many wives he took. Dog-Tooth had a big canoe made, and many more men he took from work, who did nothing and lay in the sun, save only when Dog-Tooth went in the canoe, when they paddled for him. And he made Tiger-Face head man over all the guards, so that Tiger-Face became his right arm, and when he did not like a man Tiger-Face killed that man for him. And Tiger-Face, also, made another

143

man to be his right arm, and to give commands, and to kill for him.

"But this was the strange thing: as the days went by, we who were left worked harder and harder, and yet did we get less and less to eat."

"But what of the goats and the corn and the fat roots and the fish-trap," spoke up Afraid-of-the-Dark, "what of all this? Was there not more food to be gained by man's work?"

"It is so," Long-Beard agreed. "Three men on the fish-trap got more fish than the whole tribe before there was a fish-trap. But have I not said we were fools? The more food we were able to get, the less food did we have to eat."

"But was it not plain that the many men who did not work ate it all up?" Yellow-Head demanded.

Long-Beard nodded his head sadly. "Dog-Tooth's dogs were stuffed with meat, and the men who lay in the sun and did no work were rolling in fat, and, at the same time, there were little children crying themselves to sleep with hunger biting them with every wail."

Deer-Runner was spurred by the recital of famine to tear out a chunk of bear-meat and broil it on a stick over the coals. This he devoured with smacking lips, while Long-Beard went on:

"When we grumbled, Big-Fat arose, and with the voice of God said that God had chosen the wise men to own the land and the goats and the fish-trap and the fire-brew, and that without these wise men we would all be animals, as in the days when we lived in trees.

"And there arose one who became a singer of songs for the king. Him they called the Bug, because he was small and ungainly of face and limb and excelled not in work or deed. He loved the fattest marrow bones, the choicest fish, the milk warm from the goats, the first corn that was ripe, and the snug place by the fire. And thus, becoming singer of songs to the king, he found a way to do nothing and be fat. And when the people grumbled more and more, and some threw stones at the king's grass house, the Bug sang a song of how good it was to be a Fish-Eater. In his song he told that the Fish-Eaters were the chosen of God and the finest men God had made. He sang of the Meat-Eaters as pigs and crows, and sang how fine and good it was for the Fish-Eaters to fight and die doing God's work, which was the killing of Meat-Eaters. The words of his song were like fire in us, and we clamored to be led against the Meat-Eaters. And we forgot that we were hungry, and why we had grumbled, and were glad to be led by Tiger-Face over the divide, where we killed many Meat-Eaters and were content.

"But things were no better in the Sea Valley. The only way to get food was to work for Three-Legs or Little-Belly or Pig-Jaw; for there was

144

no land that a man might plant with corn for himself. And often there were more men than Three-Legs and the others had work for. So these men went hungry, and so did their wives and children and their old mothers. Tiger-Face said they could become guards if they wanted to, and many of them did, and thereafter they did no work except to poke spears in the men who did work and who grumbled at feeding so many idlers.

"And when we grumbled, ever the Bug sang new songs. He said that Three-Legs and Pig-Jaw and the rest were strong men, and that that was why they had so much. He said that we should be glad to have strong men with us, else would we perish of our own worthlessness and the Meat-Eaters. Therefore, we should be glad to let such strong men have all they could lay hands on. And Big-Fat and Pig-Jaw and Tiger-Face and all the rest said it was true.

" 'All right,' said Long-Fang, 'then will I, too, be a strong man.' And he got himself corn and began to make fire-brew and sell it for strings of money. And, when Crooked-Eyes complained, Long-Fang said that he was himself a strong man, and that if Crooked-Eyes made any more noise he would bash his brains out for him. Whereat Crooked-Eyes was afraid and went and talked with Three-Legs and Pig-Jaw. And all three went and talked to Dog-Tooth. And Dog-Tooth spoke to Sea-Lion, and Sea-Lion sent a runner with a message to Tiger-Face. And Tiger-Face sent his guards, who burned Long-Fang's house along with the fire-brew he had made. Also, they killed him and all his family. And Big-Fat said it was good, and the Bug sang another song about how good it was to observe the law, and what a fine land the Sea Valley was, and how every man who loved the Sea Valley should go forth and kill the bad Meat-Eaters. And again his song was as fire to us, and we forgot to grumble.

"It was very strange. When Little-Belly caught too many fish, so that it took a great many to sell for a little money, he threw many of the fish back into the sea, so that more money would be paid for what was left. And Three-Legs often let many large fields lie idle so as to get more money for his corn. And the women, making so much money out of shell that much money was needed to buy with, Dog-Tooth stopped the making of money. And the women had no work, so they took the places of the men. I worked on the fish-trap, getting a string of money every five days. But my sister now did my work, getting a string of money for every ten days. The women worked cheaper, and there was less food, and Tiger-Face said for us to become guards. Only I could not become a guard because I was lame of one leg and Tiger-Face would not have me. And there were many like me. We were broken men and only fit to beg for work or to take care of the babies while the women worked."

Yellow-Head, too, was made hungry by the recital and boiled a piece of bear-meat on the coals.

"But why didn't you rise up, all of you, and kill Three-Legs and Pig-Jaw and Big-Fat and the rest and get enough to eat?" Afraid-of-the Dark demanded.

"Because we could not understand," Long-Beard answered. "There was too much to think about, and, also, there were the guards sticking spears into us, and Big-Fat talking about God, and the Bug singing new songs. And when any man did think right, and said so, Tiger-Face and the guards got him, and he was tied out to the rocks at low tide so that the rising waters drowned him.

"It was a strange thing—the money. It was like the Bug's songs. It seemed all right, but it wasn't, and we were slow to understand. Dog-Tooth began to gather the money in. He put it in a big pile, in a grass house, with guards to watch it day and night. And the more money he piled in the house the dearer money became, so that a man worked a longer time for a string of money than before. Then, too, there was always talk of war with the Meat-Eaters, and Dog-Tooth and Tiger-Face filled many houses with corn, and dried fish, and smoked goat-meat, and cheese. And with the food piled there in mountains the people had not enough to eat. But what did it matter? Whenever the people grumbled too loudly the Bug sang a new song, and Big-Fat said it was God's word that we should kill Meat-Eaters, and Tiger-Face led us over the divide to kill and be killed. I was not good enough to be a guard and lie fat in the sun, but, when we made war, Tiger-Face was glad to take me along. And when we had eaten all the food stored in the houses we stopped fighting and went back to work to pile up more food."

"Then were you all crazy," commented Deer-Runner.

"Then were we indeed all crazy," Long-Beard agreed. "It was strange, all of it. There was Split-Nose. He said everything was wrong. He said it was true that we grew strong by adding our strength together. And he said that, when we first formed the tribe, it was right that the men whose strength hurt the tribe should be shorn of their strength—men who bashed their brothers' heads and stole their brothers' wives. And now, he said, the tribe was not getting stronger, but was getting weaker, because there were men with another kind of strength that were hurting the tribe—men who had the strength of the land, like Three-Legs; who had the strength of the fish-trap, like Little-Belly; who had the strength of all the goat-meat, like Pig-Jaw. The thing to do, Split-Nose said, was to shear these men of their evil strength; to make them go to work, all of them, and to let no man eat who did not work.

"And the Bug sang another song about men like Split-Nose, who wanted to go back and live in trees.

"Yet Split-Nose said no; that he did not want to go back, but ahead; that they grew strong only as they added their strength together; and that, if the Fish-Eaters would add their strength to the Meat-Eaters, there would be no more fighting and no more watchers and no more guards, and that, with all men working, there would be so much food that each man would have to work not more than two hours a day.

"Then the Bug sang again, and he sang that Split-Nose was lazy, and he sang also the 'Song of the Bees.' It was a strange song, and those who listened were made mad, as from the drinking of strong fire-brew. The song was of a swarm of bees, and of a robber wasp who had come in to live with the bees and who was stealing all their honey. The wasp was lazy and told them there was no need to work; also, he told them to make friends with the bears, who were not honey-stealers but only very good friends. And the Bug sang in crooked words, so that those who listened knew that the swarm was the Sea Valley tribe, that the bears were the Meat-Eaters, and that the lazy wasp was Split-Nose. And, when the Bug sang that the bees listened to the wasp till the swarm was near to perishing, the people growled and snarled, and when the Bug sang that at last the good bees arose and stung the wasp to death, the people picked up stones from the ground and stoned Split-Nose to death till there was naught to be seen of him but the heap of stones they had flung on top of him. And there were many poor people who worked long and hard and had not enough to eat that helped throw the stones on Split-Nose.

"And, after the death of Split-Nose, there was but one other man that dared rise up and speak his mind, and that man was Hair-Face. 'Where is the strength of the strong?' he asked. 'We are the strong, all of us, and we are stronger than Dog-Tooth and Tiger-Face and Three-Legs and Pig-Jaw and all the rest who do nothing and eat much and weaken us by the hurt of their strength which is bad strength. Men who are slaves are not strong. If the man who first found the virtue and use of fire had used his strength we would have been his slaves, as we are the slaves to-day of Little-Belly, who found the virtue and use of the fish-trap; and of the men who found the virtue and use of the land, and the goats, and the fire-brew. Before, we lived in trees, my brothers, and no man was safe. But we fight no more with one another. We have added our strength together. Then let us fight no more with the Meat-Eaters. Let us add our strength and their strength together. Then will we be indeed strong. And then we will go out together, the Fish-Eaters and the Meat-Eaters, and we will kill the tigers and the lions and the wolves and the wild dogs, and we will pasture our goats on all the hillsides and plant our corn and fat roots in all the high

147

mountain valleys. In that day we will be so strong that all the wild animals will flee before us and perish. And nothing will withstand us, for the strength of each man will be the strength of all men in the world.'

"So said Hair-Face, and they killed him, because, they said, he was a wild man and wanted to go back and live in a tree. It was very strange. Whenever a man arose and wanted to go forward all those that stood still said he went backward and should be killed. And the poor people helped stone him, and were fools. We were all fools, except those who were fat and did no work. The fools were called wise, and the wise were stoned. Men who worked did not get enough to eat, and the men who did not work ate too much.

"And the tribe went on losing strength. The children were weak and sickly. And, because we ate not enough, strange sicknesses came among us and we died like flies. And then the Meat-Eaters came upon us. We had followed Tiger-Face too often over the divide and killed them. And now they came to repay in blood. We were too weak and sick to man the big wall. And they killed us, all of us, except some of the women, which they took away with them. The Bug and I escaped, and I hid in the wildest places, and became a hunter of meat and went hungry no more. I stole a wife from the Meat-Eaters, and went to live in the caves of the high mountains where they could not find me. And we had three sons, and each son stole a wife from the Meat-Eaters. And the rest you know, for are you not the sons of my sons?"

"But the Bug?" queried Deer-Runner. "What became of him?"

"He went to live with the Meat-Eaters and to be a singer of songs to the king. He is an old man now, but he sings the same old songs; and, when a man rises up to go forward, he sings that that man is walking backward to live in a tree."

Long-Beard dipped into the bear-carcass and sucked with toothless gums at a fist of suet.

"Some day," he said, wiping his hands on his sides, "all the fools will be dead and then all live men will go forward. The strength of the strong will be theirs, and they will add their strength together, so that, of all the men in the world, not one will fight with another. There will be no guards nor watchers on the walls. And all the hunting animals will be killed, and, as Hair-Face said, all the hillsides will be pastured with goats and all the high mountain valleys will be planted with corn and fat roots. And all men will be brothers, and no man will lie idle in the sun and be fed by his fellows. And all that will come to pass in the time when the fools are dead, and when there will be no more singers to stand still and sing the 'Song of the Bees.' Bees are not men."

148

WAR

Charmian London recorded in her massive biography of her husband that Jack "deemed one of his gems" the little story which follows. And how rightfully he deemed it! This is a gem, a diamond which is virtually unknown today, buried in the obscure files of *The Nation*, buried deeper in the scarce 1913 collection of London's stories *The Night-Born*, in which it was included with a bagful of cheap rhinestones.

Bearing a strong resemblance in mood to Ambrose Bierce's short masterpiece "An Occurrence at Owl Creek Bridge" (1891), "War" raises more questions than it answers. What war? Where did it occur? When? Who were the "alien invaders"? What was their "detested tongue"? What was the young rider's mission? What was London driving at? Is it intended as a message of pacifism, or is it aggressively warlike?

This is London's 148th short story, and he had written none better.

I

He was a young man, not more than twenty-four or five, and he might have sat his horse with the careless grace of his youth had he not been so catlike and tense. His black eyes roved everywhere, catching the movements of twigs and branches where small birds hopped; questing ever onward through the changing vistas of trees and brush, and returning always to the clumps of undergrowth on either side. And as he watched, so did he listen, though he rode on in silence, save for the boom of heavy guns from far to the west. This had been sounding monotonously in his ears for hours, and only its cessation would have aroused his notice. For he had business closer to hand. Across his saddlebow was balanced a carbine.

So tensely was he strung that a bunch of quail, exploding into flight from under his horse's nose, startled him to such an extent that

The Nation (London), 9 (July 29, 1911):635-36.

automatically, instantly, he had reined in and fetched the carbine halfway to his shoulder. He grinned sheepishly, recovered himself, and rode on. So tense was he, so bent upon the work he had to do, that the sweat stung his eyes unwiped, and unheeded rolled down his nose, and spattered his saddle pommel. The band of his cavalryman's hat was fresh-stained with sweat. The roan horse under him was likewise wet. It was high noon of a breathless day of heat. Even the birds and squirrels did not dare the sun, but sheltered in shady hiding-places among the trees.

Man and horse were littered with leaves and dusted with yellow pollen, for the open was ventured no more than was compulsory. They kept to the brush and trees, and invariably the man halted and peered out before crossing a dry glade, or a naked stretch of upland pasturings. He worked always to the north, though his way was devious, and it was from the north that he seemed most to apprehend that for which he was looking. He was no coward, but his courage was only that of the average civilized man, and he was looking to live, not die.

Up a small hillside he followed a cowpath through such dense scrub that he was forced to dismount and lead his horse. But when the path swung around to the west, he abandoned it, and headed to the north again along the oak-covered top of the ridge.

The ridge ended in a steep descent—so steep that he zigzagged back and forth across the face of the slope, sliding and stumbling among the dead leaves and matted vines, and keeping a watchful eye on the horse above, that threatened to fall down upon him. The sweat ran from him, and the pollen-dust, settling pungently in mouth and nostrils, increased his thirst. Try as he would, nevertheless the descent was noisy, and frequently he stopped, panting in the dry heat, and listening for any warning from beneath.

At the bottom he came out on a flat so densely forested that he could not make out its extent. Here the character of the woods changed, and he was able to remount. Instead of the twisted hillside oaks, tall straight trees, big-trunked and prosperous, rose from the damp, fat soil. Only here and there were thickets, easily avoided, while he encountered winding, park-like glades, where the cattle had pastured in the days before war had run them off.

His progress was more rapid now, as he came down into the valley, and at the end of half an hour he halted at an ancient rail fence on the edge of a clearing. He did not like the openness of it, yet his path lay across to the fringe of trees that marked the banks of the stream. It was a mere quarter of a mile across that open, but the thought of venturing out in it was repugnant. A rifle, a score of them, a thousand, might lurk in that fringe by the stream—and he the naked mark.

Twice he essayed to start, and twice he paused. He was appalled by his own loneliness. The pulse of war that beat from the west suggested the companionship of battling thousands; here was naught but silence, and himself, and possible death-dealing bullets from a myriad ambushes. And yet his task was to find what he feared to find. He must go on, and on, till somewhere, some time, he encountered another man, or other men, from the other side, scouting, as he was scouting, to make report, as he must make report, of having come in touch.

Changing his mind, he skirted inside the woods for a distance, and again peeped forth. This time, in the middle of the clearing, he saw a small farmhouse. There were no signs of life. No smoke curled from the chimney, not a barnyard fowl clucked or strutted. The kitchen door stood open, and he gazed so long and hard into the black aperture that it seemed almost that a farmer's wife must emerge at any moment.

He licked the pollen and dust from his dry lips, stiffened himself, mind and body, and rode out into the blazing sunshine. Nothing stirred. He went on past the house, and approached the wall of trees and bushes by the river's bank. One thought persisted maddeningly. It was of the crash in his body of a high velocity bullet. It made him feel very fragile and defenceless, and he crouched lower in the saddle.

Tethering his horse in the edge of the wood, he continued a hundred yards on foot, till he came to the stream. Twenty feet wide it was, without perceptible current, cool and inviting, and he was very thirsty. But he waited inside his screen of leafage, his eyes fixed on the screen on the opposite side. To make the wait endurable, he sat down, his carbine resting on his knees. The minutes passed, and slowly his tenseness relaxed. At last he decided there was no danger; but, just as he prepared to part the bushes and bend down to the water, a movement among the opposite bushes caught his eye.

It might be a bird. But he waited. Again there was an agitation of the bushes, and then, so suddenly that it almost startled a cry from him, the bushes parted and a face peered out. It was a face covered with several weeks' growth of ginger-colored beard. The eyes were blue and wide apart, with laughter-wrinkles in the corners, that showed despite the tired and anxious expression of the whole face.

All this he could see with microscopic clearness, for the distance was no more than twenty feet. And all this he saw in such brief time that he saw it as he lifted his carbine to his shoulder. He glanced along the sights, and knew that he was gazing upon a man who was as good as dead. It was impossible to miss at such point-blank range.

151

CURIOUS FRAGMENTS

But he did not shoot. Slowly he lowered the carbine and watched. A hand, clutching a water-bottle, became visible, and the ginger beard bent downward to fill the bottle. He could hear the gurgle of the water. Then arm and bottle and ginger beard disappeared behind the closing bushes. A long time he waited, then, with thirst unslaked, he crept back to his horse, rode slowly across the sun-washed clearing, and passed into the shelter of the woods beyond.

II

Another day, hot and breathless. A deserted farmhouse, large, with many outbuildings and an orchard, standing in a clearing. From the woods, on a roan horse, carbine across pommel, rode the young man with the quick black eyes. He breathed with relief as he gained the house. That a fight had taken place here earlier in the season was evident. Clips and empty cartridges, tarnished with verdigris, lay on the ground, which, while wet, had been torn up by the hoofs of horses. Hard by the kitchen garden were graves, tagged and numbered. From the oak tree by the kitchen door, in tattered, weather-beaten garments, hung the bodies of two men. The faces, shrivelled and defaced, bore no likeness to the faces of men. The roan horse snorted beneath them, and the rider caressed and soothed it, and tied it farther away.

Entering the house, he found the interior a wreck. He trod on empty cartridges as he walked from room to room to reconnoiter from the windows. Men had camped and slept everywhere, and, on the floor of one room, he came upon stains unmistakable where the wounded had been laid down.

Again outside, he led the horse around behind the barn, and invaded the orchard. A dozen trees were burdened with ripe apples. He filled his pockets, eating while he picked. Then a thought came to him, and he glanced at the sun, calculating the time of his return to camp. He pulled off his shirt, tying the sleeves and making a bag. This he proceeded to fill with apples.

As he was about to mount his horse, the animal suddenly pricked up its ears. The man, too, listened, and heard, faintly, the thud of hoofs on soft earth. He crept to the corner of the barn and peered out. A dozen mounted men, strung out loosely, approaching from the opposite side of the clearing, were only a matter of a hundred yards or so away. They rode on to the house. Some dismounted, while others remained in the saddle, as an earnest that

152

their stay would be short. They seemed to be holding a council, for he could hear them talking excitedly in the detested tongue of the alien invader. The time passed, but they seemed unable to reach a decision. He put the carbine away in its boot, mounted, and waited impatiently, balancing the shirt of apples on the pommel.

He heard footsteps approaching, and drove his spurs so fiercely into the roan as to force a surprised groan from the animal as it leaped forward. At the corner of the barn he saw the intruder, a mere boy of nineteen or twenty, for all of his uniform, jump back to escape being run down. At the same moment the roan swerved, and its rider caught a glimpse of the aroused men by the house. Some were springing from their horses, and he could see the rifles going to their shoulders. He passed the kitchen door, and the dried corpses swinging in the shade, compelling his foes to run around the front of the house. A rifle cracked, and a second, but he was going fast, leaning forward, low in the saddle, one hand clutching the shirt of apples, the other guiding the horse.

The top bar of the fence was four feet high, but he knew his roan, and leaped it at full career to the accompaniment of several scattered shots. Eight hundred yards straight away were the woods, and the roan was covering the distance with mighty strides. Every man was now firing. They were pumping their guns so rapidly that he no longer heard individual shots. A bullet went through his hat, but he was unaware, though he did know when another tore through the apples on the pommel. And he winced and ducked even lower when a third bullet, fired low, struck a stone between his horse's legs, and richochetted off through the air, buzzing and humming like some incredible insect.

The shots died down as the magazines were emptied, until, quickly, there was no more shooting. The young man was elated. Through that astonishing fusillade he had come unscathed. He glanced back. Yes, they had emptied their magazines. He could see several reloading. Others were running back behind the house for their horses. As he looked, two, already mounted, came back into view around the corner, riding hard. And, at the same moment, he saw the man with the unmistakable ginger beard kneel down on the ground, level his gun, and coolly take his time for the long shot.

The young man threw his spurs into the horse, crouched very low, and swerved in his flight in order to distract the other's aim. And still the shot did not come. With each jump of the horse, the woods sprang nearer. They were only two hundred yards away, and

153

still the shot was delayed.

And then he heard it, the last thing he was ever to hear, for he was dead ere he hit the ground in the long crashing fall from the saddle. And they, watching at the house, saw him fall, saw his body bounce when it struck the earth, and saw the burst of red-cheeked apples that rolled about him. They laughed at the unexpected eruption of apples, and clapped their hands in applause of the long shot by the man with the ginger beard.

THE SCARLET PLAGUE

Franklin Walker, the California scholar who has written extensively on Jack London, Frank Norris and others, has called this novelette ". . . perhaps the best example in American literature of a genre today very popular, the survival novel." ("Afterword" to *The Sea Wolf and Selected Stories.* The New American Library, 1964).

London scholar Earle Labor and others have pointed out that the story owes much to Poe's "The Masque of the Red Death," thematically as well as in some details—particularly in the symptoms of the plague. And Labor has remarked on page 111 of *Jack London: "The Scarlet Plague* is not a primitivistic re-run of *The Iron Heel.* Allowing mood to overshadow message, London creates a much more telling indictment of twentieth-century civilization than in his idea-ridden earlier novel. As occasionally happened in his fantasies, the compulsion to preach is forgotten in the heat of the poetic moment."

Originally titled *The Scarlet Death* (presumably to parallel the Black Death of the Dark Ages), this novelette is based partly on London's experiences in the great San Francisco earthquake of 1906 which helped him write vivid scenes of chaos and destruction both in this novel and in the scenes set in Chicago, after the failure of the "First Revolt," in *The Iron Heel.*

Interestingly, I. O. Evans, writing in a Preface to the 1968 British edition of the book (Arco Publications, 1968), says: "The verbosity of the narrator in his story may be based on his [London's] contacts with the professors in the universities he had visited, but so, on the other hand, may be the heroism of the bacteriologists, "killed in their laboratories even as they studied the germ of the Scarlet Death."

And Maxwell Geismar, in the often quoted chapter "Jack London: The Short Cut," in his *Rebels and Ancestors: The American Novel, 1890-1915* (1953), dismisses the book as "a rather tedious fantasy of universal destruction, written for children . . . ." Geismar also calls *The Star Rover* "an incredibly bad novel," and fails to recognize "The Red One" as a work of fantasy at all. Here his comment on *The Scarlet Plague* is pertinent, and readers completing this remarkable tale will realize that it

---

London Magazine, 28 (June, 1912):513-40.

has about the same relationship to a children's story as does William Golding's: *Lord of the Flies.*

And finally the reader may be brought up short upon reading, in this work, this sentence: "But in 1984, there was the Pantoblast Plague, a disease that broke out in a country called Brazil and that killed millions of people." One might ask if George Orwell had read *The Scarlet Plague,* and in fact he may have—either that or *The Iron Heel,* which contains a footnote saying that the futuristic city of "Asgard was not completed until 1984 A.D." Orwell demonstrated a thorough knowledge of London's work when he wrote, in 1945, an introductory essay for an edition of London's *Love of Life and Other Stories.*

I

The way led along upon what had once been the embankment of a railroad. But no train had run upon it for many years. The forest on either side swelled up the slopes of the embankment and crested across it in a green wave of trees and bushes. The trail was as narrow as a man's body, and was no more than a wild-animal runway. Occasionally, a piece of rusty iron, showing through the forest-mold, advertised that the rail and the ties still remained. In one place, a ten-inch tree, bursting through at a connection, had lifted the end of a rail clearly into view. The tie had evidently followed the rail, held to it by the spike long enough for its bed to be filled with gravel and rotten leaves, so that now the crumbling, rotten timber thrust itself up at a curious slant. Old as the road was, it was manifest that it had been of the mono-rail type.

An old man and a boy travelled along this runway. They moved slowly, for the old man was very old, a touch of palsy made his movements tremulous, and he leaned heavily upon his staff. A rude skull-cap of goatskin protected his head from the sun. From beneath this fell a scant fringe of stained and dirty-white hair. A visor, ingeniously made from a large leaf, shielded his eyes, and from under this he peered at the way of his feet on the trail. His beard, which should have been snow-white but which showed the same weather-wear and camp-stain as his hair, fell nearly to his waist in a great tangled mass. About his chest and shoulders hung a single, mangy garment of goatskin. His arms and legs, withered and skinny, betokened extreme age, as well as did their sunburn and scars and scratches betoken long years of exposure to the elements.

The boy, who led the way, checking the eagerness of his muscles to the slow progress of the elder, likewise wore a single garment—a

156

ragged-edged piece of bearskin, with a hole in the middle through which he had thrust his head. He could not have been more than twelve years old. Tucked coquettishly over one ear was the freshly severed tail of a pig. In one hand he carried a medium-sized bow and an arrow. On his back was a quiverful of arrows. From a sheath hanging about his neck on a thong, projected the battered handle of a hunting knife. He was as brown as a berry, and walked softly, with almost a catlike tread. In marked contrast with his sunburned skin were his eyes—blue, deep blue, but keen and sharp as a pair of gimlets. They seemed to bore into all about him in a way that was habitual. As he went along he smelled things, as well, his distended, quivering nostrils carrying to his brain an endless series of messages from the outside world. Also, his hearing was acute, and had been so trained that it operated automatically. Without conscious effort, he heard all the slight sounds in the apparent quiet—heard, and differentiated, and classified these sounds—whether they were of the wind rustling the leaves, of the humming of bees and gnats, of the distant rumble of the sea that drifted to him only in lulls, or of the gopher, just under his foot, shoving a pouchful of earth into the entrance of his hole.

Suddenly he became alertly tense. Sound, sight, and odor had given him a simultaneous warning. His hand went back to the old man, touching him, and the pair stood still. Ahead, at one side of the top of the embankment, arose a crackling sound, and the boy's gaze was fixed on the tops of the agitated bushes. Then a large bear, a grizzly, crashed into view, and likewise stopped abruptly, at sight of the humans. He did not like them, and growled querulously. Slowly the boy fitted the arrow to the bow, and slowly he pulled the bowstring taut. But he never removed his eyes from the bear. The old man peered from under his green leaf at the danger, and stood as quietly as the boy. For a few seconds this mutual scrutinizing went on; then, the bear betraying a growing irritability, the boy, with a movement of his head, indicated that the old man must step aside from the trail and go down the embankment. The boy followed, going backward, still holding the bow taut and ready. They waited till a crashing among the bushes from the opposite side of the embankment told them the bear had gone on. The boy grinned as he led back to the trail.

"A big un, Granser," he chuckled.

The old man shook his head.

"They get thicker every day," he complained in a thin, undependable falsetto. "Who'd have thought I'd live to see the time when a man would be afraid of his life on the way to the Cliff House? When I was a boy, Edwin, men and women and little babies used to come out here from San Francisco by tens of thousands on a nice day. And there weren't any

CURIOUS FRAGMENTS

bears then. No, sir. They used to pay money to look at them in cages, they were that rare."

"What is money, Granser?"

Before the old man could answer, the boy recollected and triumphantly shoved his hand into a pouch under his bearskin and pulled forth a battered and tarnished silver dollar. The old man's eyes glistened, as he held the coin close to them.

"I can't see," he muttered. "You look and see if you can make out the date, Edwin."

The boy laughed.

"You're a great Granser," he cried delightedly, "always making believe them little marks mean something."

The old man manifested an accustomed chagrin as he brought the coin back again close to his own eyes.

"2012," he shrilled, and then fell to cackling grotesquely. "That was the year Morgan the Fifth was appointed President of the United States by the Board of Magnates. It must have been one of the last coins minted, for the Scarlet Death came in 2013. Lord! Lord!—think of it! Sixty years ago, and I am the only person alive to-day that lived in those times. Where did you find it, Edwin?"

The boy, who had been regarding him with the tolerant curiousness one accords to the prattlings of the feeble-minded, answered promptly.

"I got it off of Hoo-Hoo. He found it when we was herdin' goats down near San José last spring. Hoo-Hoo said it was *money*. Ain't you hungry, Granser?"

The ancient caught his staff in a tighter grip and urged along the trail, his old eyes shining greedily.

"I hope Hare-Lip's found a crab . . . or two," he mumbled. "They're good eating, crabs, mighty good eating when you've no more teeth and you've got grandsons that love their old grandsire and make a point of catching crabs for him. When I was a boy—"

But Edwin, suddenly stopped by what he saw, was drawing the bowstring on a fitted arrow. He had paused on the brink of a crevasse in the embankment. An ancient culvert had here washed out, and the stream, no longer confined, had cut a passage through the fill. On the opposite side, the end of a rail projected and overhung. It showed rustily through the creeping vines which overran it. Beyond, crouching by a bush, a rabbit looked across at him in trembling hesitancy. Fully fifty feet was the distance, but the arrow flashed true; and the transfixed rabbit, crying out in sudden fright and hurt, struggled painfully away into the brush. The boy himself was a flash of brown skin and flying fur as he bounded down

158

the steep wall of the gap and up the other side. His lean muscles were springs of steel that released into graceful and efficient action. A hundred feet beyond, in a tangle of bushes, he overtook the wounded creature, knocked its head on a convenient tree-trunk, and turned it over to Granser to carry.

"Rabbit is good, very good," the ancient quavered, "but when it comes to a toothsome delicacy I prefer crab. When I was a boy—"

"Why do you say so much that ain't got no sense?" Edwin impatiently interrupted the other's threatened garrulousness.

The boy did not exactly utter these words, but something that remotely resembled them and that was more guttural and explosive and economical of qualifying phrases. His speech showed distant kinship with that of the old man, and the latter's speech was approximately an English that had gone through a bath of corrupt usage.

"What I want to know," Edwin continued, "is why you call crab 'toothsome delicacy'? Crab is crab, ain't it? No one I never heard calls it such funny things."

The old man sighed but did not answer, and they moved on in silence. The surf grew suddenly louder, as they emerged from the forest upon a stretch of sand dunes bordering the sea. A few goats were browsing among the sandy hillocks, and a skin-clad boy, aided by a wolfish-looking dog that was only faintly reminiscent of a collie, was watching them. Mingled with the roar of the surf was a continuous, deep-throated barking or bellowing, which came from a cluster of jagged rocks a hundred yards out from shore. Here huge sea-lions hauled themselves up to lie in the sun or battle with one another. In the immediate foreground arose the smoke of a fire, tended by a third savage-looking boy. Crouched near him were several wolfish dogs similar to the one that guarded the goats.

The old man accelerated his pace, sniffing eagerly as he neared the fire.

"Mussels!" he muttered ecstatically. "Mussels! And ain't that a crab, Hoo-Hoo? Ain't that a crab? My, my, you boys are good to your old grandsire."

Hoo-Hoo, who was apparently of the same age as Edwin, grinned. "All you want, Granser. I got four."

The old man's palsied eagerness was pitiful. Sitting down in the sand as quickly as his stiff limbs would let him, he poked a large rock-mussel from out of the coals. The heat had forced its shells apart, and the meat, salmon-colored, was thoroughly cooked. Between thumb and forefinger, in trembling haste, he caught the morsel and carried it to his mouth. But it was too hot, and the next moment was violently ejected. The old man

159

spluttered with the pain, and tears ran out of his eyes and down his cheeks.

The boys were true savages, possessing only the cruel humor of the savage. To them the incident was excruciatingly funny, and they burst into loud laughter. Hoo-Hoo danced up and down, while Edwin rolled gleefully on the ground. The boy with the goats came running to join in the fun.

"Set 'em to cool, Edwin, set 'em to cool," the old man besought, in the midst of his grief, making no attempt to wipe away the tears that flowed from his eyes. "And cool a crab, Edwin, too. You know your grandsire likes crabs."

From the coals arose a great sizzling, which proceeded from the many mussels bursting open their shells and exuding their moisture. They were large shellfish, running from three to six inches in length. The boys raked them out with sticks and placed them on a large piece of driftwood to cool.

"When I was a boy, we did not laugh at our elders; we respected them."

The boys took no notice, and Granser continued to babble an incoherent flow of complaint and censure. But this time he was more careful, and did not burn his mouth. All began to eat, using nothing but their hands and making loud mouth-noises and lip-smackings. The third boy, who was called Hare-Lip, slyly deposited a pinch of sand on a mussel the ancient was carrying to his mouth; and when the grit of it bit into the old fellow's mucous membrane and gums, the laughter was again uproarious. He was unaware that a joke had been played on him, and spluttered and spat until Edwin, relenting, gave him a gourd of fresh water with which to wash out his mouth.

"Where's them crabs, Hoo-Hoo?" Edwin demanded. "Granser's set upon having a snack."

Again Granser's eyes burned with greediness as a large crab was handed to him. It was a shell with legs and all complete, but the meat had long since departed. With shaky fingers and babblings of anticipation, the old man broke off a leg and found it filled with emptiness.

"The crabs, Hoo-Hoo?" he wailed. "The crabs?"

"I was foolin', Granser. They ain't no crabs. I never found one."

The boys were overwhelmed with delight at sight of the tears of senile disappointment that dribbled down the old man's cheeks. Then, unnoticed, Hoo-Hoo replaced the empty shell with a fresh-cooked crab. Already dismembered, from the cracked legs the white meat sent forth a small cloud of savory steam. This attracted the old man's nostrils, and he looked down in amazement. The change of his mood to one of joy was immediate. He snuffled and muttered and mumbled, making almost a croon of delight, as he began to eat. Of this the boys took little notice, for it was an accustomed spectacle. Nor did they notice his occasional exclamations and utterances of phrases which meant nothing to them, as, for instance, when he smacked his lips and champed his gums while muttering: "Mayonnaise! Just think—mayonnaise! And it's sixty years since the last was ever made! Two generations and never a smell of it! Why, in those days it was served in every restaurant with crab."

When he could eat no more, the old man sighed, wiped his hands on his naked legs, and gazed out over the sea. With the content of a full stomach, he waxed reminiscent.

"To think of it! I've seen this beach alive with men, women, and children on a pleasant Sunday. And there weren't any bears to eat them up, either. And right up there on the cliff was a big restaurant where you could get anything you wanted to eat. Four million people lived in San Francisco then. And now, in the whole city and county there aren't forty all told. And out there on the sea were ships and ships always to be seen, going in for the Golden Gate or coming out. And airships in the air—dirigibles and flying machines. They could travel two hundred miles an hour. The mail contracts with the New York and San Francisco Limited demanded that for the minimum. There was a chap, a Frenchman, I forget his name, who succeeded in making three hundred; but the thing was risky, too risky for conservative persons. But he was on the right clue, and he would have managed it if it hadn't been for the Great Plague. When I was a boy, there were men alive who remembered the coming of the first aeroplanes, and now I have lived to see the last of them, and that sixty years ago."

The old man babbled on, unheeded by the boys, who were long accustomed to his garrulousness, and whose vocabularies, besides, lacked the greater portion of the words he used. It was noticeable that in these rambling soliloquies his English seemed to recrudesce into better construction and phraseology. But when he talked directly with the boys it lapsed, largely, into their own uncouth and simpler forms.

"But there weren't many crabs in those days," the old man wandered on. "They were fished out, and they were great delicacies. The open season was only a month long, too. And now crabs are accessible the whole year around. Think of it—catching all the crabs you want, any time you want, in the surf of the Cliff House beach!"

A sudden commotion among the goats brought the boys to their feet. The dogs about the fire rushed to join their snarling fellow who guarded the goats, while the goats themselves stampeded in the direction of their human protectors. A half dozen forms, lean and gray, glided about on the sand hillocks or faced the bristling dogs. Edwin arched an arrow that fell short. But Hare-Lip, with a sling such as David carried into battle against Goliath, hurled a stone through the air that whistled from the speed of its flight. It fell squarely among the wolves and caused them to slink away toward the dark depths of the eucalyptus forest.

The boys laughed and lay down again in the sand, while Granser sighed ponderously. He had eaten too much, and, with hands clasped on his paunch, the fingers interlaced, he resumed his maunderings.

" 'The fleeting systems lapse like foam,' " he mumbled what was evidently a quotation. "That's it—foam, and fleeting. All man's toil upon the planet was just so much foam. He domesticated the serviceable animals, destroyed the hostile ones, and cleared the land of its wild vegetation. And then he passed, and the flood of primordial life rolled back again, sweeping his handiwork away—the weeds and the forest inundated his fields, the beasts of prey swept over his flocks, and now there are wolves on the Cliff House beach." He was appalled by the thought. "Where four million people disported themselves, the wild wolves roam to-day, and the savage progeny of our loins, with prehistoric weapons, defend themselves against the fanged despoilers. Think of it! And all because of the Scarlet Death—"

The adjective had caught Hare-Lip's ear.

"He's always saying that," he said to Edwin. "What is *scarlet?*"

" 'The scarlet of the maples can shake me like the cry of bugles going by,' " the old man quoted.

"It's red," Edwin answered the question. "And you don't know it because you come from the Chauffeur Tribe. They never did know nothing, none of them. *Scarlet* is red—I know that."

"Red is red, ain't it?" Hare-Lip grumbled. "Then what's the good of gettin' cocky and calling it scarlet?"

"Granser, what for do you always say so much what nobody knows?" he asked. "Scarlet ain't anything, but red is red. Why don't you say red, then?"

"Red is not the right word," was the reply. "The plague was scarlet. The whole face and body turned scarlet in a hour's time. Don't I know? Didn't I see enough of it? And I am telling you it was scarlet because—well, because it *was* scarlet. There is no other word for it."

"Red is good enough for me," Hare-Lip muttered obstinately. "My dad calls red red, and he ought to know. He says everybody died of the Red Death."

"Your dad is a common fellow, descended from a common fellow,"

Granser retorted heatedly. "Don't I know the beginnings of the Chauffeurs? Your grandsire was a chauffeur, a servant, and without education. He worked for other persons. But your grandmother was of good stock, only the children did not take after her. Don't I remember when I first met them catching fish at Lake Temescal?"

"What is *education?*" Edwin asked.

"Calling red scarlet," Hare-Lip sneered, then returned to the attack on Granser. "My dad told me, an' he got it from his dad afore he croaked, that your wife was a Santa Rosan, an' that she was sure no account. He said she was a *hash-slinger* before the Red Death, though I don't know what a *hash-slinger* is. You can tell me, Edwin."

But Edwin shook his head in token of ignorance.

"It is true, she was a waitress," Granser acknowledged. "But she was a good woman, and your mother was her daughter. Women were very scarce in the days after the Plague. She was the only wife I could find, even if she was a *hash-slinger,* as your father calls it. But it is not nice to talk about our progenitors that way."

"Dad says that the wife of the first Chauffeur was a *lady—*"

"What's a *lady?*" Hoo-Hoo demanded.

"A *Lady's* a Chauffeur squaw," was the quick reply of Hare-Lip.

"The first Chauffeur was Bill, a common fellow, as I said before," the old man expounded; "but his wife was a lady, a great lady. Before the Scarlet Death she was the wife of Van Warden. He was President of the Board of Industrial Magnates, and was one of the dozen men who ruled America. He was worth one billion, eight hundred millions of dollars—coins like you have there in your pouch, Edwin. And then came the Scarlet Death, and his wife became the wife of Bill, the first Chauffeur. He used to beat her, too. I have seen it myself."

Hoo-Hoo, lying on his stomach and idly digging his toes in the sand, cried out and investigated, first, his toe-nail, and next, the small hole he had dug. The other two boys joined him, excavating the sand rapidly with their hands till there lay three skeletons exposed. Two were of adults, the third being that of a part-grown child. The old man nudged along on the ground and peered at the find.

"Plague victims," he announced. "That's the way they died everywhere in the last days. This must have been a family, running away from the contagion and perishing here on the Cliff House beach. They—what are you doing, Edwin?"

This question was asked in sudden dismay, as Edwin, using the back of his hunting knife, began to knock out the teeth from the jaws of one of the skulls.

"Going to string 'em," was the response.

The three boys were now hard at it; and quite a knocking and hammering arose, in which Granser babbled on unnoticed.

"You are true savages. Already has begun the custom of wearing human teeth. In another generation you will be perforating your noses and ears and wearing ornaments of bone and shell. I know. The human race is doomed to sink back farther and farther into the primitive night ere again it begins its bloody climb upward to civilization. When we increase and feel the lack of room, we will proceed to kill one another. And then I suppose you will wear human scalp-locks at your waist, as well—as you, Edwin, who are the gentlest of my grandsons, have already begun with that vile pigtail. Throw it away, Edwin, boy; throw it away."

"What a gabble the old geezer makes," Hare-Lip remarked, when, the teeth all extracted, they began an attempt at equal division.

They were very quick and abrupt in their actions, and their speech, in moments of hot discussion over the allotment of the choicer teeth, was truly a gabble. They spoke in monosyllables and short jerky sentences that was more a gibberish than a language. And yet, through it ran hints of grammatical construction, and appeared vestiges of the conjugation of some superior culture. Even the speech of Granser was so corrupt that were it put down literally it would be almost so much nonsense to the reader. This, however, was when he talked with the boys. When he got into the full swing of babbling to himself, it slowly purged itself into pure English. The sentences grew longer and were enunciated with a rhythm and ease that was reminiscent of the lecture platform.

"Tell us about the Red Death, Granser," Hare-Lip demanded, when the teeth affair had been satisfactorily concluded.

"The Scarlet Death," Edwin corrected.

"An' don't work all that funny lingo on us," Hare-Lip went on. "Talk sensible, Granser, like a Santa Rosan ought to talk. Other Santa Rosans don't talk like you."

II

The old man showed pleasure in being thus called upon. He cleared his throat and began.

"Twenty or thirty years ago my story was in great demand. But in these days nobody seems interested—"

"There you go!" Hare-Lip cried hotly. "Cut out the funny stuff and talk sensible. What's *interested?* You talk like a baby that don't know how."

164

"Let him alone," Edwin urged, "or he'll get mad and won't talk at all. Skip the funny places. We'll catch on to some of what he tells us."

"Let her go, Granser," Hoo-Hoo encouraged; for the old man was already maundering about the disrespect for elders and the reversion to cruelty of all humans that fell from high culture to primitive conditions.

The tale began.

"There were very many people in the world in those days. San Francisco alone held four millions—"

"What is millions?" Edwin interrupted.

Granser looked at him kindly.

"I know you cannot count beyond ten, so I will tell you. Hold up your two hands. On both of them you have altogether ten fingers and thumbs. Very well. I now take this grain of sand—you hold it, Hoo-Hoo." He dropped the grain of sand into the lad's palm and went on. "Now that grain of sand stands for the ten fingers of Edwin. I add another grain. That's ten more fingers. And I add another, and another, and another, until I have added as many grains as Edwin has fingers and thumbs. That makes what I call one hundred. Remember that word—one hundred. Now I put this pebble in Hare-Lip's hand. It stands for ten grains of sand, or ten tens of fingers, or one hundred fingers. I put in ten pebbles. They stand for a thousand fingers. I take a mussel-shell, and it stands for ten pebbles, or one hundred grains of sand, or one thousand fingers. . . ."

And so on, laboriously, and with much reiteration, he strove to build up in their minds a crude conception of numbers. As the quantities increased, he had the boys holding different magnitudes in each of their hands. For still higher sums, he laid the symbols on the log of driftwood; and for symbols he was hard put, being compelled to use the teeth from the skulls for millions, and the crab-shells for billions. It was here that he stopped, for the boys were showing signs of becoming tired.

"There were four million people in San Francisco—four teeth."

The boys' eyes ranged along from the teeth and from hand to hand, down through the pebbles and sand-grains to Edwin's fingers. And back again they ranged along the ascending series in the effort to grasp such inconceivable numbers.

"That was a lot of folks, Granser," Edwin at last hazarded.

"Like sand on the beach here, like sand on the beach, each grain of sand a man, or woman, or child. Yes, my boy, all those people lived right here in San Francisco. And at one time or another all those people came out on this very beach—more people than there are grains of sand. More—more—more. And San Francisco was a noble city. And across the bay—where we camped last year, even more people lived, clear from Point

165

Richmond, on the level ground and on the hills, all the way around to San Leandro—one great city of seven million people.—Seven teeth . . . there, that's it, seven millions."

Again the boys' eyes ranged up and down from Edwin's fingers to the teeth on the log.

"The world was full of people. The census of 2010 gave eight billions for the whole world—eight crab-shells, yes, eight billions. It was not like to-day. Mankind knew a great deal more about getting food. And the more food there was, the more people there were. In the year 1800, there were one hundred and seventy millions in Europe alone. One hundred years later—a grain of sand, Hoo-Hoo—one hundred years later, at 1900, there were five hundred millions in Europe—five grains of sand, Hoo-Hoo, and this one tooth. This shows how easy was the getting of food, and how men increased. And in the year 2000, there were fifteen hundred millions in Europe. And it was the same all over the rest of the world. Eight crab-shells there, yes, eight billion people were alive on the earth when the Scarlet Death began.

"I was a young man when the Plague came—twenty-seven years old; and I lived on the other side of San Francisco Bay, in Berkeley. You remember those great stone houses, Edwin, when we came down the hills from Contra Costa? That was where I lived, in those stone houses. I was a professor of English literature."

Much of this was over the heads of the boys, but they strove to comprehend dimly this tale of the past.

"What was them stone houses for?" Hare-Lip queried.

"You remember when your dad taught you to swim?" The boy nodded. "Well, in the University of California—that is the name we had for the houses—we taught young men and women how to think, just as I have taught you now, by sand and pebbles and shells, to know how many people lived in those days. There was very much to teach. The young men and women we taught were called students. We had large rooms in which we taught. I talked to them, forty or fifty at a time, just as I am talking to you now. I told them about the books other men had written before their time, and even, sometimes, in their time—"

"Was that all you did?—just talk, talk, talk?" Hoo-Hoo demanded. "Who hunted your meat for you? and milked the goats? and caught the fish?"

"A sensible question, Hoo-Hoo, a sensible question. As I have told you, in those days food-getting was easy. We were very wise. A few men got the food for many men. The other men did other things. As you say, I talked. I talked all the time, and for this food was given me—much food,

166

fine food, beautiful food, food that I have not tasted in sixty years and shall never taste again. I sometimes think the most wonderful achievement of our tremendous civilization was food—its inconceivable abundance, its infinite variety, its marvellous delicacy. O my grandsons, life was life in those days, when we had such wonderful things to eat."

This was beyond the boys, and they let it slip by, words and thoughts, as a mere senile wandering in the narrative.

"Our food-getters were called *freemen.* This was a joke. We of the ruling classes owned all the land, all the machines, everything. These food-getters were our slaves. We took almost all the food they got, and left them a little so that they might eat, and work, and get us more food—"

"I'd have gone into the forest and got food for myself," Hare-Lip announced; "and if any man tried to take it away from me, I'd have killed him."

The old man laughed.

"Did I not tell you that we of the ruling class owned all the land, all the forest, everything? Any food-getter who would not get food for us, him we punished or compelled to starve to death. And very few did that. They preferred to get food for us, and make clothes for us, and prepare and administer to us a thousand—a mussel-shell, Hoo-Hoo—a thousand satisfactions and delights. And I was Professor Smith in those days— Professor James Howard Smith. And my lecture courses were very popular—that is, very many of the young men and women liked to hear me talk about the books other men had written.

"And I was very happy, and I had beautiful things to eat. And my hands were soft, because I did no work with them, and my body was clean all over and dressed in the softest garments—" He surveyed his mangy goatskin with disgust. "We did not wear such things in those days. Even the slaves had better garments. And we were most clean. We washed our faces and hands often every day. You boys never wash unless you fall into the water or go in swimming."

"Neither do you, Granser," Hoo-Hoo retorted.

"I know, I know. I am a filthy old man. But times have changed. No-body washes these days, and there are no conveniences. It is sixty years since I have seen a piece of soap. You do not know what soap is, and I shall not tell you, for I am telling the story of the Scarlet Death. You know what sickness is. We called it a disease. Very many of the diseases came from what we called germs. Remember that word—germs. A germ is a very small thing. It is like a woodtick, such as you find on the dogs in the spring of the year when they run in the forest. Only the germ is very small. It is so small that you cannot see it—"

167

Hoo-Hoo began to laugh.

"You're a queer un, Granser, talking about things you can't see. If you can't see 'em, how do you know they are? That's what I want to know. How do you know anything you can't see?"

"A good question, a very good question, Hoo-Hoo. But we did see—some of them. We had what we called microscopes and ultramicroscopes, and we put them to our eyes and looked through them, so that we saw things larger than they really were, and many things we could not see without the microscopes at all. Our best ultramicroscopes could make a germ look forty thousand times larger. A mussel-shell is a thousand fingers like Edwin's. Take forty mussel-shells, and by as many times larger was the germ when we looked at it through a microscope. And after that, we had other ways, by using what we called moving pictures, of making the forty-thousand-times germ many, many thousand times larger still. And thus we saw all these things which our eyes of themselves could not see. Take a grain of sand. Break it into ten pieces. Take one piece and break it into ten. Break one of those pieces into ten, and one of those into ten, and one of those into ten, and one of those into ten, and do it all day, and maybe, by sunset, you will have a piece as small as one of the germs."

The boys were openly incredulous. Hare-Lip sniffed and sneered and Hoo-Hoo snickered, until Edwin nudged them to be silent.

"The woodtick sucks the blood of the dog, but the germ, being so very small, goes right into the blood of the body, and there it has many children. In those days there would be as many as a billion—a crab-shell, please—as many as that crab-shell in one man's body. We called germs micro-organisms. When a few million, or a billion, of them were in a man, in all the blood of a man, he was sick. These germs were a disease. There were many different kinds of them—more different kinds than there are grains of sand on this beach. We knew only a few of the kinds. The micro-organic world was an invisible world, a world we could not see, and we knew very little about it. Yet we did know something. There was the *bacillus anthracis;* there was the *micrococcus;* there was the *Bacterium termo,* and the *Bacterium lactis*—that's what turns the goat milk sour even to this day, Hare-Lip; and there were *Schizomycetes* without end. And there were many others. . . ."

Here the old man launched into a disquisition on germs and their natures, using words and phrases of such extraordinary length and meaninglessness, that the boys grinned at one another and looked out over the deserted ocean till they forgot the old man was babbling on.

"But the Scarlet Death, Granser," Edwin at last suggested.

Granser recollected himself, and with a start tore himself away from

THE SCARLET PLAGUE

the rostrum of the lecture-hall, where, to another-world audience, he had been expounding the latest theory, sixty years gone, of germs and germ-diseases.

"Yes, Yes, Edwin; I had forgotten. Sometimes the memory of the past is very strong upon me, and I forget that I am a dirty old man, clad in goatskin, wandering with my savage grandsons who are goatherds in the primeval wilderness. 'The fleeting systems lapse like foam,' and so lapsed our glorious, colossal civilization. I am Granser, a tired old man. I belong to the tribe of Santa Rosans. I married into that tribe. My sons and daughters married into the Chauffeurs, the Sacramentos, and the Palo-Altos. You, Hare-Lip, are of the Chauffeurs. You, Edwin, are of the Sacramentos. And you, Hoo-Hoo, are of the Palo-Altos. Your tribe takes its name from a town that was near the seat of another great institution of learning. It was called Stanford University. Yes, I remember now. It is perfectly clear. I was telling you of the Scarlet Death. Where was I in my story?"

"You was telling about germs, the things you can't see but which make men sick," Edwin prompted.

"Yes, that's where I was. A man did not notice at first when only a few of these germs got into his body. But each germ broke in half and became two germs, and they kept doing this very rapidly so that in a short time there were many millions of them in the body. Then the man was sick. He had a disease, and the disease was named after the kind of germ that was in him. It might be measles, it might be influenza, it might be yellow fever; it might be any of thousands and thousands of kinds of diseases.

"Now this is the strange thing about these germs. There were always new ones coming to live in men's bodies. Long and long and long ago, when there were only a few men in the world, there were few diseases. But as men increased and lived closely together in great cities and civilizations, new diseases arose, new kinds of germs entered their bodies. Thus were countless millions and billions of human beings killed. And the more thickly men packed together, the more terrible were the new diseases that came to be. Long before my time, in the middle ages, there was the Black Plague that swept across Europe. It swept across Europe many times. There was tuberculosis, that entered into men wherever they were thickly packed. A hundred years before my time there was the bubonic plague. And in Africa was the sleeping sickness. The bacteriologists fought all these sicknesses and destroyed them, just as you boys fight the wolves away from your goats, or squash the mosquitoes that light on you. The bacteriologists—"

169

"But, Granser, what is a what-you-call-it?" Edwin interrupted.

"You, Edwin, are a goatherd. Your task is to watch the goats. You know a great deal about goats. A bacteriologist watches germs. That's his task, and he knows a great deal about them. So, as I was saying, the bacteriologists fought with the germs and destroyed them—sometimes. There was leprosy, a horrible disease. A hundred years before I was born, the bacteriologists discovered the germ of leprosy. They knew all about it. They made pictures of it. I have seen those pictures. But they never found a way to kill it. But in 1984, there was the Pantoblast Plague, a disease that broke out in a country called Brazil and that killed millions of people. But the bacteriologists found it out, and found the way to kill it, so that the Pantoblast Plague went no farther. They made what they called a serum, which they put into a man's body and which killed the pantoblast germs without killing the man. And in 1910, there was pellagra, and also the hookworm. These were easily killed by the bacteriologists. But in 1947 there arose a new disease that had never been seen before. It got into the bodies of babies of only ten months old or less, and it made them unable to move their hands and feet, or to eat, or anything; and the bacteriologists were eleven years in discovering how to kill that particular germ and save the babies.

"In spite of all these diseases, and of all the new ones that continued to arise, there were more and more men in the world. This was because it was easy to get food. The easier it was to get food, the more men there were; the more men there were, the more thickly were they packed together on the earth; and the more thickly they were packed, the more new kinds of germs became diseases. There were warnings. Soldervetzsky, as early as 1929, told the bacteriologists that they had no guaranty against some new disease, a thousand times more deadly than any they knew, arising and killing by the hundreds of millions and even by the billion. You see, the micro-organic world remained a mystery to the end. They knew there was such a world, and that from time to time armies of new germs emerged from it to kill men. And that was all they knew about it. For all they knew, in that invisible micro-organic world there might be as many different kinds of germs as there are grains of sand on this beach. And also, in that same invisible world it might well be that new kinds of germs came to be. It might be there that life originated—the 'abysmal fecundity,' Soldervetzsky called it, applying the words of other men who had written before him. . . ."

It was at this point that Hare-Lip rose to his feet, an expression of huge contempt on his face.

"Granser," he announced, "you make me sick with your gabble.

170

Why don't you tell about the Red Death? If you ain't going to, say so, an' we'll start back for camp."

The old man looked at him and silently began to cry. The weak tears of age rolled down his cheeks, and all the feebleness of his eighty-seven years showed in his grief-stricken countenance.

"Sit down," Edwin counselled soothingly. "Granser's all right. He's just gettin' to the Scarlet Death, ain't you, Granser? He's just goin' to tell us about it right now. Sit down, Hare-Lip. Go ahead, Granser."

III

The old man wiped the tears away on his grimy knuckles and took up the tale in a tremulous, piping voice that soon strengthened as he got the swing of the narrative.

"It was in the summer of 2013 that the Plague came. I was twenty-seven years old, and well do I remember it. Wireless dispatches—"

Hare-Lip spat loudly his disgust, and Granser hastened to make amends.

"We talked through the air in those days, thousands and thousands of miles. And the word came of a strange disease that had broken out in New York. There were seventeen millions of people living then in that noblest city of America. Nobody thought anything about the news. It was only a small thing. There had been only a few deaths. It seemed, though, that they had died very quickly, and that one of the first signs of the disease was the turning red of the face and all the body. Within twenty-four hours came the report of the first case in Chicago. And on the same day, it was made public that London, the greatest city in the world, next to Chicago, had been secretly fighting the plague for two weeks and censoring the news dispatches—that is, not permitting the word to go forth to the rest of the world that London had the plague.

"It looked serious, but we in California, like everywhere else, were not alarmed. We were sure that the bacteriologists would find a way to overcome this new germ, just as they had overcome other germs in the past. But the trouble was the astonishing quickness with which this germ destroyed human beings, and the fact that it inevitably killed any human body it entered. No one ever recovered. There was the old Asiatic cholera, when you might eat dinner with a well man in the evening, and the next morning, if you got up early enough, you would see him being hauled by your window in the death-cart. But this new plague was quicker than that—much quicker. From the moment of the first signs of it, a man would be dead in an hour. Some lasted for several hours. Many died within ten or fifteen minutes of the appearance of the first signs.

"The heart began to beat faster and the heat of the body to increase. Then came the scarlet rash, spreading like wildfire over the face and body. Most persons never noticed the increase in heat and heart-beat, and the first they knew was when the scarlet rash came out. Usually, they had convulsions at the time of the appearance of the rash. But these convulsions did not last long and were not very severe. If one lived through them, he became perfectly quiet, and only did he feel a numbness swiftly creeping up his body from the feet. The heels became numb first, then the legs, and hips, and when the numbness reached as high as his heart he died. They did not rave or sleep. Their minds always remained cool and calm up to the moment their heart numbed and stopped. And another strange thing was the rapidity of decomposition. No sooner was a person dead than the body seemed to fall to pieces, to fly apart, to melt away even as you looked at it. That was one of the reasons the plague spread so rapidly. All the billions of germs in a corpse were so immediately released.

"And it was because of all this that the bacteriologists had so little chance in fighting the germs. They were killed in their laboratories even as they studied the germ of the Scarlet Death. They were heroes. As fast as they perished, others stepped forth and took their places. It was in London that they first isolated it. The news was telegraphed everywhere. Trask was the name of the man who succeeded in this, but within thirty hours he was dead. Then came the struggle in all the laboratories to find something that would kill the plague germs. All drugs failed. You see, the problem was to get a drug, or serum, that would kill the germs in the body and not kill the body. They tried to fight it with other germs, to put into the body of a sick man germs that were the enemies of the plague germs—"

"And you can't see these germ-things, Granser," Hare-Lip objected, "and here you gabble, gabble, gabble about them as if they was anything, when they're nothing at all. Anything you can't see, ain't, that's what. Fighting things that ain't with things that ain't! They must have been all fools in them days. That's why they croaked. I ain't goin' to believe in such rot, I tell you that."

Granser promptly began to weep, while Edwin hotly took up his defense.

"Look here, Hare-Lip, you believe in lots of things you can't see."

Hare-Lip shook his head.

"You believe in dead men walking about. You never seen one dead man walk about."

"I tell you I seen 'em, last winter, when I was wolf-hunting with dad."

THE SCARLET PLAGUE

"Well, you always spit when you cross running water," Edwin challenged.

"That's to keep off bad luck," was Hare-Lip's defence.

"You believe in bad luck?"

"Sure."

"An' you ain't never seen bad luck," Edwin concluded triumphantly. "You're just as bad as Granser and his germs. You believe in what you don't see. Go on, Granser."

Hare-Lip, crushed by this metaphysical defeat, remained silent, and the old man went on. Often and often, though this narrative must not be clogged by the details, was Granser's tale interrupted while the boys squabbled among themselves. Also, among themselves they kept up a constant, low-voiced exchange of explanation and conjecture, as they strove to follow the old man into his unknown and vanished world.

"The Scarlet Death broke out in San Francisco. The first death came on a Monday morning. By Thursday they were dying like flies in Oakland and San Francisco. They died everywhere—in their beds, at their work, walking along the street. It was on Tuesday that I saw my first death—Miss Collbran, one of my students, sitting right there before my eyes, in my lecture-room. I noticed her face while I was talking. It had suddenly turned scarlet. I ceased speaking and could only look at her, for the first fear of the plague was already on all of us and we knew that it had come. The young women screamed and ran out of the room. So did the young men run out, all but two. Miss Collbran's convulsions were very mild and lasted less than a minute. One of the young men fetched her a glass of water. She drank only a little of it, and cried out:

" 'My feet! All sensation has left them.'

"After a minute she said, 'I have no feet. I am unaware that I have any feet. And my knees are cold. I can scarcely feel that I have knees.'

"She lay on the floor, a bundle of notebooks under her head. And we could do nothing. The coldness and the numbness crept up past her hips to her heart, and when it reached her heart she was dead. In fifteen minutes, by the clock—I timed it—she was dead, there, in my own classroom, dead. And she was a very beautiful, strong, healthy young woman. And from the first sign of the plague to her death only fifteen minutes elapsed. That will show you how swift was the Scarlet Death.

"Yet in those few minutes I remained with the dying woman in my classroom, the alarm had spread over the university; and the students, by thousands, all of them, had deserted the lecture-room and laboratories. When I emerged, on my way to make report to the President of the Faculty, I found the university deserted. Across the campus were several

173

stragglers hurrying for their homes. Two of them were running.

"President Hoag I found in his office, all alone, looking very old and very gray, with a multitude of wrinkles in his face that I had never seen before. At the sight of me, he pulled himself to his feet and tottered away to the inner office, banging the door after him and locking it. You see, he knew I had been exposed, and he was afraid. He shouted to me through the door to go away. I shall never forget my feelings as I walked down the silent corridors and out across that deserted campus. I was not afraid. I had been exposed, and I looked upon myself as already dead. It was not that, but a feeling of awful depression that impressed me. Everything had stopped. It was like the end of the world to me—my world. I had been born within sight and sound of the university. It had been my predestined career. My father had been a professor there before me, and his father before him. For a century and a half had this university, like a splendid machine, been running steadily on. And now, in an instant, it had stopped. It was like seeing the sacred flame die down on some thrice-sacred altar. I was shocked, unutterably shocked.

"When I arrived home, my housekeeper screamed as I entered, and fled away. And when I rang, I found the housemaid had likewise fled. I investigated. In the kitchen I found the cook on the point of departure. But she screamed, too, and in her haste dropped a suitcase of her personal belongings and ran out of the house and across the grounds, still screaming. I can hear her scream to this day. You see, we did not act in this way when ordinary diseases smote us. We were always calm over such things, and sent for the doctors and nurses who knew just what to do. But this was different. It struck so suddenly, and killed so swiftly, and never missed a stroke. When the scarlet rash appeared on a person's face, that person was marked by death. There was never a known case of a recovery.

"I was alone in my big house. As I have told you often before, in those days we could talk with one another over wires or through the air. The telephone bell rang, and I found my brother talking to me. He told me that he was not coming home for fear of catching the plague from me, and that he had taken our two sisters to stop at Professor Bacon's home. He advised me to remain where I was, and wait to find out whether or not I had caught the plague.

"To all of this I agreed, staying in my house and for the first time in my life attempting to cook. And the plague did not come out on me. By means of the telephone I could talk with whomsoever I pleased and get the news. Also, there were the newspapers, and I ordered all of them to be thrown up to my door so that I could know what was happening with the rest of the world.

"New York City and Chicago were in chaos. And what happened with them was happening in all the large cities. A third of the New York police were dead. Their chief was also dead, likewise the mayor. All law and order had ceased. The bodies were lying in the streets unburied. All railroads and vessels carrying food and such things into the great city had ceased running, and mobs of the hungry poor were pillaging the stores and warehouses. Murder and robbery and drunkenness were everywhere. Already the people had fled from the city by millions—at first the rich, in their private motor-cars and dirigibles, and then the great mass of the population, on foot, carrying the plague with them, themselves starving and pillaging the farmers and all the towns and villages on the way.

"The man who sent this news, the wireless operator, was alone with his instrument on the top of a lofty building. The people remaining in the city—he estimated them at several hundred thousand—had gone mad from fear and drink, and on all sides of him great fires were raging. He was a hero, that man who stayed by his post—an obscure newspaperman, most likely.

"For twenty-four hours, he said, no transatlantic airships had arrived, and no more messages were coming from England. He did state, though, that a message from Berlin—that's in Germany—announced that Hoffmeyer, a bacteriologist of the Metchnikoff School, had discovered the serum for the plague. That was the last word, to this day, that we of America ever received from Europe. If Hoffmeyer discovered the serum, it was too late, or otherwise, long ere this, explorers from Europe would have come looking for us. We can only conclude that what happened in America happened in Europe, and that, at the best, some several score may have survived the Scarlet Death on that whole continent.

"For one day longer the dispatches continued to come from New York. Then they, too, ceased. The man who had sent them, perched in his lofty building, had either died of the plague or been consumed in the great conflagrations he had described as raging around him. And what had occurred in New York had been duplicated in all the other cities. It was the same in San Francisco, and Oakland, and Berkeley. By Thursday the people were dying so rapidly that their corpses could not be handled, and dead bodies lay everywhere. Thursday night the panic outrush for the country began. Imagine, my grandsons, people, thicker than the salmon-run you have seen on the Sacramento River, pouring out of the cities by millions, madly over the country, in vain attempt to escape the ubiquitous death. You see, they carried the germs with them. Even the airships of the rich, fleeing for mountain and desert fastnesses, carried the germs.

175

"Hundreds of these airships escaped to Hawaii, and not only did they bring the plague with them, but they found the plague already there before them. This we learned by the dispatches, until all order in San Francisco vanished, and there were no operators left at their posts to receive or send. It was amazing, astounding, this loss of communication with the world. It was exactly as if the world had ceased, been blotted out. For sixty years that world has no longer existed for me. I know there must be such places as New York, Europe, Asia, and Africa; but not one word has been heard of them—not in sixty years. With the coming of the Scarlet Death the world fell apart, absolutely, irretrievably. Ten thousand years of culture and civilization passed in the twinkling of an eye, 'lapsed like foam.'

"I was telling about the airships of the rich. They carried the plague with them and no matter where they fled, they died. I never encountered but one survivor of any of them—Mungerson. He was afterwards a Santa Rosan, and he married my eldest daughter. He came into the tribe eight years after the plague. He was then nineteen years old, and he was compelled to wait twelve years more before he could marry. You see, there were no unmarried women, and some of the older daughters of the Santa Rosans were already bespoken. So he was forced to wait until my Mary had grown to sixteen years. It was his son, Gimp-Leg, who was killed last year by the mountain lion.

"Mungerson was eleven years old at the time of the plague. His father was one of the Industrial Magnates, a very wealthy, powerful man. It was on his airship, the *Condor,* that they were fleeing, with all the family, for the wilds of British Columbia, which is far to the north of here. But there was some accident, and they were wrecked near Mount Shasta. You have heard of that mountain. It is far to the north. The plague broke out amongst them, and this boy of eleven was the only survivor. For eight years he was alone, wandering over a deserted land and looking vainly for his own kind. And at last, travelling south, he picked up with us, the Santa Rosans.

"But I am ahead of my story. When the great exodus from the cities around San Francisco Bay began, and while the telephones were still working, I talked with my brother. I told him this flight from the cities was insanity, that there were no symptoms of the plague in me, and that the thing for us to do was to isolate ourselves and our relatives in some safe place. We decided on the Chemistry Building, at the university, and we planned to lay in a supply of provisions, and by force of arms to prevent any other persons from forcing their presence upon us after we had retired to our refuge.

176

"All this being arranged, my brother begged me to stay in my own house for at least twenty-four hours more, on the chance of the plague developing in me. To this I agreed, and he promised to come for me next day. We talked on over the details of the provisioning and the defending of the Chemistry Building until the telephone died. It died in the midst of our conversation. That evening there were no electric lights, and I was alone in my house in the darkness. No more newspapers were being printed, so I had no knowledge of what was taking place outside. I heard sounds of rioting and of pistol shots, and from my windows I could see the glare in the sky of some conflagration in the direction of Oakland. It was a night of terror. I did not sleep a wink. A man—why and how I do not know—was killed on the sidewalk in front of the house. I heard the rapid reports of an automatic pistol, and a few minutes later the wounded wretch crawled up to my door, moaning and crying out for help. Arming myself with two automatics, I went to him. By the light of a match I ascertained that while he was dying of the bullet wounds, at the same time the plague was on him. I fled indoors, whence I heard him moan and cry out for half an hour longer.

"In the morning, my brother came to me. I had gathered into a handbag what things of value I purposed taking, but when I saw his face I knew that he would never accompany me to the Chemistry Building. The plague was on him. He intended shaking my hand, but I went back hurriedly before him.

"Look at yourself in the mirror," I commanded.

"He did so, and at sight of his scarlet face, the color deepening as he looked at it, he sank down nervelessly in a chair.

" 'My God!' he said. 'I've got it. Don't come near me. I am a dead man.'

"Then the convulsions seized him. He was two hours in dying, and he was conscious to the last, complaining about the coldness and loss of sensation in his feet, his calves, his thighs, until at last it was his heart and he was dead.

"That was the way the Scarlet Death slew. I caught up my handbag and fled. The sights in the streets were terrible. One stumbled on bodies everywhere. Some were not yet dead. And even as you looked, you saw men sink down with the death fastened upon them. There were numerous fires burning in Berkeley, while Oakland and San Francisco were apparently being swept by vast conflagrations. The smoke of the burning filled the heavens, so that the mid-day was as a gloomy twilight, and, in the shifts of wind, sometimes the sun shone through dimly, a dull red orb. Truly, my grandsons, it was like the last days of the end of the world.

177

"There were numerous stalled motor-cars, showing that the gasoline and the engine supplies of the garages had given out. I remember one such car. A man and a woman lay back dead in the seats, and on the pavement near it were two more women and a child. Strainge and terrible sights there were on every hand. People slipped by silently, furtively, like ghosts—white-faced women carrying infants in their arms; fathers leading children by the hand; singly, and in couples, and in families—all fleeing out of the city of death. Some carried supplies of food, others blankets and valuables, and there were many who carried nothing.

"There was a grocery store—a place where food was sold. The man to whom it belonged—I knew him well—a quiet, sober, but stupid and obstinate fellow, was defending it. The windows and doors had been broken in, but he, inside, hiding behind a counter, was discharging his pistol at a number of men on the sidewalk who were breaking in. In the entrance were several bodies—of men, I decided, whom he had killed earlier in the day. Even as I looked on from a distance, I saw one of the robbers break the windows of the adjoining store, a place where shoes were sold, and deliberately set fire to it. I did not go to the groceryman's assistance. The time for such acts had already passed. Civilization was crumbling, and it was each for himself.

IV

"I went away hastily, down a cross-street, and at the first corner I saw another tragedy. Two men of the working class had caught a man and a woman with two children, and were robbing them. I knew the man by sight though I had never been introduced to him. He was a poet whose verses I had long admired. Yet I did not go to his help, for at the moment I came upon the scene there was a pistol shot, and I saw him sinking to the ground. The woman screamed, and she was felled with a fist-blow by one of the brutes. I cried out threateningly, whereupon they discharged their pistols at me and I ran away around the corner. Here I was blocked by an advancing conflagration. The buildings on both sides were burning, and the street was filled with smoke and flame. From somewhere in that murk came a woman's voice calling shrilly for help. But I did not go to her. A man's heart turned to iron amid such scenes, and one heard all too many appeals for help.

"Returning to the corner, I found the two robbers were gone. The poet and his wife lay dead on the pavement. It was a shocking sight. The two children had vanished—whither I could not tell. And I knew, now, why it was that the fleeing persons I encountered slipped along so furtively and with such white faces. In the midst of our civilization, down in our slums and labor-ghettos, we had bred a race of barbarians, of savages; and now, in the time of our calamity, they turned upon us like the wild beasts they were and destroyed us. And they destroyed themselves as well. They inflamed themselves with strong drink and committed a thousand atrocities, quarreling and killing one another in the general madness. One group of workingmen I saw, of the better sort, who had banded together, and, with their women and children in their midst, the sick and aged in litters and being carried, and with a number of horses pulling a truck-load of provisions, they were fighting their way out of the city. They made a fine spectacle as they came down the street through the drifting smoke, though they nearly shot me when I first appeared in their path. As they went by, one of their leaders shouted out to me in apologetic explanation. He said they were killing the robbers and looters on sight, and that they had thus banded together as the only means by which to escape the prowlers.

"It was here that I saw for the first time what I was soon to see so often. One of the marching men had suddenly shown the unmistakable mark of the plague. Immediately those about him drew away, and he, without a remonstrance, stepped out of his place to let them pass on. A woman, most probably his wife, attempted to follow him. She was leading a little boy by the hand. But the husband commanded her sternly to go on, while others laid hands on her and restrained her from following him. This I saw, and I saw the man also, with his scarlet blaze of face, step into a doorway on the opposite side of the street. I heard the report of his pistol, and saw him sink lifeless to the ground.

"After being turned aside twice again by advancing fires, I succeeded in getting through to the university. On the edge of the campus I came upon a party of university folk who were going in the direction of the Chemistry Building. They were all family men, and their families were with them, including the nurses and the servants. Professor Badminton greeted me, and I had difficulty in recognizing him. Somewhere he had gone through flames, and his beard was singed off. About his head was a bloody bandage, and his clothes were filthy. He told me he had been cruelly beaten by prowlers, and that his brother had been killed the previous night, in the defence of their dwelling.

"Midway across the campus, he pointed suddenly to Mrs. Swinton's face. The unmistakable scarlet was there. Immediately all the other women set up a screaming and began to run away from her. Her two children were with a nurse, and these also ran with the women. But her husband, Doctor Swinton, remained with her.

179

" 'Go on, Smith,' he told me. 'Keep an eye on the children. As for me, I shall stay with my wife. I know she is as already dead, but I can't leave her. Afterwards, if I escape, I shall come to the Chemistry Building, and do you watch for me and let me in.'

"I left him bending over his wife and soothing her last moments, while I ran to overtake the party. We were the last to be admitted to the Chemistry Building. After that, with our automatic rifles we maintained our isolation. By our plans, we had arranged for a company of sixty to be in this refuge. Instead, every one of the number originally planned had added relatives and friends and whole families until there were over four hundred souls. But the Chemistry Building was large, and, standing by itself, was in no danger of being burned by the great fires that raged everywhere in the city.

"A large quantity of provisions had been gathered, and a food committee took charge of it, issuing rations daily to the various families and groups that arranged themselves into messes. A number of committees were appointed, and we developed a very efficient organization. I was on the committee of defence, though for the first day no prowlers came near. We could see them in the distance, however, and by the smoke of their fires knew that several camps of them were occupying the far edge of the campus. Drunkenness was rife, and often we heard them singing ribald songs or insanely shouting. While the world crashed to ruin about them and all the air was filled with the smoke of its burning, these low creatures gave rein to their bestiality and fought and drank and died. And after all, what did it matter? Everybody died anyway, the good and the bad, the efficients and the weaklings, those that loved to live and those that scorned to live. They passed. Everything passed.

"When twenty-four hours had gone by and no signs of the plague were apparent, we congratulated ourselves and set about digging a well. You have seen the great iron pipes which in those days carried water to all the city-dwellers. We feared that the fires in the city would burst the pipes and empty the reservoirs. So we tore up the cement floor of the central court of the Chemistry Building and dug a well. There were many young men, undergraduates, with us, and we worked night and day on the well. And our fears were confirmed. Three hours before we reached water, the pipes went dry.

"A second twenty-four hours passed, and still the plague did not appear among us. We thought we were saved. But we did not know what I afterwards decided to be true, namely, that the period of the incubation of the plague germs in a human's body was a matter of a number of days. It slew so swiftly when once it manifested itself, that we were led to believe

180

that the period of incubation was equally swift. So, when two days had left us unscathed, we were elated with the idea that we were free of the contagion.

"But the third day disillusioned us. I can never forget the night preceding it. I had charge of the night guards from eight to twelve, and from the roof of the building I watched the passing of all man's glorious works. So terrible were the local conflagrations that all the sky was lighted up. One could read the finest print in the red glare. All the world seemed wrapped in flames. San Francisco spouted smoke and fire from a score of vast conflagrations that were like so many active volcanoes. Oakland, San Leandro, Haywards—all were burning; and to the northward, clear to Point Richmond, other fires were at work. It was an awe-inspiring spectacle. Civilization, my grandsons, civilization was passing in a sheet of flame and a breath of death. At ten o'clock that night, the great powder magazines at Point Pinole exploded in rapid succession. So terrific were the concussions that the strong building rocked as in an earthquake, while every pane of glass was broken. It was then that I left the roof and went down the long corridors, from room to room, quieting the alarmed women and telling them what had happened.

"An hour later, at a window on the ground floor, I heard pandemonium break out in the camps of the prowlers. There were cries and screams, and shots from many pistols. As we afterward conjectured, this fight had been precipitated by an attempt on the part of those that were well to drive out those that were sick. At any rate, a number of the plague-stricken prowlers escaped across the campus and drifted against our doors. We warned them back, but they cursed us and discharged a fusillade from their pistols. Professor Merryweather, at one of the windows, was instantly killed, the bullet striking him squarely between the eyes. We opened fire in turn, and all the prowlers fled away with the exception of three. One was a woman. The plague was on them and they were reckless. Like foul fiends, there in the red glare from the skies, with faces blazing, they continued to curse us and fire at us. One of the men I shot with my own hand. After that the other man and the woman, still cursing us, lay down under our windows, where we were compelled to watch them die of the plague.

"The situation was critical. The explosions of the powder magazines had broken all the windows of the Chemistry Building, so that we were exposed to the germs from the corpses. The sanitary committee was called upon to act, and it responded nobly. Two men were required to go out and remove the corpses, and this meant the probable sacrifice of their own lives, for, having performed the task, they were not to be permitted to

181

re-enter the building. One of the professors, who was a bachelor, and one of the undergraduates volunteered. They bade good-bye to us and went forth. They were heroes. They gave up their lives that four hundred others might live. After they had performed their work, they stood for a moment, at a distance, looking at us wistfully. Then they waved their hands in farewell and went away slowly across the campus toward the burning city.

"And yet it was all useless. The next morning the first one of us was smitten with the plague—a little nurse-girl in the family of Professor Stout. It was no time for weak-kneed, sentimental policies. On the chance that she might be the only one, we thrust her forth from the building and commanded her to be gone. She went away slowly across the campus, wringing her hands and crying pitifully. We felt like brutes, but what were we to do? There were four hundred of us, and individuals had to be sacrificed.

"In one of the laboratories three families had domiciled themselves, and that afternoon we found among them no less than four corpses and seven cases of the plague in all its different stages.

"Then it was that the horror began. Leaving the dead lie, we forced the living ones to segregate themselves in another room. The plague began to break out among the rest of us, and as fast as the symptoms appeared, we sent the stricken ones to these segregated rooms. We compelled them to walk there by themselves, so as to avoid laying hands on them. It was heartrending. But still the plague raged among us, and room after room was filled with the dead and dying. And so we who were yet clean retreated to the next floor and to the next, before this sea of the dead, that, room by room and floor by floor, inundated the building.

"The place became a charnel house, and in the middle of the night the survivors fled forth, taking nothing with them except arms and ammunition and a heavy store of tinned foods. We camped on the opposite side of the campus from the prowlers, and, while some stood guard, others of us volunteered to scout into the city in quest of horses, motor-cars, carts, and wagons, or anything that would carry our provisions and enable us to emulate the banded workingmen I had seen fighting their way out to the open country.

"I was one of these scouts; and Doctor Hoyle, remembering that his motor-car had been left behind in his home garage, told me to look for it. We scouted in pairs, and Dombey, a young undergraduate, accompanied me. We had to cross half a mile of the residence portion of the city to get to Doctor Hoyle's home. Here the buildings stood apart, in the midst of trees and grassy lawns, and here the fires had played freaks, burning whole

182

blocks, skipping blocks and often skipping a single house in a block. And here, too, the prowlers were still at their work. We carried our automatic pistols openly in our hands, and looked desperate enough, forsooth, to keep them from attacking us. But at Doctor Hoyle's house the thing happened. Untouched by fire, even as we came to it the smoke of flames burst forth.

"The miscreant who had set fire to it staggered down the steps and out along the driveway. Sticking out of his coat pockets were bottles of whiskey, and he was very drunk. My first impulse was to shoot him, and I have never ceased regretting that I did not. Staggering and maundering to himself, with bloodshot eyes, and a raw and bleeding slash down one side of his bewhiskered face, he was altogether the most nauseating specimen of degradation and filth I had ever encountered. I did not shoot him, and he leaned against a tree on the lawn to let us go by. It was the most absolute, wanton act. Just as we were opposite him, he suddenly drew a pistol and shot Dombey through the head. The next instant I shot him. But it was too late. Dombey expired without a groan, immediately. I doubt if he even knew what had happened to him.

"Leaving the two corpses, I hurried on past the burning house to the garage, and there found Doctor Hoyle's motor-car. The tanks were filled with gasoline, and it was ready for use. And it was in this car that I threaded the streets of the ruined city and came back to the survivors on the campus. The other scouts returned, but none had been so fortunate. Professor Fairmead had found a Shetland pony, but the poor creature, tied in a stable and abandoned for days, was so weak from want of food and water that it could carry no burden at all. Some of the men were for turning it loose, but I insisted that we should lead it along with us, so that, if we got out of food, we would have it to eat.

"There were forty-seven of us when we started, many being women and children. The President of the Faculty, an old man to begin with, and now hopelessly broken by the awful happenings of the past week, rode in the motor-car with several young children and the aged mother of Professor Fairmead. Wathope, a young professor of English, who had a grievous bullet-wound in his leg, drove the car. The rest of us walked, Professor Fairmead leading the pony.

"It was what should have been a bright summer day, but the smoke from the burning world filled the sky, through which the sun shone murkily, a dull and lifeless orb, blood-red and ominous. But we had grown accustomed to that blood-red sun. With the smoke it was different. It bit into our nostrils and eyes, and there was not one of us whose eyes were not bloodshot. We directed our course to the southeast through the endless miles of suburban residences, travelling along where the first swells of low hills rose from the flat of the central city. It was by this way, only, that we could expect to gain the country.

"Our progress was painfully slow. The women and children could not walk fast. They did not dream of walking, my grandsons, in the way all people walk to-day. In truth, none of us knew how to walk. It was not until after the plague that I learned really to walk. So it was that the pace of the slowest was the pace of all, for we dared not separate on account of the prowlers. There were not so many now of these human beasts of prey. The plague had already well diminished their numbers, but enough still lived to be a constant menace to us. Many of the beautiful residences were untouched by fire, yet smoking ruins were everywhere. The prowlers, too, seemed to have got over their insensate desire to burn, and it was more rarely that we saw houses freshly on fire.

"Several of us scouted among the private garages in search of motor-cars and gasoline. But in this we were unsuccessful. The first great flights from the cities had swept all such utilities away. Calgan, a fine young man, was lost in this work. He was shot by prowlers while crossing a lawn. Yet this was our only casualty, though, once, a drunken brute deliberately opened fire on all of us. Luckily, he fired wildly, and we shot him before he had done any hurt.

"At Fruitvale, still in the heart of the magnificent residence section of the city, the plague again smote us. Professor Fairmead was the victim. Making signs to us that his mother was not to know, he turned aside into the grounds of a beautiful mansion. He sat down forlornly on the steps of the front veranda, and I, having lingered, waved him a last farewell. That night, several miles beyond Fruitvale and still in the city, we made camp. And that night we shifted camp twice to get away from our dead. In the morning there were thirty of us. I shall never forget the President of the Faculty. During the morning's march his wife, who was walking, betrayed the fatal symptoms, and when she drew aside to let us go on, he insisted on leaving the motor-car and remaining with her. There was quite a discussion about this, but in the end we gave in. It was just as well, for we knew not which ones of us, if any, might ultimately escape.

"That night, the second of our march, we camped beyond Haywards in the first stretches of country. And in the morning there were eleven of us that lived. Also, during the night, Wathope, the professor with the wounded leg, deserted us in the motor-car. He took with him his sister and his mother and most of our tinned provisions. It was that day, in the afternoon, while resting by the wayside, that I saw the last airship I shall ever see. The smoke was much thinner here in the country, and I first

184

sighted the ship drifting and veering helplessly at an elevation of two thousand feet. What had happened I could not conjecture, but even as we looked we saw her bow dip down lower and lower. Then the bulkheads of the various gas-chambers must have burst, for, quite perpendicular, she fell like a plummet to the earth. And from that day to this I have not seen another airship. Often and often, during the next few years, I scanned the sky for them hoping against hope that somewhere in the world civilization had survived. But it was not to be. What happened with us in California must have happened with everybody everywhere.

"Another day, and at Niles there were three of us. Beyond Niles, in the middle of the highway, we found Wathope. The motor-car had broken down, and there, on the rugs which they had spread on the ground, lay the bodies of his sister, his mother, and himself.

"Wearied by the unusual exercise of continual walking, that night I slept heavily. In the morning I was alone in the world. Canfield and Parsons, my last companions, were dead of the plague. Of the four hundred that sought shelter in the Chemistry Building, and of the forty-seven that began the march, I alone remained—I and the Shetland pony. Why this should be so there is no explaining. I did not catch the plague, that is all. I was immune. I was merely the one lucky man in a million—just as every survivor was one in a million, or, rather, in several millions, for the proportion was at least that.

V

"For two days I sheltered in a pleasant grove where there had been no deaths. In those two days, while badly depressed and believing that my turn would come at any moment, nevertheless I rested and recuperated. So did the pony. And on the third day, putting what small store of tinned provisions I possessed on the pony's back, I started on across a very lonely land. Not a live man, woman, child, did I encounter, though the dead were everywhere. Food, however, was abundant. The land then was not as it is now. It was all cleared of trees and brush, and it was cultivated. The food for millions of mouths was growing, ripening, and going to waste. From the fields and orchards I gathered vegetables, fruits, and berries. Around the deserted farmhouses I got eggs and caught chickens. And frequently I found supplies of tinned provisions in the store-rooms.

"A strange thing was what was taking place with all the domestic animals. Everywhere they were going wild and preying on one another. The chickens and ducks were the first to be destroyed, while the pigs were the first to go wild, followed by the cats. Nor were the dogs long in adapting themselves to the changed conditions. There was a veritable plague of dogs. They devoured the corpses, barked and howled during the nights, and in the daytime slunk about in the distance. As the time went by, I noticed a change in their behavior. At first they were apart from one another, very suspicious and very prone to fight. But after a not very long while they began to come together and run in packs. The dog, you see, always was a social animal, and this was true before ever he came to be domesticated by man. In the last days of the world before the plague, there were many many very different kinds of dogs—dogs without hair and dogs with warm fur, dogs so small that they would make scarcely a mouthful for other dogs that were as large as mountain lions. Well, all the small dogs, and the weak types, were killed by their fellows. Also, the very large ones were not adapted for the wild life and bred out. As a result, the many different kinds of dogs disappeared, and there remained, running in packs, the medium-sized wolfish dogs that you know to-day."

"But the cats don't run in packs, Granser," Hoo-Hoo objected.

"The cat was never a social animal. As one writer in the nineteenth century said, the cat walks by himself. He always walked by himself, from before the time he was tamed by man, down through the long ages of domestication, to to-day when once more he is wild.

"The horses also went wild, and all the fine breeds we had degenerated into the small mustang horse you know to-day. The cows likewise went wild, as did the pigeons and the sheep. And that a few of the chickens survived you know yourself. But the wild chicken of to-day is quite a different thing from the chickens we had in those days.

"But I must go on with my story. I travelled through a deserted land. As the time went by I began to yearn more and more for human beings. But I never found one, and I grew lonelier and lonelier. I crossed Livermore Valley and the mountains between it and the great valley of the San Joaquin. You have never seen that valley, but it is very large and it is the home of the wild horse. There are great droves there, thousands and tens of thousands. I revisited it thirty years after, so I know. You think there are lots of wild horses down here in the coast valleys, but they are as nothing compared with those of the San Joaquin. Strange to say, the cows, when they went wild, went back into the lower mountains. Evidently they were better able to protect themselves there.

"In the country districts the ghouls and prowlers had been less in evidence, for I found many villages and towns untouched by fire. But they were filled by the pestilential dead, and I passed by without exploring them. It was near Lathrop that, out of my loneliness, I picked up a pair of collie dogs that were so newly free that they were urgently willing to

186

return to their allegiance to man. These collies accompanied me for many years, and the strains of them are in those very dogs there that you boys have to-day. But in sixty years the collie strain has worked out. These brutes are more like domesticated wolves than anything else."

Hare-Lip rose to his feet, glanced to see that the goats were safe, and looked at the sun's position in the afternoon sky, advertising impatience at the prolixity of the old man's tale. Urged to hurry by Edwin, Granser went on.

"There is little more to tell. With my two dogs and my pony, and riding a horse I had managed to capture, I crossed the San Joaquin and went on to a wonderful valley in the Sierras called Yosemite. In the great hotel there I found a prodigious supply of tinned provisions. The pasture was abundant, as was the game, and the river that ran through the valley was full of trout. I remained there three years in an utter loneliness that none but a man who has once been highly civilized can understand. Then I could stand it no more. I felt that I was going crazy. Like the dog, I was a social animal and I needed my kind. I reasoned that since I had survived the plague, there was a possibility that others had survived. Also, I reasoned that after three years the plague germs must all be gone and the land be clean again.

"With my horse and dogs and pony, I set out. Again I crossed the San Joaquin Valley, the mountains beyond, and came down into Livermore Valley. The change in those three years was amazing. All the land had been splendidly tilled, and now I could scarcely recognize it, such was the sea of rank vegetation that had overrun the agricultural handiwork of man. You see, the wheat, the vegetables, and orchard trees had always been cared for and nursed by man, so that they were soft and tender. The weeds and wild bushes and such things, on the contrary, had always been fought by man, so that they were tough and resistant. As a result, when the hand of man was removed, the wild vegetation smothered and destroyed practically all the domesticated vegetation. The coyotes were greatly increased, and it was at this time that I first encountered wolves, straying in twos and threes and small packs down from the regions where they had always persisted.

"It was at Lake Temescal, not far from the one-time city of Oakland, that I came upon the first live human beings. Oh, my grandsons, how can I describe to you my emotion, when, astride my horse and dropping down the hillside to the lake, I saw the smoke of a campfire rising through the trees. Almost did my heart stop beating. I felt that I was going crazy. Then I heard the cry of a babe—a human babe. And dogs barked, and my dogs answered. I did not know but what I was the one

187

human alive in the whole world. It could not be true that here were others—smoke, and the cry of a babe.

"Emerging on the lake, there, before my eyes, not a hundred yards away, I saw a man, a large man. He was standing on an outjutting rock and fishing. I was overcome. I stopped my horse. I tried to call out but could not. I waved my hand. It seemed to me that the man looked at me, but he did not appear to wave. Then I laid my head on my arms there in the saddle. I was afraid to look again, for I knew it was an hallucination, and I knew that if I looked the man would be gone. And so precious was the hallucination, that I wanted it to persist yet a little while. I knew, too, that as long as I did not look it would persist.

"Thus I remained, until I heard my dogs snarling, and a man's voice. What do you think the voice said? I will tell you. It said: *'Where in hell did you come from?'*

"Those were the words, the exact words. That was what your other grandfather said to me, Hare-Lip, when he greeted me there on the shore of Lake Temescal fifty-seven years ago. And they were the most ineffable words I have ever heard. I opened my eyes, and there he stood before me, a large, dark, hairy man, heavy-jawed, slant-browed, fierce-eyed. How I got off my horse I do not know. But it seemed that the next I knew I was clasping his hand with both of mine and crying. I would have embraced him, but he was ever a narrow-minded, suspicious man, and he drew away from me. Yet did I cling to his hand and cry."

Granser's voice faltered and broke at the recollection, and the weak tears streamed down his cheeks while the boys looked on and giggled.

"Yet did I cry," he continued, "and desire to embrace him, though the Chauffeur was a brute, a perfect brute—the most abhorrent man I have ever known. His name was . . . strange, how I have forgotten his name. Everybody called him Chauffeur—it was the name of his occupation, and it stuck. That is how, to this day, the tribe he founded is called the Chauffeur Tribe.

"He was a violent, unjust man. Why the plague germs spared him I can never understand. It would seem, in spite of our old metaphysical notions about absolute justice, that there is no justice in the universe. Why did he live?—an iniquitous, moral monster, a blot on the face of nature, a cruel, relentless, bestial cheat as well. All he could talk about was motor-cars, machinery, gasoline, and garages—and especially, and with huge delight, of his mean pilferings and sordid swindlings of the persons who had employed him in the days before the coming of the plague. And yet he was spared, while hundreds of millions, yea, billions, of better men were destroyed.

188

"I went on with him to his camp, and there I saw her, Vesta, the one woman. It was glorious and . . . pitiful. There she was, Vesta Van Warden, the young wife of John Van Warden, clad in rags, with marred and scarred and toil-calloused hands, bending over the campfire and doing scullion work—she, Vesta, who had been born to the purple of the greatest baronage of wealth the world has ever known. John Van Warden, her husband, worth one billion, eight hundred millions and President of the Board of Industrial Magnates, had been the ruler of America. Also, sitting on the International Board of Control, he had been one of the seven men who ruled the world. And she herself had come of equally noble stock. Her father, Philip Saxon, had been President of the Board of Industrial Magnates up to the time of his death. This office was in process of becoming hereditary, and had Philip Saxon had a son that son would have succeeded him. But his only child was Vesta, the perfect flower of generations of the highest culture this planet has ever produced. It was not until the engagement between Vesta and Van Warden took place, that Saxon indicated the latter as his successor. It was, I am sure, a political marriage. I have reason to believe that Vesta never really loved her husband in the mad passionate way of which the poets used to sing. It was more like the marriages that obtained among crowned heads in the days before they were displaced by the Magnates.

"And there she was, boiling fish-chowder in a soot-covered pot, her glorious eyes inflamed by the acrid smoke of the open fire. Hers was a sad story. She was the one survivor in a million, as I had been, as the Chauffeur had been. On a crowning eminence of the Alameda Hills, overlooking San Francisco Bay, Van Warden had built a vast summer palace. It was surrounded by a park of a thousand acres. When the plague broke out, Van Warden sent her there. Armed guards patrolled the boundaries of the park, and nothing entered in the way of provisions or even mail matter that was not first fumigated. And yet did the plague enter, killing the guards at their posts, the servants at their tasks, sweeping away the whole army of retainers—or, at least, all of them who did not flee to die elsewhere. So it was that Vesta found herself the sole living person in the palace that had become a charnel house.

"Now the Chauffeur had been one of the servants that ran away. Returning, two months afterward, he discovered Vesta in a little summer pavilion where there had been no deaths and where she had established herself. He was a brute. She was afraid, and she ran away and hid among the trees. That night, on foot, she fled into the mountains—she, whose tender feet and delicate body had never known the bruise of stones nor the scratch of briars. He followed, and that night he caught her. He struck

189

her. Do you understand? He beat her with those terrible fists of his and made her his slave. It was she who had to gather the firewood, build the fires, cook, and do all the degrading camp-labor—she, who had never performed a menial act in her life. These things he compelled her to do, while he, a proper savage, elected to lie around camp and look on. He did nothing, absolutely nothing, except on occasion to hunt meat or catch fish."

"Good for Chauffeur," Hare-Lip commented in an undertone to the other boys. "I remember him before he died. He was a corker. But he did things, and he made things go. You know, Dad married his daughter, an' you ought to see the way he knocked the spots outa Dad. The Chauffeur was a son-of-a-gun. He made us kids stand around. Even when he was croakin', he reached out for me, once, an' laid my head open with that long stick he kept always beside him."

Hare-Lip rubbed his bullet head reminiscently, and the boys returned to the old man, who was maundering ecstatically about Vesta, the squaw of the founder of the Chauffeur Tribe.

"And so I say to you that you cannot understand the awfulness of the situation. The Chauffeur was a servant, understand, a servant. And he cringed, with bowed head, to such as she. She was a lord of life, both by birth and by marriage. The destinies of millions, such as he, she carried in the hollow of her pink-white hand. And, in the days before the plague, the slightest contact with such as he would have been pollution. Oh, I have seen it. Once, I remember, there was Mrs. Goldwin, wife of one of the great magnates. It was on a landing stage, just as she was embarking in her private dirigible, that she dropped her parasol. A servant picked it up and made the mistake of handing it to her—to her, one of the greatest royal ladies of the land! She shrank back, as though he were a leper, and indicated her secretary to receive it. Also, she ordered her secretary to ascertain the creature's name and to see that he was immediately discharged from service. And such a woman was Vesta Van Warden. And her the Chauffeur beat and made his slave.

"—Bill—that was it; Bill, the Chauffeur. That was his name. He was a wretched, primitive man, wholly devoid of the finer instincts and chivalrous promptings of a cultured soul. No, there is no absolute justice, for to him fell that wonder of womanhood, Vesta Van Warden. The grievousness of this you will never understand, my grandsons; for you are yourselves primitive little savages, unaware of aught else but savagery. Why should Vesta not have been mine? I was a man of culture and refinement, a professor in a great university. Even so, in the time before the plague, such was her exalted position, she would not have deigned to know that I

190

existed. Mark, then, the abysmal degradation to which she fell at the hands of the Chauffeur. Nothing less than the destruction of all mankind had made it possible that I should know her, look in her eyes, converse with her, touch her hand—ay, and love her and know that her feelings toward me were very kindly. I have reason to believe that she, even she, would have loved me, there being no other man in the world except the Chauffeur. Why, when it destroyed eight billions of souls, did not the plague destroy just one more man, and that man the Chauffeur?

"Once, when the Chauffeur was away fishing, she begged me to kill him. With tears in her eyes she begged me to kill him. But he was a strong and violent man, and I was afraid. Afterwards, I talked with him. I offered him my horse, my pony, my dogs, all that I possessed, if he would give Vesta to me. And he grinned in my face and shook his head. He was very insulting. He said that in the old days he had been a servant, had been dirt under the feet of men like me and of women like Vesta, and that now he had the greatest lady in the land to be servant to him and cook his food and nurse his brats. 'You had your day before the plague,' he said; 'but this is my day, and a damned good day it is. I wouldn't trade back to the old times for anything.' Such words he spoke, but they are not his words. He was a vulgar, low minded man, and vile oaths fell continually from his lips.

"Also, he told me that if he caught me making eyes at his woman he'd wring my neck and give her a beating as well. What was I to do? I was afraid. He was a brute. That first night, when I discovered the camp, Vesta and I had great talk about the things of our vanished world. We talked of art, and books, and poetry; and the Chauffeur listened and grinned and sneered. He was bored and angered by our way of speech which he did not comprehend, and finally he spoke up and said: 'And this is Vesta Van Warden, one-time wife of Van Warden the Magnate—a high and stuck-up beauty, who is now my squaw. Eh, Professor Smith, times is changed, times is changed. Here, you, woman, take off my moccasins, and lively about it. I want Professor Smith to see how well I have you trained.'

"I saw her clench her teeth, and the flame of revolt rise in her face. He drew back his gnarled fist to strike, and I was afraid, and sick at heart. I could do nothing to prevail against him. So I got up to go, and not be witness to such indignity. But the Chauffeur laughed and threatened me with a beating if I did not stay and behold. And I sat there, perforce, by the campfire on the shore of Lake Temescal, and saw Vesta, Vesta Van Warden, kneel and remove the moccasins of that grinning, hairy, ape-like human brute.

"—Oh, you do not understand, my grandsons. You have never

known anything else, and you do not understand.

" 'Halter-broke and bridle-wise,' the Chauffeur gloated, while she performed that dreadful, menial task. 'A trifle balky at times, Professor, a trifle balky; but a clout alongside the jaw makes her as meek and gentle as a lamb.'

"And another time he said: 'We've got to start all over and replenish the earth and multiply. You're handicapped, Professor. You ain't got no wife, and we're up against a regular Garden-of-Eden proposition. But I ain't proud. I'll tell you what, Professor.' He pointed at their little infant, barely a year old. 'There's your wife, though you'll have to wait till she grows up. It's rich, ain't it? We're all equals here, and I'm the biggest toad in the splash. But I ain't stuck up—not I. I do you the honor, Professor Smith, the very great honor of betrothing to you my and Vesta Van Warden's daughter. Ain't it cussed bad that Van Warden ain't here to see?'

VI

"I lived three weeks of infinite torment there in the Chauffeur's camp. And then, one day, tiring of me, or of what to him was my bad effect on Vesta, he told me that the year before, wandering through the Contra Costa Hills to the Straits of Carquinez, across the Straits he had seen a smoke. This meant that there were still other human beings, and that for three weeks he had kept this inestimably precious information from me. I departed at once, with my dogs and horses, and journeyed across the Contra Costa Hills to the Straits. I saw no smoke on the other side, but at Port Costa discovered a small steel barge on which I was able to embark my animals. Old canvas which I found served me for a sail, and a southerly breeze fanned me across the Straits and up to the ruins of Vallejo. Here, on the outskirts of the city, I found evidences of a recently occupied camp. Many clam-shells showed me why these humans had come to the shores of the Bay. This was the Santa Rosa Tribe, and I followed its track along the old railroad right of way across the salt marshes to Sonoma Valley. Here, at the old brickyard at Glen Ellen, I came upon the camp. There were eighteen souls all told. Two were old men, one of whom was Jones, a banker. The other was Harrison, a retired pawnbroker, who had taken for wife the matron of the State Hospital for the Insane at Napa. Of all the persons of the city of Napa, and of all the other towns and villages in that rich and populous valley, she had been the only survivor. Next, there were the three young men—Cardiff and Hale, who had been farmers, and Wainwright, a common day-laborer. All three had found wives. To Hale, a crude, illiterate farmer, had fallen Isadore, the greatest prize, next

192

to Vesta, of the women who came through the plague. She was one of the world's most noted singers, and the plague had caught her at San Francisco. She has talked with me for hours at a time, telling me of her adventures, until, at last, rescued by Hale in the Mendocino Forest Reserve, there had remained nothing for her to do but become his wife. But Hale was a good fellow, in spite of his illiteracy. He had a keen sense of justice and right-dealing, and she was far happier with him than was Vesta with the Chauffeur.

"The wives of Cardiff and Wainwright were ordinary women, accustomed to toil, with strong constitutions—just the type for the wild new life which they were compelled to live. In addition were two adult idiots from the feeble-minded home at Eldredge, and five or six young children and infants born after the formation of the Santa Rosa Tribe. Also, there was Bertha. She was a good woman, Hare-Lip, in spite of the sneers of your father. Her I took for wife. She was the mother of your father, Edwin, and of yours, Hoo-Hoo. And it was our daughter, Vera, who married your father, Hare-Lip—your father, Sandow, who was the oldest son of Vesta Van Warden and the Chauffeur.

"And so it was that I became the nineteenth member of the Santa Rosa Tribe. There were only two outsiders added after me. One was Mungerson, descended from the Magnates, who wandered alone in the wilds of Northern California for eight years before he came south and joined us. He it was who waited twelve years more before he married my daughter, Mary. The other was Johnson, the man who founded the Utah Tribe. That was where he came from, Utah, a country that lies very far away from here, across the great deserts, to the east. It was not until twenty-seven years after the plague that Johnson reached California. In all that Utah region he reported but three survivors, himself one, and all men. For many years these three men lived and hunted together, until at last, desperate, fearing that with them the human race would perish utterly from the planet, they headed westward on the possibility of finding women survivors in California. Johnson alone came through the great desert, where his two companions died. He was forty-six years old when he joined us, and he married the fourth daughter of Isadore and Hale, and his eldest son married your aunt, Hare-Lip, who was the third daughter of Vesta and the Chauffeur. Johnson was a strong man, with a will of his own. And it was because of this that he seceded from the Santa Rosans and formed the Utah Tribe at San José. It is a small tribe—there are only nine in it; but, though he is dead, such was his influence and the strength of his breed, that it will grow into a strong tribe and play a leading part in the recivilization of the planet.

193

"There are only two other tribes that we know of—the Los Angelitos and the Carmelitos. The latter started from one man and woman. He was called Lopez, and he was descended from the ancient Mexicans and was very black. He was a cowherd in the ranges beyond Carmel, and his wife was a maidservant in the great Del Monte Hotel. It was seven years before we first got in touch with the Los Angelitos. They have a good country down there, but it is too warm. I estimate the present population of the world at between three hundred and fifty and four hundred—provided, of course, that there are no scattered little tribes elsewhere in the world. If there be such, we have not heard from them. Since Johnson crossed the desert from Utah, no word nor sign has come from the East or anywhere else. The great world which I knew in my boyhood and early manhood is gone. It has ceased to be. I am the last man who was alive in the days of the plague and who knows the wonders of that far-off time. We, who mastered the planet—its earth, and sea, and sky—and who were as very gods, now live in primitive savagery along the water courses of this California country.

"But we are increasing rapidly—your sister, Hare-Lip, already has four children. We are increasing rapidly and making ready for a new climb toward civilization. In time, pressure of population will compel us to spread out, and a hundred generations from now we may expect our descendants to start across the Sierras, oozing slowly along, generation by generation, over the great continent to the colonization of the East—a new Aryan drift around the world.

"But it will be slow, very slow; we have so far to climb. We fell so hopelessly far. If only one physicist or one chemist had survived! But it was not to be, and we have forgotten everything. The Chauffeur started working in iron. He made the forge which we use to this day. But he was a lazy man, and when he died he took with him all he knew of metals and machinery. What was I to know of such things? I was a classical scholar, not a chemist. The other men who survived were not educated. Only two things did the Chauffeur accomplish—the brewing of strong drink and the growing of tobacco. It was while he was drunk, once, that he killed Vesta. I firmly believe that he killed Vesta in a fit of drunken cruelty though he always maintained that she fell into the lake and was drowned.

"And, my grandsons, let me warn you against the medicine-men. They call themselves *doctors*, travestying what was once a noble profession, but in reality they are medicine-men, devil-devil men, and they make for superstition and darkness. They are cheats and liars. But so debased and degraded are we, that we believe their lies. They, too, will increase in numbers as we increase, and they will strive to rule us. Yet are

194

they liars and charlatans. Look at young Cross-Eyes, posing as a doctor, selling charms against sickness, giving good hunting, exchanging promises of fair weather for good meat and skins, sending the death-stick, performing a thousand abominations. Yet I say to you, that when he says he can do these things, he lies. I, Professor Smith, Professor James Howard Smith, say that he lies. I have told him so to his teeth. Why has he not sent me the death-stick? Because he knows that with me it is without avail. But you, Hare-Lip, so deeply are you sunk in black superstition that did you awake this night and find the death-stick beside you, you would surely die. And you would die, not because of any virtues in the stick, but because you are a savage with the dark and clouded mind of a savage.

"The doctors must be destroyed, and all that was lost must be discovered over again. Wherefore, earnestly, I repeat unto you certain things which you must remember and tell to your children after you. You must tell them that when water is made hot by fire, there resides in it a wonderful thing called steam, which is stronger than ten thousand men and which can do all man's work for him. There are other very useful things. In the lightning flash resides a similarly strong servant of man, which was of old his slave and which some day will be his slave again.

"Quite a different thing is the alphabet. It is what enables me to know the meaning of fine markings, whereas you boys know only rude picture-writing. In that dry cave on Telegraph Hill, where you see me often go when the tribe is down by the sea, I have stored many books. In them is great wisdom. Also, with them, I have placed a key to the alphabet, so that one who knows picture-writing may also know print. Some day men will read again; and then, if no accident has befallen my cave, they will know that Professor James Howard Smith once lived and saved for them the knowledge of the ancients.

"There is another little device that men inevitably will rediscover. It is called gunpowder. It was what enabled us to kill surely and at long distances. Certain things which are found in the ground, when combined in the right proportions, will make this gunpowder. What these things are, I have forgotten, or else I never knew. But I wish I did know. Then would I make powder, and then would I certainly kill Cross-Eyes and rid the land of superstition—"

"After I am man-grown I am going to give Cross-Eyes all the goats, and meat, and skins I can get, so that he'll teach me to be a doctor," Hoo-Hoo asserted. "And when I know, I'll make everybody else sit up and take notice. They'll get down in the dirt to me, you bet."

The old man nodded his head solemnly, and murmured:

"Strange it is to hear the vestiges and remnants of the complicated

195

Aryan speech falling from the lips of a filthy little skin-clad savage. All the world is topsy-turvy. And it has been topsy-turvy ever since the plague."

"You won't make me sit up," Hare-Lip boasted to the would-be medicine-man. "If I paid you for a sending of the death-stick and it didn't work, I'd bust in your head—understand, you Hoo-Hoo, you?"

"I'm going to get Granser to remember this here gunpowder stuff," Edwin said softly, "and then I'll have you all on the run. You, Hare-Lip, will do my fighting for me and get my meat for me, and you, Hoo-Hoo, will send the death-stick for me and make everybody afraid. And if I catch Hare-Lip trying to bust your head, Hoo-Hoo, I'll fix him with that same gunpowder. Granser ain't such a fool as you think, and I'm going to listen to him and some day I'll be boss over the whole bunch of you."

The old man shook his head sadly, and said:

"The gunpowder will come. Nothing can stop it—the same old story over and over. Man will increase, and men will fight. The gunpowder will enable men to kill millions of men, and in this way only, by fire and blood, will a new civilization, in some remote day, be evolved. And of what profit will it be? Just as the old civilization passed, so will the new. It may take fifty thousand years to build, but it will pass. All things pass. Only remain cosmic force and matter, ever in flux, ever acting and reacting and realizing the eternal types—the priest, the soldier, and the king. Out of the mouths of babes comes the wisdom of all the ages. Some will fight, some will rule, some will pray; and all the rest will toil and suffer sore while on their bleeding carcasses is reared again, and yet again, without end, the amazing beauty and surpassing wonder of the civilized state. It were just as well that I destroyed those cave-stored books—whether they remain or perish, all their old truths will be discovered, their old lies lived and handed down. What is the profit—"

Hare-Lip leaped to his feet, giving a quick glance at the pasturing goats and the afternoon sun.

"Gee!" he muttered to Edwin. "The old geezer gets more long-winded every day. Let's pull for camp."

While the other two, aided by the dogs, assembled the goats and started them for the trail through the forest, Edwin stayed by the old man and guided him in the same direction. When they reached the old right of way, Edwin stopped suddenly and looked back. Hare-Lip and Hoo-Hoo and the dogs and the goats passed on. Edwin was looking at a small herd of wild horses which had come down on the hard sand. There were at least twenty of them, young colts and yearlings and mares, led by a beautiful stallion which stood in the foam at the edge of the surf, with arched neck and bright wild eyes, sniffing the salt air from off the sea.

"What is it?" Granser queried.

"Horses," was the answer. "First time I ever seen 'em on the beach. It's the mountain lions getting thicker and thicker and driving 'em down."

The low sun shot red shafts of light, fanshaped, up from a cloud-tumbled horizon. And close at hand, in the white waste of shore-lashed waters, the sea-lions, bellowing their old primeval chant, hauled up out of the sea on the black rocks and fought and loved.

"Come on, Granser," Edwin prompted.

And old man and boy, skin-clad and barbaric, turned and went along the right of way into the forest in the wake of the goats.

THE RED ONE

It is fitting to end a collection of Jack London's short fiction—particularly his fantasy fiction—with "The Red One," one of his strongest stories, written toward the close of his life (he died six months to the day after completing it). In writing "The Red One" and the very fine "Like Argus of the Ancient Times" (1917), a nonfantasy story of the Klondike, London did seem to be, as Irving Stone has observed, rearing up for a last show of strength.

Charmian London wrote that the story "evidences the author's profound meditation upon reaching out of the most primordial toward the most cosmic," (*Book of Jack London,* 2:334), and that may be the case. One thing is clear: with no "pseudo-scientific" accouterments whatever, no atmosphere of scientific credibility, London created an extraordinary, greatly neglected science-fiction-fantasy tale of shuddering impact.

Recent research has shown that the plot for this story came from London's poet-friend George Sterling, who also helped describe the great red orb of the title.

There it was! The abrupt liberation of sound, as he timed it with his watch, Bassett likened to the trump of an archangel. Walls of cities, he meditated, might well fall down before so vast and compelling a summons. For the thousandth time vainly he tried to analyze the tone-quality of that enormous peal that dominated the land far into the strongholds of the surrounding tribes. The mountain gorge which was its source rang to the rising tide of it until it brimmed over and flooded earth and sky and air. With the wantonness of a sick man's fancy, he likened it to the mighty cry of some Titan of the Elder World vexed with misery or wrath. Higher and higher it arose, challenging and demanding in such profounds of volume that it seemed intended for ears beyond the narrow confines of the solar

Cosmopolitan, 65 (October, 1918):34-41, 132, 135-38.

system. There was in it, too, the clamor of protest in that there were no ears to hear and comprehend its utterance.

—Such the sick man's fancy. Still he strove to analyze the sound. Sonorous as thunder was it, mellow as a golden bell, thin and sweet as a thrummed taut cord of silver—no; it was none of these, nor a blend of these. There were no words nor semblances in his vocabulary and experience with which to describe the totality of that sound.

Time passed. Minutes merged into quarters of hours, and quarters of hours into half hours, and still the sound persisted, ever changing from its initial vocal impulse yet never receiving fresh impulse—fading, dimming, dying as enormously as it had sprung into being. It became a confusion of troubled mutterings and babblings and colossal whisperings. Slowly it withdrew, sob by sob, into whatever great bosom had birthed it, until it whimpered deadly whispers of wrath and as equally seductive whispers of delight, striving still to be heard, to convey some cosmic secret, some understanding of infinite import and value. It dwindled to a ghost of sound that had lost its menace and promise, and became a thing that pulsed on in the sick man's consciousness for minutes after it had ceased. When he could hear it no longer, Bassett glanced at his watch. An hour had elapsed ere that archangel's trump had subsided into tonal nothingness.

Was this, then, *his* dark tower?—Bassett pondered, remembering his Browning and gazing at his skeleton-like and fever-wasted hands. And the fancy made him smile—of Childe Roland bearing a slug-horn to his lips with an arm as feeble as his was. Was it months, or years, he asked himself, since he first heard that mysterious call on the beach at Ringmanu? To save himself he could not tell. The long sickness had been most long. In conscious count of time he knew of months, many of them; but he had no way of estimating the long intervals of delirium and stupor. And how fared Captain Bateman of the blackbirder *Nari?* he wondered; and had Captain Bateman's drunken mate died of delirium tremens yet?

From which vain speculations, Bassett turned idly to review all that had occurred since that day on the beach of Ringmanu when he first heard the sound and plunged into the jungle after it. Sagawa had protested. He could see him yet, his queer little monkeyish face eloquent with fear, his back burdened with specimen cases, in his hands Bassett's butterfly net and naturalist's shotgun, as he quavered in Bêche-de-mer English: "Me fella too much fright along bush. Bad fella boy too much stop'm along bush."

Bassett smiled sadly at the recollection. The little New Hanover boy had been frightened, but had proved faithful, following him without hesitancy into the bush in the quest after the source of the wonderful sound. No fire-hollowed tree-trunk, that, throbbing war through the jungle

199

depths, had been Bassett's conclusion. Erroneous had been his next conclusion, namely, that the source or cause could not be more distant than an hour's walk and that he would easily be back by mid-afternoon to be picked up by the *Nari's* whaleboat.

"That big fella noise no good, all the same devil-devil," Sagawa had adjudged. And Sagawa had been right. Had he not had his head hacked off within the day? Bassett shuddered. Without doubt Sagawa had been eaten as well by the bad fella boys too much that stopped along the bush. He could see him, as he had last seen him stripped of the shotgun and all the naturalist's gear of his master, lying on the narrow trail where he had been decapitated barely the moment before. Yes, within a minute the thing had happened. Within a minute, looking back, Bassett had seen him trudging patiently along under his burdens. Then Bassett's own trouble had come upon him. He looked at the cruelly healed stumps of the first and second fingers of his left hand, then rubbed them softly into the indentation in the back of his skull. Quick as had been the flash of the long-handled tomahawk, he had been quick enough to duck away his head and partially to deflect the stroke with his up-flung hand. Two fingers and a nasty scalp-wound had been the price he paid for his life. With one barrel of his ten-gauge shotgun he had blown the life out of the bushman who had so nearly got him; with the other barrel he had peppered the bushmen bending over Sagawa, and had the pleasure of knowing that the major portion of the charge had gone into the one who leaped away with Sagawa's head. Everything had occurred in a flash. Only himself, the slain bushman, and what remained of Sagawa, were in the narrow. wild-pig run of a path. From the dark jungle on either side came no rustle of movement or sound of life. And he had suffered distinct and dreadful shock. For the first time in his life he had killed a human being, and he knew nausea as he contemplated the mess of his handiwork.

Then had begun the chase. He retreated up the pig-run before his hunters, who were between him and the beach. How many there were, he could not guess. There might have been one, or a hundred, for aught he saw of them. That some of them took to the trees and travelled along through the jungle roof he was certain; but at the most he never glimpsed more than an occasional flitting of shadows. No bowstrings twanged that he could hear; but every little while, whence discharged he knew not, tiny arrows whispered past him or struck tree-boles and fluttered to the ground beside him. They were bone-tipped and feather-shafted, and the feathers, torn from the breasts of humming-birds, iridesced like jewels.

Once—and now, after the long lapse of time, he chuckled gleefully at the recollection—he had detected a shadow above him that came to instant

200

rest as he turned his gaze upward. He could make out nothing, but, deciding to chance it, had fired at it a heavy charge of number five shot. Squalling like an infuriated cat, the shadow crashed down through tree-ferns and orchids and thudded upon the earth at his feet, and, still squalling its rage and pain, had sunk its human teeth into the ankle of his stout tramping boot. He, on the other hand, was not idle, and with his free foot had done what reduced the squalling to silence. So inured to savagery had Bassett since become, that he chuckled again with the glee of the recollection.

What a night had followed! Small wonder that he had accumulated such a virulence and variety of fevers, he thought, as he recalled that sleepless night of torment, when the throb of his wounds was as nothing compared with the myriad stings of the mosquitoes. There had been no escaping them, and he had not dared to light a fire. They had literally pumped his body full of poison, so that, with the coming of day, eyes swollen almost shut, he had stumbled blindly on, not caring much when his head should be hacked off and his carcass started on the way of Sagawa's to the cooking fire. Twenty-four hours had made a wreck of him—of mind as well as body. He had scarcely retained his wits at all, so maddened was he by the tremendous inoculation of poison he had received. Several times he fired his shotgun with effect into the shadows that dogged him. Stinging day insects and gnats added to his torment, while his bloody wounds attracted hosts of loathsome flies that clung sluggishly to his flesh and had to be brushed off and crushed off.

Once, in that day, he heard again the wonderful sound, seemingly more distant, but rising imperiously above the nearer war-drums in the bush. Right there was where he had made his mistake. Thinking that he had passed beyond it and that, therefore, it was between him and the beach of Ringmanu, he had worked back toward it when in reality he was penetrating deeper and deeper into the mysterious heart of the unexplored island. That night, crawling in among the twisted roots of a banyan tree, he had slept from exhaustion while the mosquitoes had had their will of him.

Followed days and nights that were vague as nightmares in his memory. One clear vision he remembered was of suddenly finding himself in the midst of a bush village and watching the old men and children fleeing into the jungle. All had fled but one. From close at hand and above him, a whimpering as of some animal in pain and terror had startled him. And looking up he had seen her—a girl, or young woman, rather, suspended by one arm in the cooking sun. Perhaps for days she had so hung. Her swollen protruding tongue spoke as much. Still alive, she gazed

201

at him with eyes of terror. Past help, he decided, as he noted the swellings of her legs which advertised that the joints had been crushed and the great bones broken. He resolved to shoot her, and there the vision terminated. He could not remember whether he had or not, any more than could he remember how he chanced to be in that village or how he succeeded in getting away from it.

Many pictures, unrelated, came and went in Bassett's mind as he reviewed that period of his terrible wanderings. He remembered invading another village of a dozen houses and driving all before him with his shotgun save for one old man, too feeble to flee, who spat at him and whined and snarled as he dug open a ground-oven and from amid the hot stones dragged forth a roasted pig that steamed its essence deliciously through its green-leaf wrappings. It was at this place that a wantonness of savagery had seized upon him. Having feasted, ready to depart with a hind quarter of the pig in his hand, he deliberately fired the grass thatch of a house with his burning glass.

But seared deepest of all in Bassett's brain, was the dank and noisome jungle. It actually stank with evil, and it was always twilight. Rarely did a shaft of sunlight penetrate its matted roof a hundred feet overhead. And beneath that roof was an aerial ooze of vegetation, a monstrous, parasitic dripping of decadent life-forms that rooted in death and lived on death. And through all this he drifted, ever pursued by the flitting shadows of the anthropophagi, themselves ghosts of evil that dared not face him in battle but that knew, soon or late, that they would feed on him. Bassett remembered that at the time, in lucid moments, he had likened himself to a wounded bull pursued by plains' coyotes too cowardly to battle with him for the meat of him, yet certain of the inevitable end of him when they would be full gorged. As the bull's horns and stamping hoofs kept off the coyotes, so his shotgun kept off these Solomon Islanders, these twilight shades of bushmen of the island of Guadalcanal.

Came the day of the grass lands. Abruptly, as if cloven by the sword of God in the hand of God, the jungle terminated. The edge of it, perpendicular and as black as the infamy of it, was a hundred feet up and down. And, beginning at the edge of it, grew the grass—sweet, soft, tender, pasture grass that would have delighted the eyes and beasts of any husbandman and that extended, on and on, for leagues and leagues of velvet verdure, to the backbone of the great island, the towering mountain range flung up by some ancient earth-cataclysm, serrated and gullied but not yet erased by the erosive tropic rains. But the grass! He had crawled into it a dozen yards, buried his face in it, smelled it, and broken down in a fit of involuntary weeping.

And, while he wept, the wonderful sound had pealed forth—if by *peal*, he had often thought since, an adequate description could be given of the enunciation of so vast a sound so melting sweet. Sweet it was as no sound ever heard. Vast it was, of so mighty a resonance that it might have proceeded from some brazen-throated monster. And yet it called to him across that leagues-wide savannah, and was like a benediction to his long-suffering, pain-wracked spirit.

He remembered how he lay there in the grass, wet-cheeked but no longer sobbing, listening to the sound and wondering that he had been able to hear it on the beach of Ringmanu. Some freak of air pressures and air currents, he reflected, had made it possible for the sound to carry so far. Such conditions might not happen again in a thousand days or ten thousand days; but the one day it had happened had been the day he landed from the *Nari* for several hours' collecting. Especially had he been in quest of the famed jungle butterfly, a foot across from wing-tip to wing-tip, as velvet-dusky of lack of color as was the gloom of the roof, of such lofty arboreal habits that it resorted only to the jungle roof and could be brought down only by a dose of shot. It was for this purpose that Sagawa had carried the twenty-gauge shotgun.

Two days and nights he had spent crawling across that belt of grass land. He had suffered much, but pursuit had ceased at the jungle-edge. And he would have died of thirst had not a heavy thunderstorm revived him on the second day.

And then had come Balatta. In the first shade, where the savannah yielded to the dense mountain jungle, he had collapsed to die. At first she had squealed with delight at sight of his helplessness, and was for beating his brain out with a stout forest branch. Perhaps it was his very utter helplessness that had appealed to her, and perhaps it was her human curiosity that made her refrain. At any rate, she had refrained, for he opened his eyes again under the impending blow, and saw her studying him intently. What especially struck her about him were his blue eyes and white skin. Coolly she had squatted on her hams, spat on his arm, and with her finger-tips scrubbed away the dirt of days and nights of muck and jungle that sullied the pristine whiteness of his skin.

And everything about her had struck him especially, although there was nothing conventional about her at all. He laughed weakly at the recollection, for she had been as innocent of garb as Eve before the fig-leaf adventure. Squat and lean at the same time, asymmetrically limbed, string-muscled as if with lengths of cordage, dirt-caked from infancy save for casual showers, she was as unbeautiful a prototype of woman as he, with a scientist's eye, had ever gazed upon. Her breasts advertised at the one time her maturity and youth; and, if by nothing else, her sex was advertised by the one article of finery with which she was adorned, namely a pig's tail, thrust through a hole in her left ear-lobe. So lately had the tail been severed, that its raw end still oozed blood that dried upon her shoulder like so much candle-droppings. And her face! A twisted and wizened complex of apish features, perforated by upturned, sky-open, Mongolian nostrils, by a mouth that sagged from a huge upper-lip and faded precipitately into a retreating chin, and by peering querulous eyes that blinked as blink the eyes of denizens of monkey-cages.

Not even the water she brought him in a forest-leaf, and the ancient and half-putrid chunk of roast pig, could redeem in the slightest the grotesque hideousness of her. When he had eaten weakly for a space, he closed his eyes in order not to see her, although again and again she poked them open to peer at the blue of them. Then had come the sound. Nearer, much nearer, he knew it to be; and he knew equally well, despite the weary way he had come, that it was still many hours distant. The effect of it on her had been startling. She cringed under it, with averted face, moaning and chattering with fear. But after it had lived its full life of an hour, he closed his eyes and fell asleep with Balatta brushing the flies from him.

When he awoke it was night, and she was gone. But he was aware of renewed strength, and, by then too thoroughly inoculated by the mosquito poison to suffer further inflammation, he closed his eyes and slept an unbroken stretch till sun-up. A little later Balatta had returned, bringing with her a half dozen women who, unbeautiful as they were, were patently not so unbeautiful as she. She evidenced by her conduct that she considered him her find, her property, and the pride she took in showing him off would have been ludicrous had his situation not been so desperate.

Later, after what had been to him a terrible journey of miles, when he collapsed in front of the devil-devil house in the shadow of the breadfruit tree, she had shown very lively ideas on the matter of retaining possession of him. Ngurn, whom Bassett was to know afterward as the devil-devil doctor, priest, or medicine man of the village, had wanted his head. Others of the grinning and chattering monkey-men, all as stark of clothes and bestial of appearance as Balatta, had wanted his body for the roasting oven. At that time he had not understood their language, if by *language* might be dignified the uncouth sounds they made to represent ideas. But Bassett had thoroughly understood the matter of debate, especially when the men pressed and prodded and felt of the flesh of him as if he were so much commodity in a butcher's stall.

THE RED ONE

Balatta had been losing the debate rapidly, when the accident happened. One of the men, curiously examining Bassett's shotgun, managed to cock and pull a trigger. The recoil of the butt into the pit of the man's stomach had not been the most sanguinary result, for the charge of shot, at a distance of a yard, had blown the head of one of the debaters into nothingness.

Even Balatta joined the others in flight, and, ere they returned, his senses already reeling from the oncoming fever-attack, Bassett had regained possession of the gun. Whereupon, although his teeth chattered with the ague and his swimming eyes could scarcely see, he held onto his fading consciousness until he could intimidate the bushmen with the simple magics of compass, watch, burning glass, and matches. At the last, with due emphasis of solemnity and awfulness, he had killed a young pig with his shotgun and promptly fainted.

Bassett flexed his arm muscles in quest of what possible strength might reside in such weakness, and dragged himself slowly and totteringly to his feet. He was shockingly emaciated; yet, during the various convalescences of the many months of his long sickness, he had never regained quite the same degree of strength as this time. What he feared was another relapse such as he had already frequently experienced. Without drugs, without even quinine, he had managed so far to live through a combination of the most pernicious and most malignant of malarial and black-water fevers. But could he continue to endure? Such was his everlasting query. For, like the genuine scientist he was, he would not be content to die until he had solved the secret of the sound.

Supported by a staff, he staggered the few steps to the devil-devil house where death and Ngurn reigned in gloom. Almost as infamously dark and evil-stinking as the jungle was the devil-devil house—in Bassett's opinion. Yet therein was usually to be found his favorite crony and gossip, Ngurn, always willing for a yarn or a discussion, the while he sat in the ashes of death and in a slow smoke shrewdly revolved curing human heads suspended from the rafters. For, through the months' interval of consciousness of his long sickness, Bassett had mastered the psychological simplicities and lingual difficulties of the language of the tribe of Ngurn and Balatta, and Gngngn—the latter the addle-headed young chief who was ruled by Ngurn, and who, whispered intrigue had it, was the son of Ngurn.

"Will the Red One speak to-day?" Bassett asked, by this time so accustomed to the old man's gruesome occupation as to take even an interest in the progress of the smoke-curing.

With the eye of an expert Ngurn examined the particular head he was at work upon.

"It will be ten days before I can say 'finish,' " he said. "Never has any man fixed heads like these."

Bassett smiled inwardly at the old fellow's reluctance to talk with him of the Red One. It had always been so. Never, by any chance, had Ngurn or any other member of the weird tribe divulged the slightest hint of any physical characteristic of the Red One. Physical the Red One must be, to emit the wonderful sound, and though it was called the Red One, Bassett could not be sure that red represented the color of it. Red enough were the deeds and powers of it, from what abstract clues he had gleaned. Not alone, had Ngurn informed him, was the Red One more bestial powerful than the neighbor tribal gods, ever a-thirst for the red blood of living human sacrifices, but the neighbor gods themselves were sacrificed and tormented before him. He was the god of a dozen allied villages similar to this one, which was the central and commanding village of the federation. By virtue of the Red One many alien villages had been devastated and even wiped out, the prisoners sacrificed to the Red One. This was true to-day, and it extended back into old history carried down by word of mouth through the generations. When he, Ngurn, had been a young man, the tribes beyond the grass lands had made a war raid. In the counter raid, Ngurn and his fighting folk had made many prisoners. Of children alone over five score living had been bled white before the Red One, and many, many more men and women.

The Thunderer, was another of Ngurn's names for the mysterious deity. Also at times was he called The Loud Shouter, The God-Voiced, The Bird-Throated, The One with the Throat Sweet as the Throat of the Honey-Bird, The Sun Singer, and The Star-Born.

Why The Star-Born? In vain Bassett interrogated Ngurn. According to that old devil-devil doctor, the Red One had always been, just where he was at present, forever singing and thundering his will over men. But Ngurn's father, wrapped in decaying grass-matting and hanging even then over their heads among the smoky rafters of the devil-devil house, had held otherwise. That departed wise one had believed that the Red One came from out of the starry night, else why—so his argument had run—had the old and forgotten ones passed his name down as the Star-Born? Bassett could not but recognize something cogent in such argument. But Ngurn affirmed the long years of his long life, wherein he had gazed upon many starry nights, yet never had he found a star on grass land or in jungle depth—and he had looked for them. True, he had beheld shooting stars (this in reply to Bassett's contention); but likewise had he beheld the phosphorescence of fungoid growths and rotten meat and fireflies on dark nights, and the flames of wood-fires and of blazing candle-nuts; yet what

206

were flame and blaze and glow when they had flamed, and blazed and glowed? Answer: memories, memories only, of things which had ceased to be, like memories of matings accomplished, of feasts forgotten, of desires that were the ghosts of desires, flaring, flaming, burning, yet unrealized in achievement of easement and satisfaction. Where was the appetite of yesterday? the roasted flesh of the wild pig the hunter's arrow failed to slay? the maid, unwed and dead, ere the young man knew her?

A memory was not a star, was Ngurn's contention. How could a memory be a star? Further, after all his long life he still observed the starry night-sky unaltered. Never had he noted the absence of a single star from its accustomed place. Besides, stars were fire, and the Red One was not fire—which last involuntary betrayal told Bassett nothing.

"Will the Red One speak to-morrow?" he queried.

Ngurn shrugged his shoulders as who should say.

"And the day after?—and the day after that?" Bassett persisted.

"I would like to have the curing of your head," Ngurn changed the subject. "It is different from any other head. No devil-devil has a head like it. Besides, I would cure it well. I would take months and months. The moons would come and the moons would go, and the smoke would be very slow, and I should myself gather the materials for the curing smoke. The skin would not wrinkle. It would be as smooth as your skin now."

He stood up, and from the dim rafters grimed with the smoking of countless heads, where day was no more than a gloom, took down a matting-wrapped parcel and began to open it.

"It is a head like yours," he said, "but it is poorly cured."

Bassett had pricked up his ears at the suggestion that it was a white man's head; for he had long since come to accept that these jungle-dwellers, in the midmost center of the great island, had never had intercourse with white men. Certainly he had found them without the almost universal Bêche-de-mer English of the west South Pacific. Nor had they knowledge of tobacco, nor of gunpowder. Their few precious knives, made from lengths of hoop-iron, and their few and more precious tomahawks, made from cheap trade hatchets, he had surmised they had captured in war from the bushmen of the jungle beyond the grass lands, and that they, in turn, had similarly gained them from the salt water men who fringed the coral beaches of the shore and had contact with the occasional white men.

"The folk in the out beyond do not know how to cure heads," old Ngurn explained, as he drew forth from the filthy matting and placed in Bassett's hands an indubitable white man's head.

Ancient it was beyond question; white it was as the blond hair

207

attested. He could have sworn it once belonged to an Englishman, and to an Englishman of long before by token of the heavy gold circlets still threaded in the withered earlobes.

"Now your head . . ." the devil-devil doctor began on his favorite topic.

"I'll tell you what," Bassett interrupted, struck by a new idea. "When I die I'll let you have my head to cure, if, first, you take me to look upon the Red One."

"I will have your head anyway when you are dead," Ngurn rejected the proposition. He added, with the brutal frankness of the savage: "Besides, you have not long to live. You are almost a dead man now. You will grow less strong. In not many months I shall have you here turning and turning in the smoke. It is pleasant, through the long afternoons, to turn the head of one you have known as well as I know you. And I shall talk to you and tell you the many secrets you want to know. Which will not matter, for you will be dead."

"Ngurn," Bassett threatened in sudden anger. "You know the Baby Thunder in the Iron that is mine." (This was in reference to his all-potent and all-awful shotgun.) "I can kill you any time, and then you will not get my head."

"Just the same, will Gngngn, or some one else of my folk get it," Ngurn complacently assured him. "And just the same will it turn and turn here in the devil-devil house in the smoke. The quicker you slay me with your Baby Thunder, the quicker will your head turn in the smoke."

And Bassett knew he was beaten in the discussion.

What was the Red One?—Bassett asked himself a thousand times in the succeeding week, while he seemed to grow stronger. What was the source of the wonderful sound? What was this Sun Singer, this Star-Born One, this mysterious deity, as bestial-conducted as the black and kinky-headed and monkey-like human beasts who worshiped it, and whose silver-sweet, bull-mouthed singing and commanding he had heard at the taboo distance for so long?

Ngurn had he failed to bribe with the inevitable curing of his head when he was dead. Gngngn, imbecile and chief that he was, was too imbecilic, too much under the sway of Ngurn, to be considered. Remained Balatta, who, from the time she found him and poked his blue eyes open to recrudescence of her grotesque, female hideousness, had continued his adorer. Woman she was, and he had long known that the only way to win from her treason to her tribe was through the woman's heart of her.

Bassett was a fastidious man. He had never recovered from the initial horror caused by Balatta's female awfulness. Back in England, even at best,

208

the charm of woman, to him, had never been robust. Yet now, resolutely, as only a man can do who is capable of martyring himself for the cause of science, he proceeded to violate all the fineness and delicacy of his nature by making love to the unthinkably disgusting bushwoman.

He shuddered, but with averted face hid his grimaces and swallowed his gorge as he put his arm around her dirt-crusted shoulders and felt the contact of her rancid-oily and kinky hair with his neck and chin. But he nearly screamed when she succumbed to that caress so at the very first of the courtship and mowed and gibbered and squealed little, queer, piglike gurgly noises of delight. It was too much. And the next he did in the singular courtship was to take her down to the stream and give her a vigorous scrubbing.

From then on he devoted himself to her like a true swain as frequently and for as long at a time as his will could override his repugnance. But marriage, which she ardently suggested, with due observance of tribal custom, he balked at. Fortunately, taboo rule was strong in the tribe. Thus, Ngurn could never touch bone, or flesh, or hide of crocodile. This had been ordained at his birth. Gngngn was denied ever the touch of woman. Such pollution, did it chance to occur, could be purged only by the death of the offending female. It had happened once, since Bassett's arrival, when a girl of nine, running in play, stumbled and fell against the sacred chief. And the girl-child was seen no more. In whispers, Balatta told Bassett that she had been three days and nights in dying before the Red One. As for Balatta, the breadfruit was taboo to her. For which Bassett was thankful. The taboo might have been water.

For himself, he fabricated a special taboo. Only could he marry, he explained, when the Southern Cross rode highest in the sky. Knowing his astronomy, he thus gained a reprieve of nearly nine months; and he was confident that within that time he would either be dead or escaped to the coast with full knowledge of the Red One and of the source of the Red One's wonderful voice. At first he had fancied the Red One to be some colossal statue, like Memnon, rendered vocal under certain temperature conditions of sunlight. But when, after a war raid, a batch of prisoners was brought in and the sacrifice made at night, in the midst of rain, when the sun could play no part, the Red One had been more vocal than usual, Bassett discarded that hypothesis.

In company with Balatta, sometimes with men and parties of women, the freedom of the jungle was his for three quadrants of the compass. But the fourth quadrant, which contained the Red One's abiding place, was taboo. He made more thorough love to Balatta—also saw to it that she scrubbed herself more frequently. Eternal female she was, capable of any treason for the sake of love. And, though the sight of her was provocative of nausea and the contact of her provocative of despair, although he could not escape her awfulness in his dream-haunted nightmares of her, he nevertheless was aware of the cosmic verity of sex that animated her and that made her own life of less value than the happiness of her lover with whom she hoped to mate. Juliet or Balatta? Where was the intrinsic difference? The soft and tender product of ultra-civilization, or her bestial prototype of a hundred thousand years before her?—there was no difference.

Bassett was a scientist first, a humanist afterward. In the jungle-heart of Guadalcanal he put the affair to the test, as in the laboratory he would have put to the test any chemical reaction. He increased his feigned ardor for the bushwoman, at the same time increasing the imperiousness of his will of desire over her to be led to look upon the Red One face to face. It was the old story, he recognized, that the woman must pay, and it occurred when the two of them, one day, were catching the unclassified and unnamed little black fish, an inch long, half-eel and half-scaled, rotund with salmon-golden roe, that frequented the fresh water and that were esteemed, raw and whole, fresh or putrid, a perfect delicacy. Prone in the muck of the decaying jungle-floor, Balatta threw herself, clutching his ankles with her hands, kissing his feet and making slubbery noises that chilled his backbone up and down again. She begged him to kill her rather than exact this ultimate love-payment. She told him of the penalty of breaking the taboo of the Red One—a week of torture, living, the details of which she yammered out from her face in the mire until he realized that he was yet a tyro in knowledge of the frightfulness the human was capable of wreaking on the human.

Yet did Bassett insist on having his man's will satisfied, at the woman's risk, that he might solve the mystery of the Red One's singing, though she should die long and horribly and screaming. And Balatta, being mere woman, yielded. She led him into the forbidden quadrant. An abrupt mountain shouldering in from the north to meet a similar intrusion from the south, tormented the stream in which they had fished into a deep and gloomy gorge. After a mile along the gorge, the way plunged sharply upward until they crossed a saddle of raw limestone which attracted his geologist's eye. Still climbing, although he paused often from sheer physical weakness, they scaled forest-clad heights until they emerged on a naked mesa of tableland. Bassett recognized the stuff of its composition as black volcanic sand, and knew that a pocket magnet could have captured a full load of the sharply angular grains he trod upon.

And then, holding Balatta by the hand and leading her onward, he came to it—a tremendous pit, obviously artificial, in the heart of the plateau. Old history, the South Seas Sailing Directions, scores of remembered data and connotations swift and furious, surged through his brain. It was Mendana who had discovered the islands and named them Solomon's, believing that he had found that monarch's fabled mines. They had laughed at the old navigator's childlike credulity; and yet here stood himself, Bassett, on the rim of an excavation for all the world like the diamond pits of South Africa.

But no diamond this that he gazed upon. Rather was it a pearl, with the depth of iridescence of a pearl; but of a size all pearls of earth and time welded into one, could not have totalled; and of a color undreamed of any pearl, or of anything else, for that matter, for it was the color of the Red One. And the Red One himself Bassett knew it to be on the instant. A perfect sphere, fully two hundred feed in diameter, the top of it was a hundred feet below the level of the rim. He likened the color quality of it to lacquer. Indeed, he took it to be some sort of lacquer applied by man, but a lacquer too marvelously clever to have been manufactured by the bush-folk. Brighter than bright cherry-red, its richness of color was as if it were red builded upon red. It glowed and iridesced in the sunlight as if gleaming up from underlay under underlay of red.

In vain Balatta strove to dissuade him from descending. She threw herself in the dirt; but, when he continued down the trail that spiralled the pit-wall, she followed, cringing and whimpering her terror. That the red sphere had been dug out as a precious thing, was patent. Considering the paucity of members of the federated twelve villages and their primitive tools and methods, Bassett knew that the toil of a myriad generations could scarcely have made that enormous excavation.

He found the pit bottom carpeted with human bones, among which, battered and defaced, lay village gods of wood and stone. Some, covered with obscene totemic figures and designs, were carved from solid tree trunks forty or fifty feet in length. He noted the absence of the shark and turtle gods, so common among the shore villages, and was amazed at the constant recurrence of the helmet motive. What did these jungle savages of the dark heart of Guadalcanal know of helmets? Had Mendana's men-at-arms worn helmets and penetrated here centuries before? And if not, then whence had the bush-folk caught the motive?

Advancing over the litter of gods and bones, Balatta whimpering at his heels, Bassett entered the shadow of the Red One and passed on under its gigantic overhand until he touched it with his finger-tips. No lacquer that. Nor was the surface smooth as it should have been in the case of lacquer. On the contrary, it was corrugated and pitted, with here and there

211

patches that showed signs of heat and fusing. Also, the substance of it was metal, though unlike any metal or combination of metals he had ever known. As for the color itself, he decided it to be no application. It was the intrinsic color of the metal itself.

He moved his finger-tips, which up to that had merely rested, along the surface, and felt the whole gigantic sphere quicken and live and respond. It was incredible! So light a touch on so vast a mass! Yet did it quiver under the finger-tip caress in rhythmic vibrations that became whisperings and rustlings and mutterings of sound—but of sound so different; so elusive thin that it was shimmeringly sibillant; so mellow that it was maddening sweet, piping like an elfin horn, which last was just what Bassett decided would be like a peal from some bell of the gods reaching earthward from across space.

He looked to Balatta with swift questioning; but the voice of the Red One he had evoked had flung her face-downward and moaning among the bones. He returned to contemplation of the prodigy. Hollow it was, and of no metal known on earth, was his conclusion. It was right-named by the ones of old-time as the Star-Born. Only from the stars could it have come, and no thing of chance was it. It was a creation of artifice and mind. Such perfection of form, such hollowness that it certainly possessed, could not be the result of mere fortuitousness. A child of intelligences, remote and unguessable, working corporally in metals, it indubitably was. He stared at it in amaze, his brain a racing wild-fire of hypotheses to account for this far-journeyer who had adventured the night of space, threaded the stars, and now rose before him and above him, exhumed by patient anthropophagi, pitted and lacquered by its fiery bath in two atmospheres.

But was the color a lacquer of heat upon some familiar metal? Or was it an intrinsic quality of the metal itself? He thrust in the blade-point of his pocket-knife to test the constitution of the stuff. Instantly the entire sphere burst into a mighty whispering, sharp with protest, almost twanging goldenly if a whisper could possibly be considered to twang, rising higher, sinking deeper, the two extremes of the registry of sound threatening to complete the circle and coalesce into the bull-mouthed thundering he had so often heard beyond the taboo distance.

Forgetful of safety, of his own life itself, entranced by the wonder of the unthinkable and unguessable thing, he raised his knife to strike heavily from a long stroke, but was prevented by Balatta. She upreared on her knees in an agony of terror, clasping his knees and supplicating him to desist. In the intensity of her desire to impress him, she put her forearm between her teeth and sank them to the bone.

He scarcely observed her act, although he yielded automatically to

212

his gentler instincts and withheld the knife-hack. To him, human life had dwarfed to microscopic proportions before this colossal portent of higher life from within the distances of the sidereal universe. As had she been a dog, he kicked the ugly little bushwoman to her feet and compelled her to start with him on an encirclement of the base. Part way around, he encountered horrors. Even, among the others, did he recognize the sun-shrivelled remnant of the nine-years girl who had accidentally broken Chief Gngngn's personality taboo. And, among what was left of these that had passed, he encountered what was left of one who had not yet passed. Truly had the bush-folk named themselves into the name of the Red One, seeing in him their own image which they strove to placate and please with such red offerings.

Farther around, always treading the bones and images of humans and gods that constituted the floor of this ancient charnel house of sacrifice, he came upon the device by which the Red One was made to send his call singing thunderingly across the jungle-belts and grass lands to the far beach of Ringmanu. Simple and primitive was it as was the Red One's consummate artifice. A great king-post, half a hundred feet in length, seasoned by centuries of superstitious care, carven into dynasties of gods, each superimposed, each helmeted, each seated in the open mouth of a crocodile, was slung by ropes, twisted of climbing vegetable parasites, from the apex of a tripod of three great forest trunks, themselves carved into grinning and grotesque adumbrations of man's modern concepts of art and god. From the striker king-post, were suspended ropes of climbers to which men could apply their strength and direction. Like a battering ram, this king-post could be driven end-onward against the mighty, red-iridescent sphere.

Here was where Ngurn officiated and functioned religiously for himself and the twelve tribes under him. Basset laughed aloud, almost with madness, at the thought of this wonderful messenger, winged with intelligence across space, to fall into a bushman stronghold and be worshiped by apelike, man-eating and head-hunting savages. It was as if God's Word had fallen into the muck mire of the abyss underlying the bottom of hell; as if Jehovah's Commandments had been presented on carved stone to the monkeys of the monkey cage at the Zoo; as if the Sermon on the Mount had been preached in a roaring bedlam of lunatics.

The slow weeks passed. The nights, by election, Bassett spent on the ashen floor of the devil-house, beneath the ever-swinging, slow-curing heads. His reason for this was that it was taboo to the lesser sex of woman, and therefore, a refuge for him from Balatta, who grew more persecutingly

213

and perilously loverly as the Southern Cross rode higher in the sky and marked the imminence of her nuptials. His days Bassett spent in a hammock swung under the shade of the great breadfruit tree before the devil-devil house. There were breaks in this program, when, in the comas of his devastating fever-attacks, he lay for days and nights in the house of heads. Ever he struggled to combat the fever, to live, to continue to live, to grow strong and stronger against the day when he would be strong enough to dare the grass lands and the belted jungle beyond, and win to the beach, and to some labor-recruiting, blackbirding ketch or schooner, and on to civilization and the men of civilization, to whom he could give news of the message from other worlds that lay, darkly worshiped by beastmen, in the black heart of Guadalcanal's midmost center.

On other nights, lying late under the breadfruit tree, Bassett spent long hours watching the slow setting of the western stars beyond the black wall of jungle where it had been thrust back by the clearing for the village. Possessed of more than a cursory knowledge of astronomy, he took a sick man's pleasure in speculating as to the dwellers on the unseen worlds of those incredibly remote suns, to haunt whose houses of light, life came forth, a shy visitant, from the rayless crypts of matter. He could no more apprehend limits to time than bounds to space. No subversive radium speculations had shaken his steady scientific faith in the conservation of energy and the indestructibility of matter. Always and forever must there have been stars. And surely, in that cosmic ferment, all must be comparatively alike, comparatively of the same substance, or substances, save for the freaks of the ferment. All must obey, or compose, the same laws that ran without infraction through the entire experience of man. Therefore, he argued and agreed, must worlds and life be appanages to all the suns as they were appanages to the particular sun of his own solar system.

Even as he lay here, under the breadfruit tree, an intelligence that stared across the starry gulfs, so must all the universe be exposed to the ceaseless scrutiny of innumerable eyes, like his, though grantedly different, with behind them, by the same token, intelligences that questioned and sought the meaning and the construction of the whole. So reasoning, he felt his soul go forth in kinship with that august company, that multitude whose gaze was forever upon the arras of infinity.

Who were they, what were they, those far distant and superior ones who had bridged the sky with their gigantic, red-iridescent, heaven-singing message? Surely, and long since, had they, too, trod the path on which man had so recently, by the calendar of the cosmos, set his feet. And to be able to send such a message across the pit of space, surely they had

214

reached those heights to which man, in tears and travail and bloody sweat, in darkness and confusion of many counsels, was so slowiy struggling. And what were they on their heights? Had they won Brotherhood? Or had they learned that the law of love imposed the penalty of weakness and decay? Was strife, life? Was the rule of all the universe the pitiless rule of natural selection? And, and most immediately and poignantly, were their far conclusions, their long-won wisdoms, shut even then in the huge, metallic heart of the Red One, waiting for the first earth-man to read? Of one thing he was certain: No drop of red dew shaken from the lion-mane of some sun in torment, was the sounding sphere. It was of design, not chance, and it contained the speech and wisdom of the stars.

What engines and elements and mastered forces, what lore and mysteries and destiny-controls, might be there! Undoubtedly, since so much could be enclosed in so little a thing as the foundation stone of a public building, this enormous sphere should contain vast histories, profounds of research achieved beyond man's wildest guesses, laws and formulae that, easily mastered, would make man's life on earth, individual and collective, spring up from its present mire to inconceivable heights of purity and power. It was Time's greatest gift to blindfold, insatiable, and sky-aspiring man. And to him, Bassett, had been vouchsafed the lordly fortune to be the first to receive this message from man's interstellar kin!

No white man, much less no outland man of the other bush-tribes, had gazed upon the Red One and lived. Such the law expounded by Ngurn to Bassett. There was such a thing as blood brotherhood, Bassett, in return, had often argued in the past. But Ngurn had stated solemnly no. Even the blood brotherhood was outside the favor of the Red One. Only a man born within the tribe could look upon the Red One and live. But now, his guilty secret known only to Balatta, whose fear of immolation before the Red One fast-sealed her lips, the situation was different. What he had to do was recover from the abominable fevers that weakened him and gain to civilization. Then would he lead an expedition back, and, although the entire population of Guadalcanal be destroyed, extract from the heart of the Red One the message of the world from other worlds.

But Bassett's relapses grew more frequent, his brief convalescences less and less vigorous, his periods of coma longer, until he came to know, beyond the last promptings of the optimism inherent in so tremendous a constitution as his own, that he would never live to cross the grass lands, perforate the perilous coast jungle, and reach the sea. He faded as the Southern Cross rose higher in the sky, till even Balatta knew that be would be dead ere the nuptial date determined by his taboo. Ngurn made pilgrimage personally and gathered the smoke materials for the curing of

215

Bassett's head, and to him made proud announcement and exhibition of the artistic perfectness of his intention when Bassett should be dead. As for himself, Bassett was not shocked. Too long and too deeply had life ebbed down in him to bite him with fear of its impending extinction. He continued to persist, alternating periods of unconsciousness with periods of semi-consciousness, dreamy and unreal, in which he idly wondered whether he had ever truly beheld the Red One or whether it was a nightmare fancy of delirium.

Came the day when all mists and cobwebs dissolved, when he found his brain clear as a bell, and took just appraisement of his body's weakness. Neither hand nor foot could he lift. So little control of his body did he have, that he was scarcely aware of possessing one. Lightly indeed his flesh sat upon his soul, and his soul, in its briefness of clarity, knew by its very clarity, that the black of cessation was near. He knew the end was close; knew that in all truth he had with his eyes beheld the Red One, the messenger between the worlds; knew that he would never live to carry that message to the world—that message, for aught to the contrary, which might already have waited man's hearing in the heart of Guadalcanal for ten thousand years. And Bassett stirred with resolve, calling Ngurn to him, out under the shade of the breadfruit tree, and with the old devil-devil doctor discussing the terms and arrangements of his last life effort, his final adventure in the quick of the flesh.

"I know the law, O Ngurn," he concluded the matter. "Whoso is not of the folk may not look upon the Red One and live. I shall not live anyway. Your young men shall carry me before the face of the Red One, and I shall look upon him, and hear his voice, and thereupon die, under your hand, O Ngurn. Thus will the three things be satisfied: the law, my desire, and your quicker possession of my head for which all your preparations wait."

To which Ngurn consented, adding:

"It is better so. A sick man who cannot get well is foolish to live on for so little a while. Also, is it better for the living that he should go. You have been much in the way of late. Not but what it was good for me to talk to such a wise one. But for moons of days we have held little talk. Instead, you have taken up room in the house of heads, making noises like a dying pig, or talking much and loudly in your own language which I do not understand. This has been a confusion to me, for I like to think on the great things of the light and dark as I turn the heads in the smoke. Your much noise has thus been a disturbance to the long-learning and hatching of the final wisdom that will be mine before I die. As for you, upon whom the dark has already brooded, it is well that you die now. And I promise

216

you, in the long days to come when I turn your head in the smoke, no man of the tribe shall come in to disturb us. And I will tell you many secrets, for I am an old man and very wise, and I shall be adding wisdom to wisdom as I turn your head in the smoke."

So a litter was made, and, borne on the shoulders of half a dozen of the men, Bassett departed on the last little adventure that was to cap the total adventure, for him, of living. With a body of which he was scarcely aware, for even the pain had been exhausted out of it, and with a bright clear brain that accommodated him to a quiet ecstasy of sheer lucidness of thought, he lay back on the lurching litter and watched the fading of the passing world, beholding for the last time the breadfruit tree before the devil-devil house, the dim day beneath the matted jungle roof, the gloomy gorge between the shouldering mountains, the saddle of raw limestone, and the mesa of black, volcanic sand.

Down the spiral path of the pit they bore him, encircling the sheening glowing Red One that seemed ever imminent to iridesce from color and light into sweet singing and thunder. And over bones and logs of immolated men and gods they bore him, past the horrors of other immolated ones that yet lived, to the three-king-post tripod and the huge king-post striker.

Here Bassett, Helped by Ngurn and Balatta, weakly sat up, swaying weakly from the hips, and with clear, unfaltering, all-seeing eyes gazed upon the Red One.

"Once, O Ngurn," he said, not taking his eyes from the sheening, vibrating surface whereon and wherein all the shades of cherry-red played unceasingly, ever a-quiver to change into sound, to become silken rustlings, silvery whisperings, golden thrummings of chords, velvet pipings of elfland, mellow-distances of thunderings.

"I wait," Ngurn prompted after a long pause, the long-handled tomahawk unassumingly ready in his hand.

"Once, O Ngurn," Bassett repeated, "let the Red One speak so that I may see it speak as well as hear it. Then strike, thus, when I raise my hand; for, when I raise my hand, I shall drop my head forward and make place for the stroke at the base of my neck. But, O Ngurn, I, who am about to pass out of the light of day forever, would like to pass with the wonder-voice of the Red One singing greatly in my ears."

"And I promise you that never will a head be so well cured as yours," Ngurn assured him, at the same time signalling the tribesmen to man the propelling ropes suspended from the king-post striker. "Your head shall be my greatest piece of work in the curing of heads."

Bassett smiled quietly at the old one's conceit, as the great carved

217

CURIOUS FRAGMENTS

log, drawn back through two-score feet of space, was released. The next moment he was lost in ecstasy at the abrupt and thunderous liberation of sound. But such thunder! Mellow it was with preciousness of all sounding metals. Archangels spoke in it; it was magnificently beautiful before all other sounds; it was invested with the intelligence of supermen of planets of other suns; it was the voice of God, seducing and commanding to be heard. And—the everlasting miracle of that interstellar metal! Bassett, with his own eyes, saw color and colors transform into sound till the whole visible surface of the vast sphere was a-crawl and titillant and vaporous with what he could not tell was color or was sound. In that moment the interstices of matter were his, and the interfusings and intermating transfusings of matter and force.

Time passed. At the last Bassett was brought back from his ecstasy by an impatient movement of Ngurn. He had quite forgotten the old devil-devil one. A quick flash of fancy brought a husky chuckle into Bassett's throat. His shotgun lay beside him in the litter. All he had to do, muzzle to head, was press the trigger and blow his head into nothingness.

But why cheat him? was Bassett's next thought. Head-hunting, cannibal beast of a human that was as much ape as human, nevertheless Old Ngurn had, according to his lights, played squarer than square. Ngurn was in himself a fore-runner of ethics and contract, of consideration, and gentleness in man. No, Bassett decided; it would be a ghastly pity and an act of dishonor to cheat the old fellow at the last. His head was Ngurn's, and Ngurn's head to cure it would be.

And Bassett, raising his hand in signal, bending forward his head as agreed so as to expose cleanly the articulation to his taut spinal cord, forgot Balatta, who was merely a woman, a woman merely and only and undesired. He knew, without seeing, when the razor-edged hatchet rose in the air behind him. And for that instant, ere the end, there fell upon Bassett the shadow of the Unknown, a sense of impending marvel of the rending of walls before the imaginable. Almost, when he knew the blow had started and just ere the edge of steel bit the flesh and nerves, it seemed that he gazed upon the serene face of the Medusa, Truth.—And, simultaneous with the bite of the steel on the onrush of the dark, in a flashing instant of fancy, he saw the vision of his head turning slowly, always turning, in the devil-devil house beside the breadfruit tree.

Waikiki, Honolulu,
May 22, 1916.

JACK LONDON:
A CHRONOLOGY

1876 Born at 615 Third Street, San Francisco, California, January 12. Son of Flora Wellman (born Massillon, Ohio, August 17, 1843) and William Henry Chaney (born near present-day Chesterville, Maine, January 13, 1821). Chaney, an itinerant astrologer, lives with Flora Wellman 1874-75 but deserts his common-law wife upon learning of her pregnancy and later (1897) denies to London that he can have been his father.

On September 7 Flora (who uses the name Chaney) marries John London, a native of Pennsylvania and a Union Army veteran, a widower with two daughters. John London accepts Flora's son as his own, and he is named John Griffith London, the middle name deriving from a favorite nephew of Flora Wellman's, Griffith Everhard.

1891 Completes grammar school. Works in a cannery.

1892 Purchases the sloop *Razzle-Dazzle* with $300 borrowed from his former wet nurse "Mammy Jenny" Prentiss and becomes "Prince of the Oyster Pirates" on San Francisco Bay.

Serves as officer in the fish patrol of San Francisco Bay.

1893 Serves several months aboard the sealing schooner *Sophie Sutherland* in Bering Sea and the North Pacific. Returns in summer, and November 12 wins first prize in the *San Francisco Call*'s Best Descriptive Article contest for "Story of a Typhoon Off the Coast of Japan."

1894 Joins the western detachment of Coxey's Army—Kelly's Army—to march to Washington, D.C. Leaves the ragtag "army" in the Midwest and rides the rails eastward. Is arrested for vagrancy in Niagara Falls, N.Y., in June and serves one month in the Erie County Penitentiary. These experiences he will later chronicle in *The Road* (1907).

1895 Finishes public school education at Oakland High School, where he writes sketches and stories for the student magazine *Aegis*.

1896 Joins Socialist Labor party. Passes entrance examinations and attends the University of California at Berkeley for one semester.

1897 Joins Klondike gold rush and spends the winter in the Yukon.
John London dies in Oakland October 14.

1898 Returns from Alaska by 2,000 mile boat trip down the Yukon River.

1899 Publishes first "professional" story, "To the Man on Trail," in *Overland Monthly*. Begins writing for a living.
December 21 signs contract with Houghton Mifflin Co. for a book of short stories.

1900 "An Odyssey of the North" is published in the *Atlantic Monthly*. Marries Bessie Maddern April 7; on the same day his first published book, *The Son of the Wolf*, a collection of northland fiction, appears.

1901 First daughter, Joan, is born.

1902 Travels to London where he lives six weeks in the city's East End ghetto and there gathers material for his brilliant sociological study *The People of the Abyss* (a phrase credited to H. G. Wells).
Second daughter, Bess, is born.
First novel, *A Daughter of the Snows*, is published by Lippincott.

1903 W. H. Chaney dies January 8.
The Kempton-Wace Letters, an epistolary exchange with coauthor Anna Strunsky on the subject of love, is published by Macmillan.
Separates from Bessie London.
The Call of the Wild is published, an instantaneous success.

1904 Sails for Japan and Korea as war correspondent for the Hearst syndicate in the Russo-Japanese War.
The Sea Wolf is published.

1905 Divorces Bessie Maddern London. Marries Charmian Kittredge November 20 in Chicago.
Purchases ranch near Glen Ellen, California.
Lectures in Midwest and East.

1906 Lectures at Yale in January on "The Coming Crisis."
Reports on the San Francisco earthquake and fire, April 18, for *Collier's*.
Begins building the *Snark* (named after Lewis Carroll's creation), to sail around the world.
White Fang, written as a companion volume to *The Call of the Wild*, is published.

1907 Sails April 23 from San Francisco in *Snark*, visiting Hawaii—including the leper colony at Molokai—the Marquesas, and Tahiti.

1908 Returns to California aboard the *Mariposa* to straighten out financial affairs. Continues *Snark* voyage to Samoa, Fiji Islands, New Hebrides, and the Solomon Islands.

1908 *The Iron Heel* is published.

1909 Is hospitalized in Sydney, Australia, with a series of tropical ailments. Abandons *Snark* voyage and returns to California on the Scotch collier *Tymeric* via Pitcairn Island, Ecuador, Panama, New Orleans, and Arizona. Arrives home on July 24.

      Martin Eden, a semiautobiographical novel, is published.

1910 Devotes energies and funds to building up his "Beauty Ranch."

      Wolf House, London's baronial mansion, is begun.

      Birth and death of the Londons' first child, a daughter named Joy.

1911 With his wife and servant drives a four-horse carriage through northern California and Oregon.

1912 Sails March 2 from Baltimore around Cape Horn to Seattle aboard the four-masted barque *Dirigo,* a 148-day voyage.

      The Londons' second baby lost in miscarriage.

1913 Wolf House August 21 is mysteriously destroyed by fire, a $70,000 loss, probably arson.

      John Barleycorn, semiautobiographical novel-treatise on alcoholism, is published.

1914 Becomes correspondent for *Collier's* at $1100 a week, in Mexican revolution.

1915 Returns to Hawaii, this time for health purposes.

      His last great work, *The Star Rover,* is published.

      Is warned by doctors of his excesses in drink and diet.

1916 Resigns from Socialist party "because of its lack of fire and fight, and its loss of emphasis on the class struggle."

      Dies 7:45 P.M. November 22, of uremic poisoning. Suicide, as suggested by biographical novelist Irving Stone (in *Sailor on Horseback*), by a calculated lethal dose of morphine and atropine sulphates, a possibility but in no way conclusive.

1922 Flora Wellman London dies January 4.

1947 Bessie Maddern London dies September 7.

1955 Charmian Kittredge London dies January 13.

1965 *Letters from Jack London,* most important of all source books on London's life and thought, is published by Odyssey Press.

1970 *Jack London Reports,* a collection of London's war correspondence, prizefight reporting, and miscellaneous newspaper writing, is published by Doubleday, edited by King Hendricks and Irving Shepard.

1971 Joan London dies January 18.

SUGGESTED READING

Arthur Calder-Marshall, Ed. *The Bodley Head Jack London* (London: The Bodley Head, 1963), four volumes.

Earle Labor. *Jack London* (New York: Twayne Publishers, 1974).

Earle Labor, Ed. *Great Short Works of Jack London* (New York: Harper & Row, 1965).

Sam Moskowitz. *Explorers of the Infinite* (New York: World Publishing Co., 1963).

Charmian London. *The Book of Jack London* (New York: The Century Co., 1921), two volumes.

Joan London. *Jack London and His Times* (New York: Doubleday, Doran & Co., 1939; re-issued with new Introductory material by University of Washington Press [Seattle], 1968).

Irving Shepard and King Hendricks, Eds. *Letters from Jack London* (New York: The Odyssey Press, 1965).

Irving Stone. *Sailor on Horseback: The Biography of Jack London* (New York: Houghton, Mifflin Co., 1938).

Dale L. Walker. *The Alien Worlds of Jack London* (Grand Rapids, Mich.: Wolf House Books, 1973).

Dale L. Walker and James E. Sisson III. *The Fiction of Jack London: A Chronological Bibliography* (El Paso, Texas: Texas Western Press of The University of Texas at El Paso, 1972).

Franklin Walker. *Jack London and the Klondike* (San Marino, Calif.: The Huntington Library, 1966).

Hensley Woodbridge, John London, George H. Tweney. *Jack London: A Bibliography* (Millwood, N.J.: Kraus Reprint Co., 1973; originally published by Talisman Press, Georgetown, Calif., 1966).

DALE L. WALKER has been interested in Jack London for over twenty-five years and has published twenty articles, two bibliographies, and two short books on London. In addition, Walker is coauthor (with Richard O'Connor) of *The Lost Revolutionary: A Biography of John Reed* (1967); and author of *C. L. Sonnichsen: Grassroots Historian* (1972), and *Death Was the Black Horse: The Story of Rough Rider Buckey O'Neill* (1975). He lives with his wife Alice McCord Walker and their five children in El Paso, where he studies Jack London and Victorian British military history. He is director of the news bureau for the University of Texas at El Paso.

PHILIP JOSÉ FARMER ranks among the finest science fiction writers in America today. He has twice won the coveted Hugo Award—in 1971 for best novel (*To Your Scattered Bodies Go*), and in 1967 for best novella (*Riders of the Purple Wage*). A man of limitless imagination, Farmer's always innovative and pathmarking works include two recent full-length biographies of fictional characters (complete with detailed genealogical tables): *Tarzan Alive: A Definitive Biography of Lord Greystoke* (1972), and *Doc Savage: His Apocalyptic Life* (1973).